VOLUME
3

ISSUES
5

PAGES
160

LOEB ★ McGUINNESS

HULK

MARVEL COMICS ★ PRESENTS ★

★ STARRING: ★

WRITER JEPH LOEB

— VS. —

PENCILER ED McGUINNESS

★ INKERS ★

DEXTER VINES
(ROUNDS 1 & 2)

MARK FARMER
(ROUNDS 3 & 4)

TOM PALMER
(ROUND 5)

RICHARD STARKINGS
and COMICRAFT'S
ALBERT DESCHESNE

★ CORNERMEN ★

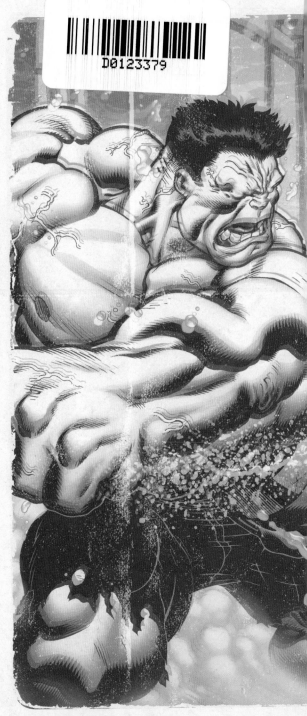

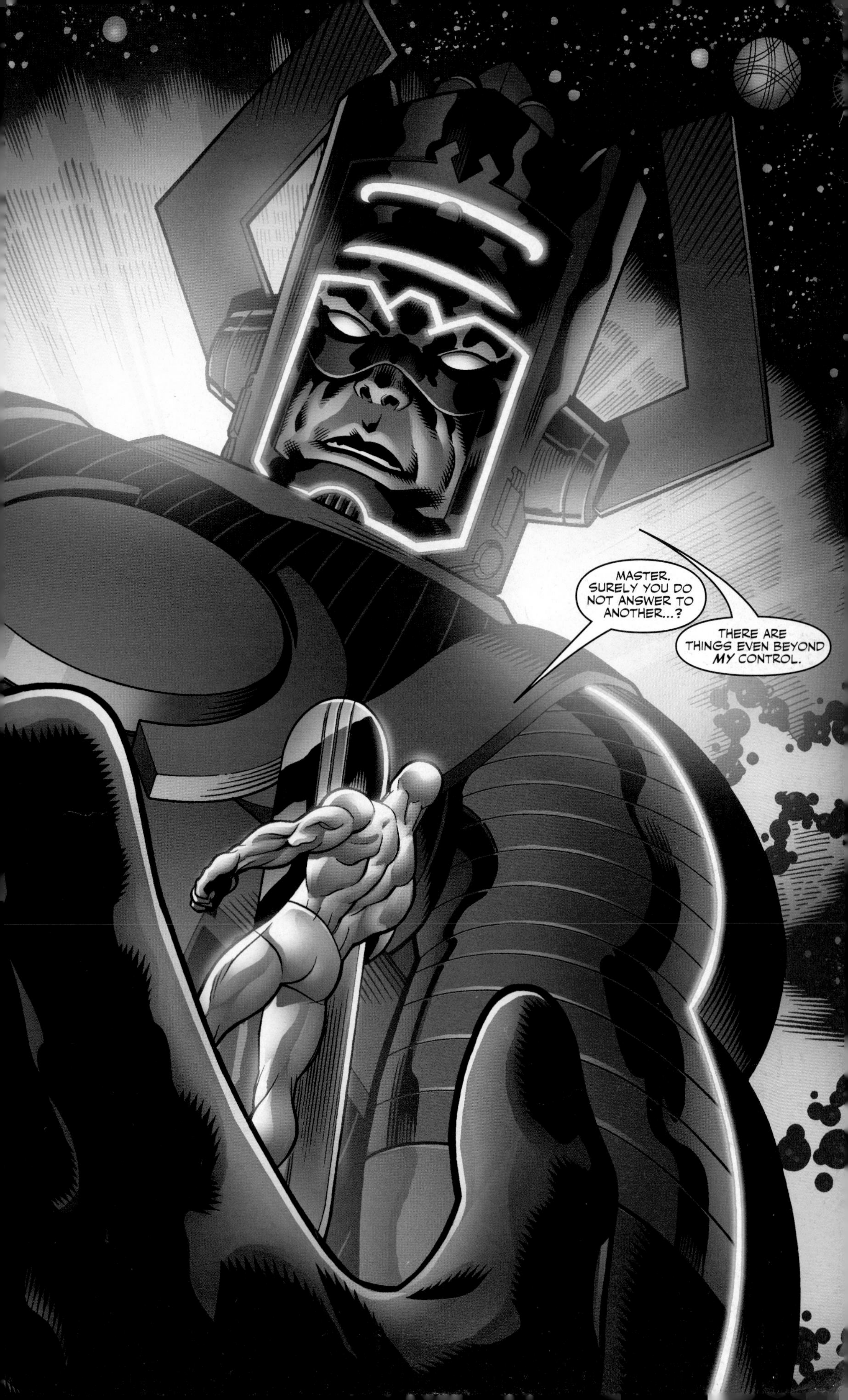
MASTER. SURELY YOU DO NOT ANSWER TO ANOTHER...?
THERE ARE THINGS EVEN BEYOND MY CONTROL.

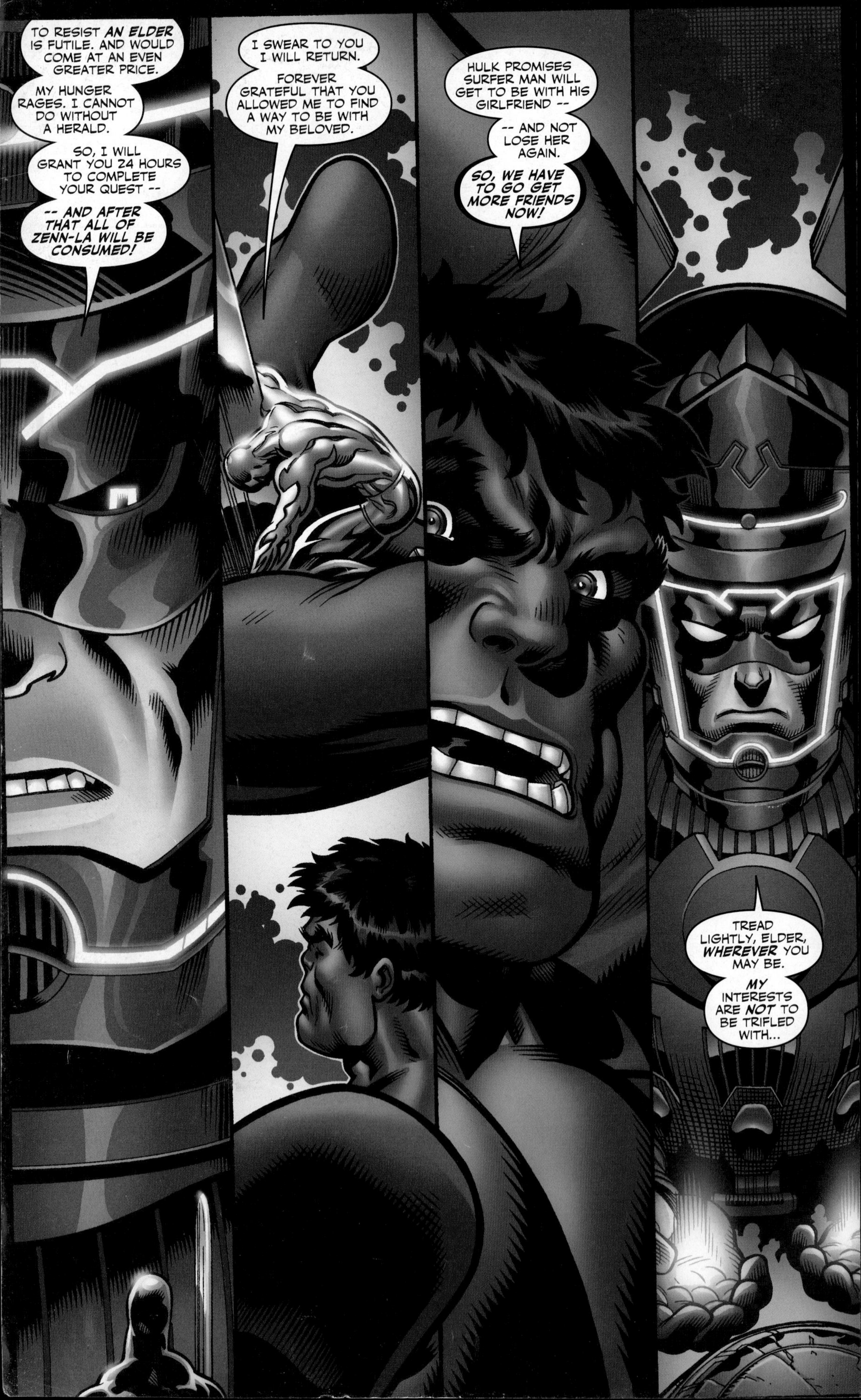
TO RESIST AN ELDER IS FUTILE. AND WOULD COME AT AN EVEN GREATER PRICE.
MY HUNGER RAGES. I CANNOT DO WITHOUT A HERALD.
SO, I WILL GRANT YOU 24 HOURS TO COMPLETE YOUR QUEST --
-- AND AFTER THAT ALL OF ZENN-LA WILL BE CONSUMED!
I SWEAR TO YOU I WILL RETURN.
FOREVER GRATEFUL THAT YOU ALLOWED ME TO FIND A WAY TO BE WITH MY BELOVED.
HULK PROMISES SURFER MAN WILL GET TO BE WITH HIS GIRLFRIEND --
-- AND NOT LOSE HER AGAIN.
SO, WE HAVE TO GO GET MORE FRIENDS NOW!
TREAD LIGHTLY, ELDER, WHEREVER YOU MAY BE.
MY INTERESTS ARE NOT TO BE TRIFLED WITH...

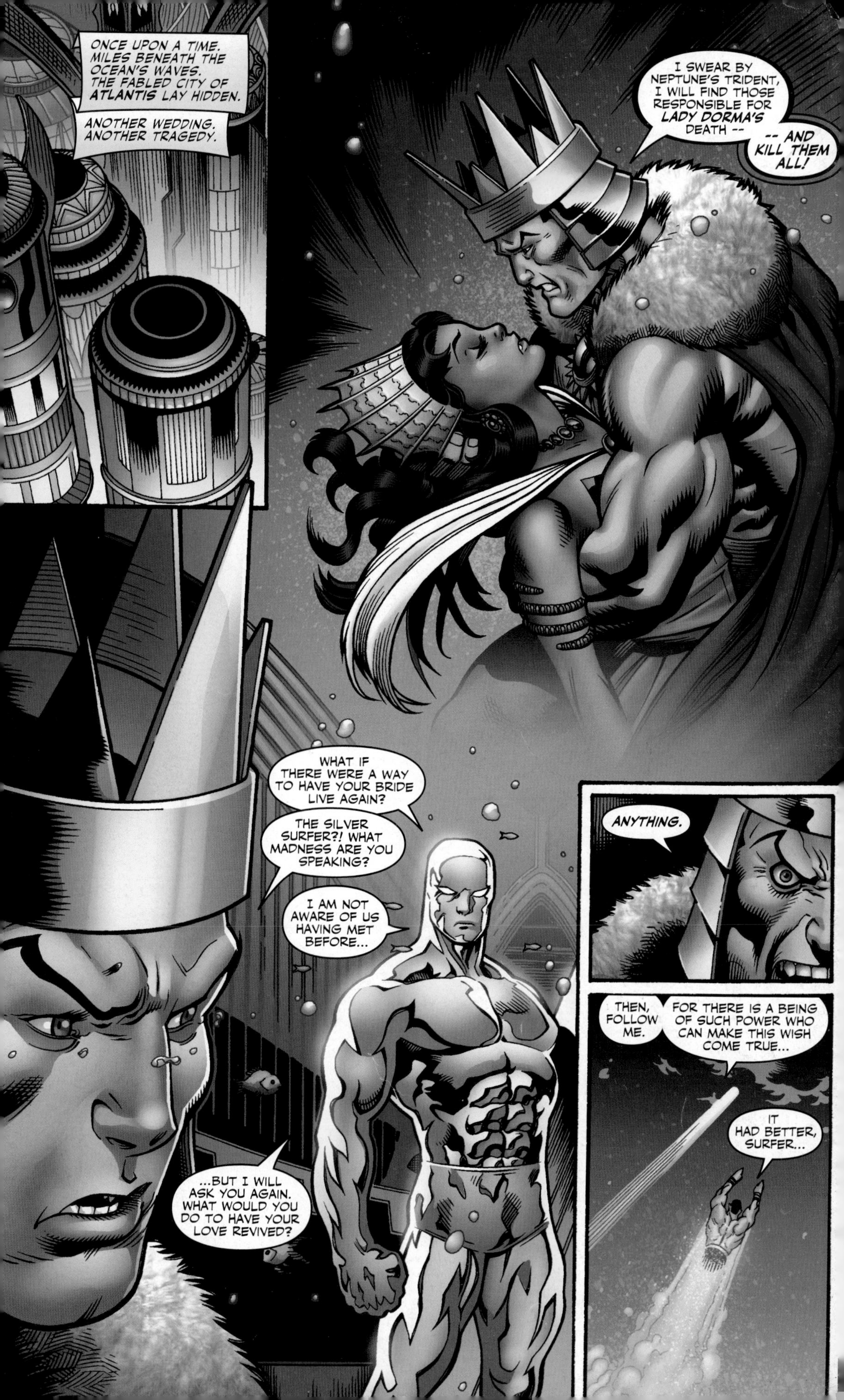
ONCE UPON A TIME. MILES BENEATH THE OCEAN'S WAVES. THE FABLED CITY OF ATLANTIS LAY HIDDEN.
ANOTHER WEDDING. ANOTHER TRAGEDY.
I SWEAR BY NEPTUNE'S TRIDENT, I WILL FIND THOSE RESPONSIBLE FOR LADY DORMA'S DEATH --
-- AND KILL THEM ALL!
WHAT IF THERE WERE A WAY TO HAVE YOUR BRIDE LIVE AGAIN?
THE SILVER SURFER?! WHAT MADNESS ARE YOU SPEAKING?
I AM NOT AWARE OF US HAVING MET BEFORE...
...BUT I WILL ASK YOU AGAIN. WHAT WOULD YOU DO TO HAVE YOUR LOVE REVIVED?
ANYTHING.
THEN, FOLLOW ME.
FOR THERE IS A BEING OF SUCH POWER WHO CAN MAKE THIS WISH COME TRUE...
IT HAD BETTER, SURFER...

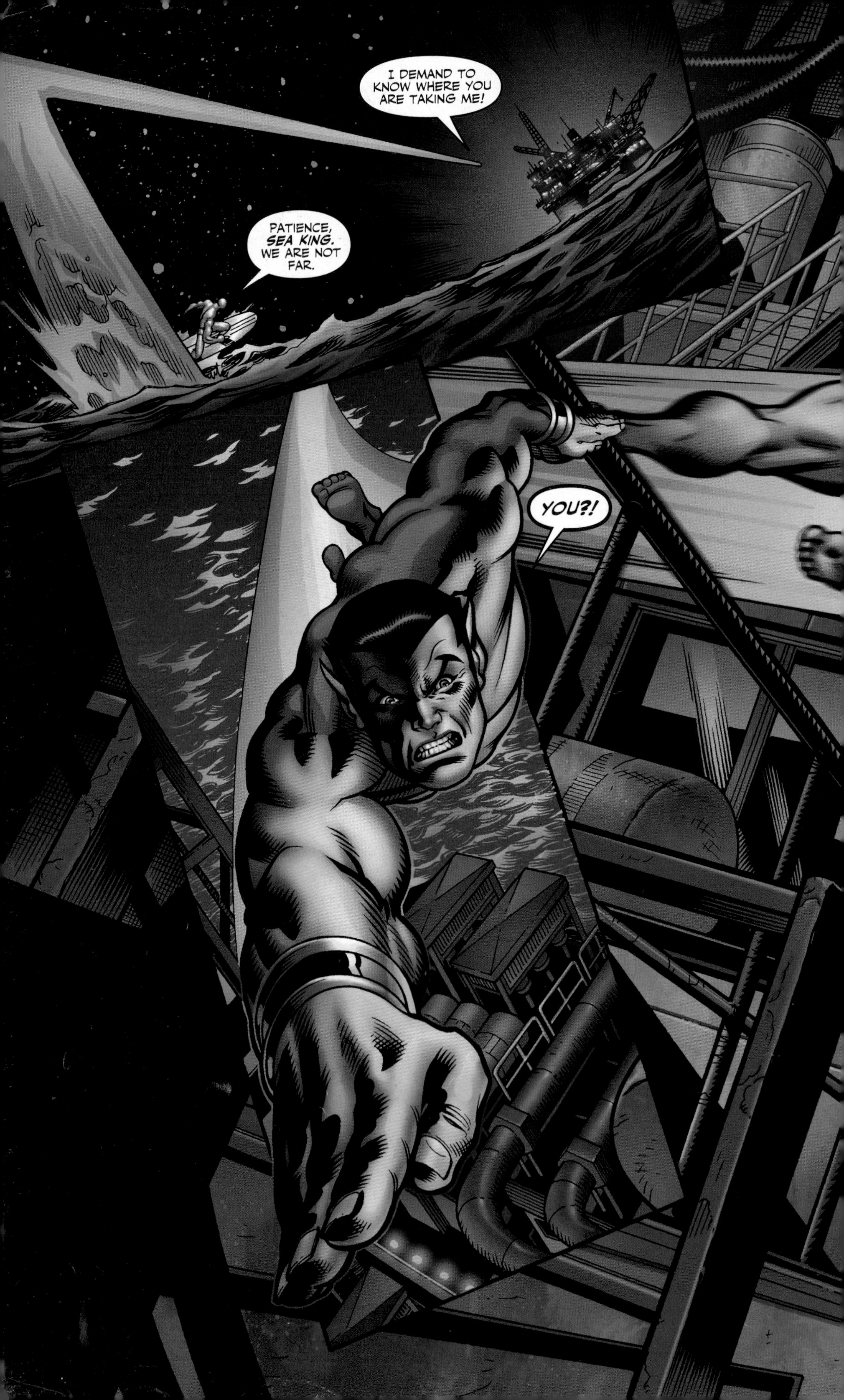
I DEMAND TO KNOW WHERE YOU ARE TAKING ME!
PATIENCE, SEA KING. WE ARE NOT FAR.
YOU?!

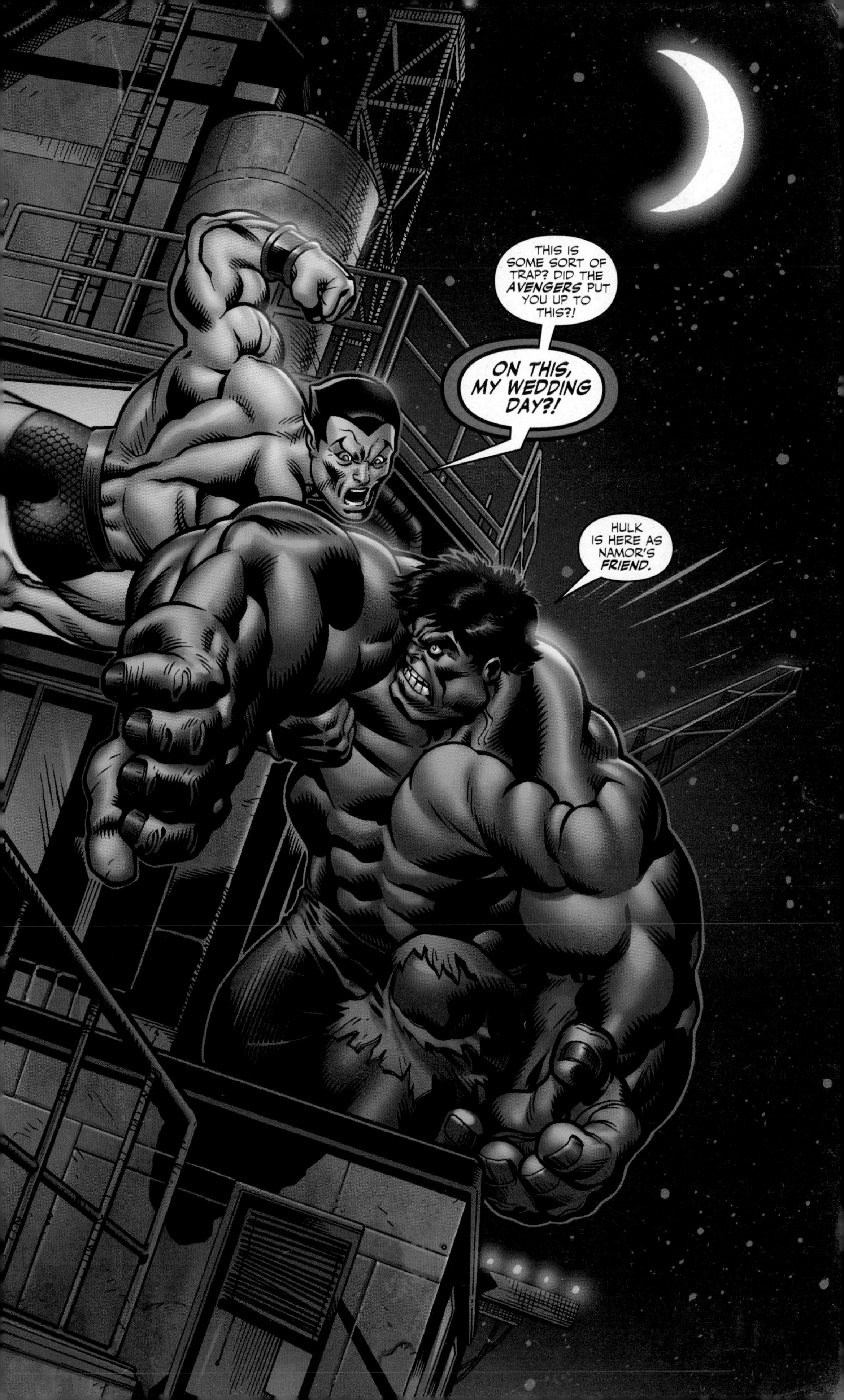
THIS IS SOME SORT OF TRAP? DID THE AVENGERS PUT YOU UP TO THIS?!
ON THIS, MY WEDDING DAY?!
HULK IS HERE AS NAMOR'S FRIEND.

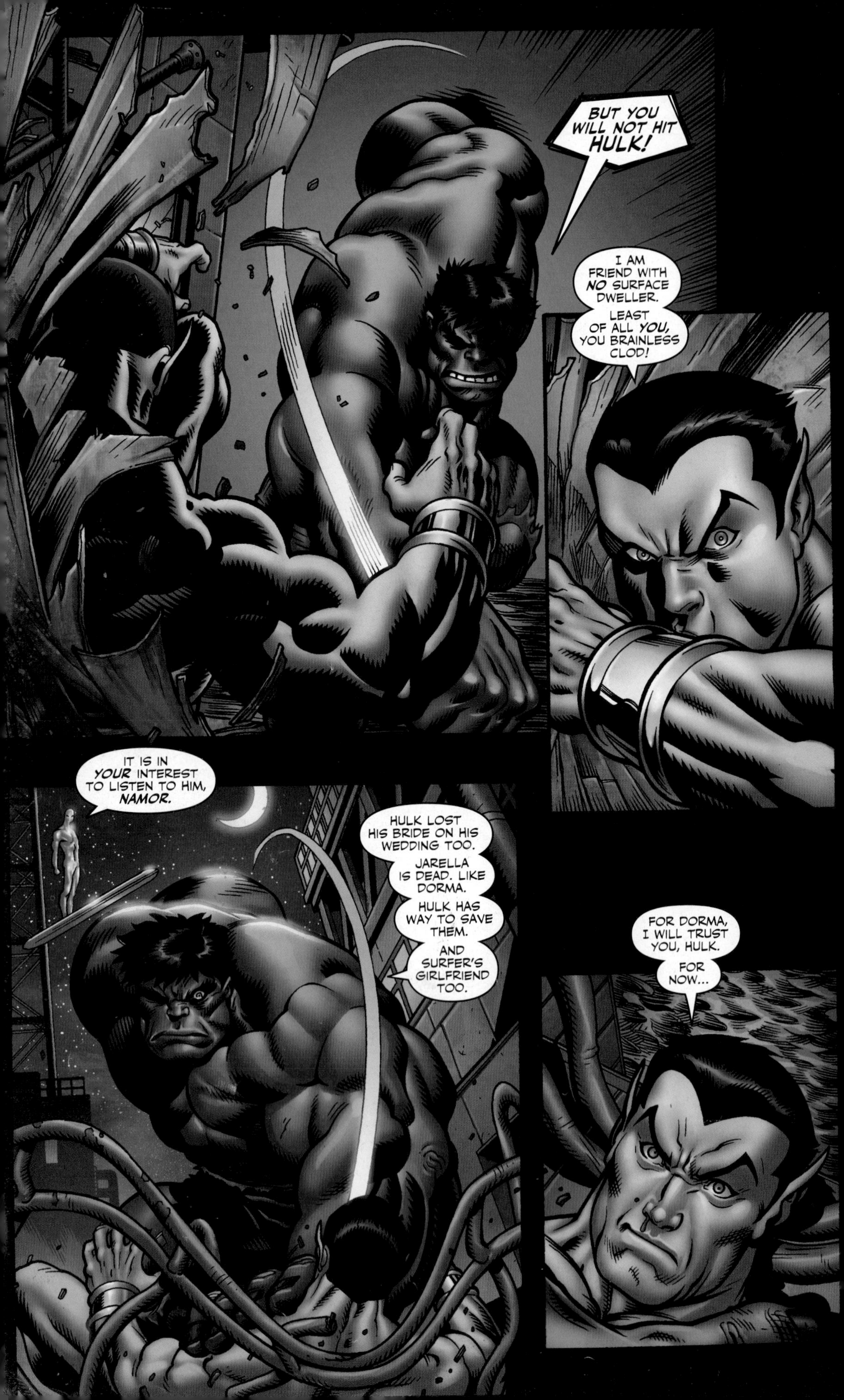
BUT YOU WILL NOT HIT HULK!
I AM FRIEND WITH NO SURFACE DWELLER.
LEAST OF ALL YOU, YOU BRAINLESS CLOD!
IT IS IN YOUR INTEREST TO LISTEN TO HIM, NAMOR.
HULK LOST HIS BRIDE ON HIS WEDDING TOO.
JARELLA IS DEAD. LIKE DORMA.
HULK HAS WAY TO SAVE THEM.
AND SURFER'S GIRLFRIEND TOO.
FOR DORMA, I WILL TRUST YOU, HULK.
FOR NOW...

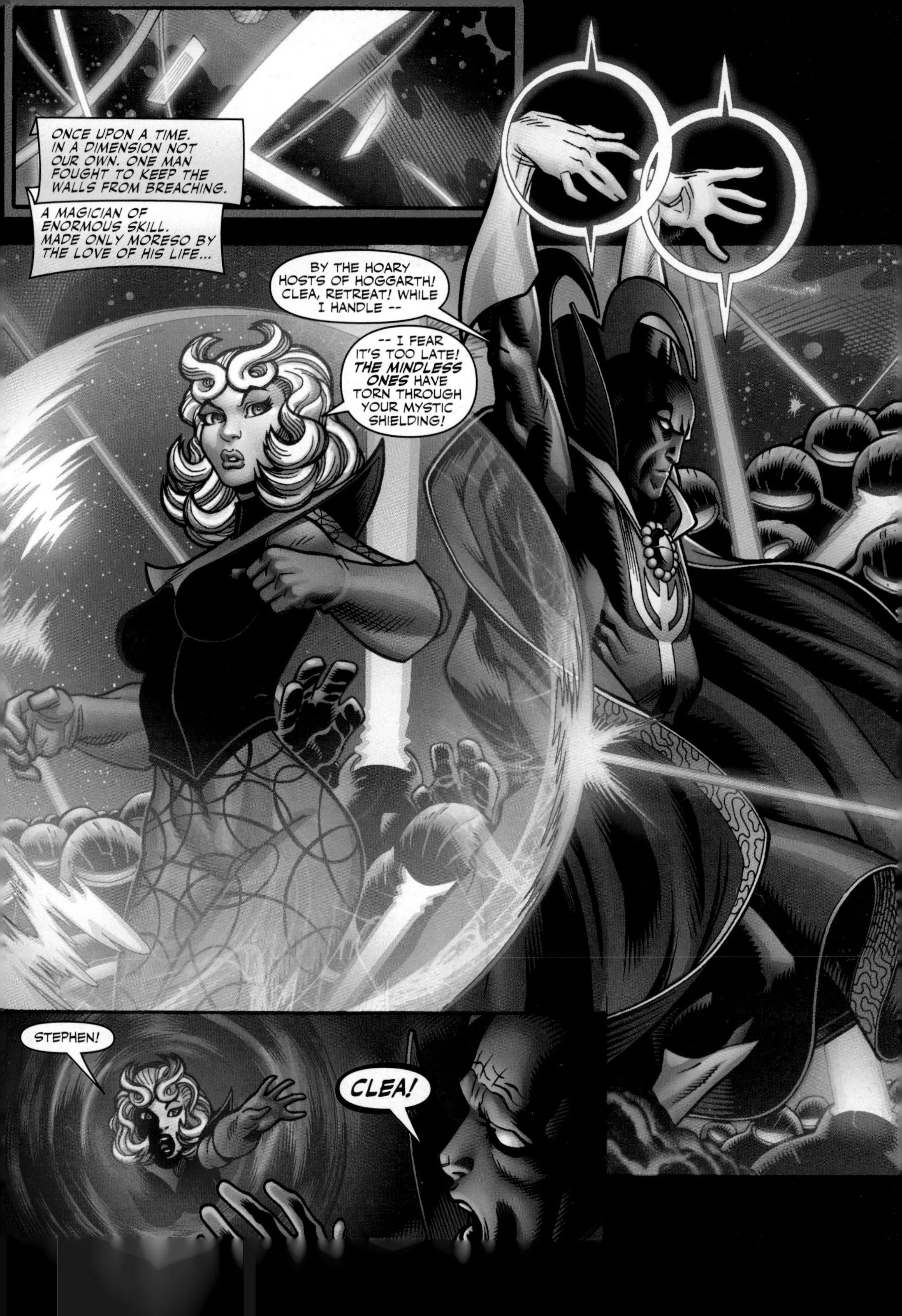
ONCE UPON A TIME. IN A DIMENSION NOT OUR OWN. ONE MAN FOUGHT TO KEEP THE WALLS FROM BREACHING.
A MAGICIAN OF ENORMOUS SKILL. MADE ONLY MORESO BY THE LOVE OF HIS LIFE...
BY THE HOARY HOSTS OF HOGGARTH! CLEA, RETREAT! WHILE I HANDLE --
-- I FEAR IT'S TOO LATE! THE MINDLESS ONES HAVE TORN THROUGH YOUR MYSTIC SHIELDING!
STEPHEN!
CLEA!

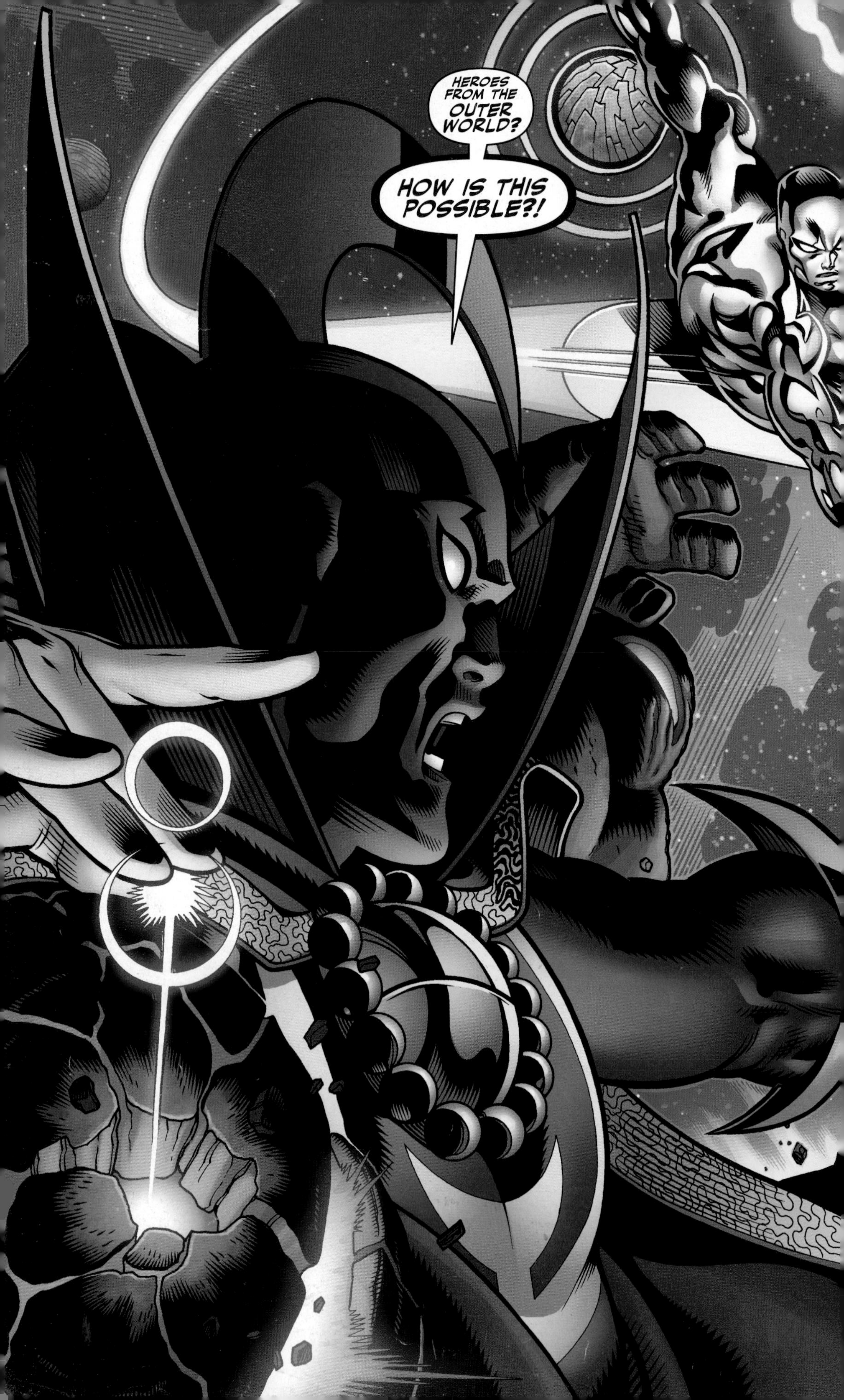
HEROES FROM THE OUTER WORLD?
HOW IS THIS POSSIBLE?!

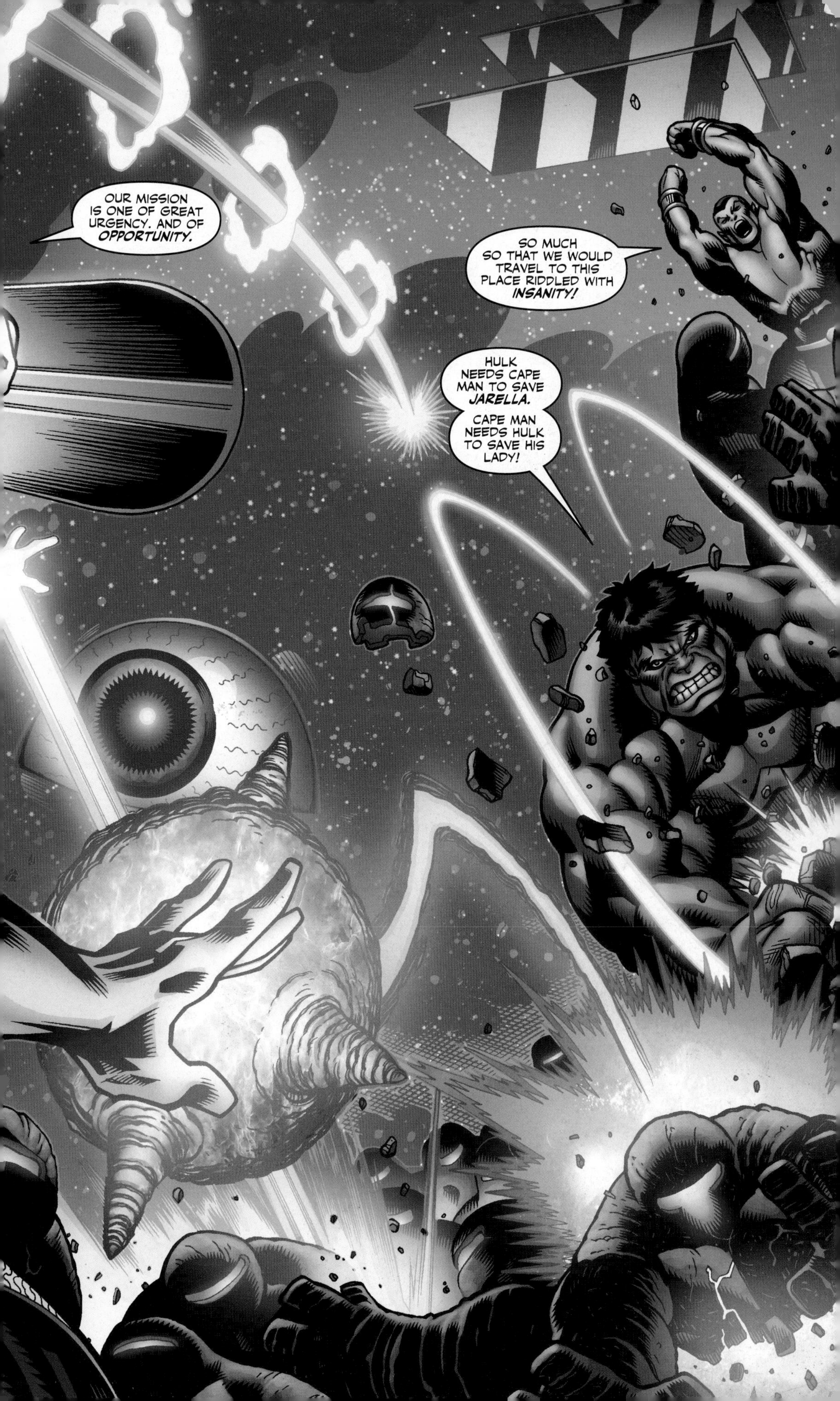
OUR MISSION IS ONE OF GREAT URGENCY. AND OF *OPPORTUNITY.*
SO MUCH SO THAT WE WOULD TRAVEL TO THIS PLACE RIDDLED WITH ***INSANITY!***
HULK NEEDS CAPE MAN TO SAVE ***JARELLA.***
CAPE MAN NEEDS HULK TO SAVE HIS LADY!

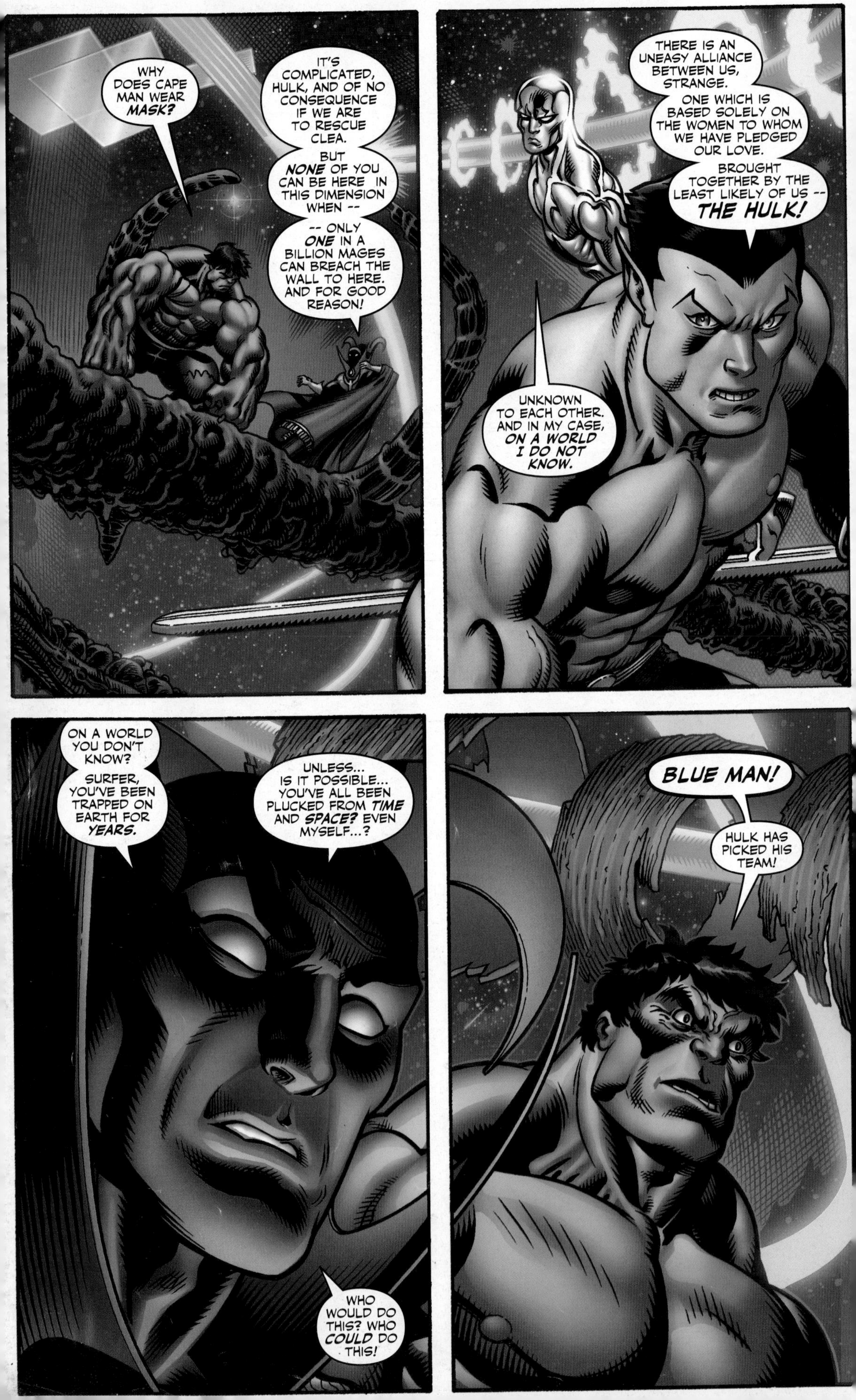

WHY DOES CAPE MAN WEAR MASK?
IT'S COMPLICATED, HULK, AND OF NO CONSEQUENCE IF WE ARE TO RESCUE CLEA.
BUT NONE OF YOU CAN BE HERE IN THIS DIMENSION WHEN --
-- ONLY ONE IN A BILLION MAGES CAN BREACH THE WALL TO HERE. AND FOR GOOD REASON!
THERE IS AN UNEASY ALLIANCE BETWEEN US, STRANGE.
ONE WHICH IS BASED SOLELY ON THE WOMEN TO WHOM WE HAVE PLEDGED OUR LOVE.
BROUGHT TOGETHER BY THE LEAST LIKELY OF US -- THE HULK!
UNKNOWN TO EACH OTHER. AND IN MY CASE, ON A WORLD I DO NOT KNOW.
ON A WORLD YOU DON'T KNOW?
SURFER, YOU'VE BEEN TRAPPED ON EARTH FOR YEARS.
UNLESS... IS IT POSSIBLE... YOU'VE ALL BEEN PLUCKED FROM TIME AND SPACE? EVEN MYSELF...?
WHO WOULD DO THIS? WHO COULD DO THIS!
BLUE MAN!
HULK HAS PICKED HIS TEAM!

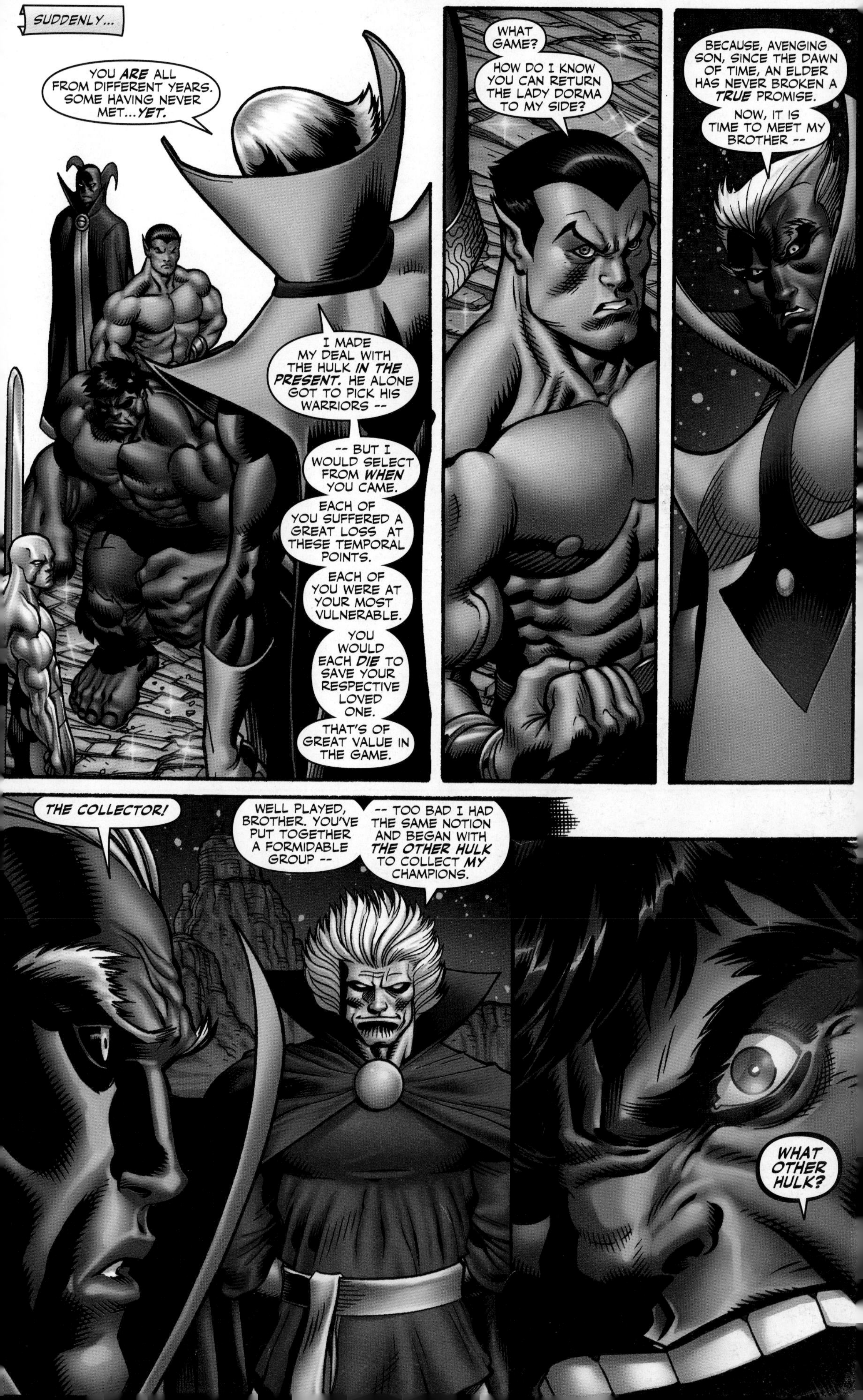
SUDDENLY...
YOU ARE ALL FROM DIFFERENT YEARS. SOME HAVING NEVER MET...YET.
I MADE MY DEAL WITH THE HULK IN THE PRESENT. HE ALONE GOT TO PICK HIS WARRIORS --
-- BUT I WOULD SELECT FROM WHEN YOU CAME.
EACH OF YOU SUFFERED A GREAT LOSS AT THESE TEMPORAL POINTS.
EACH OF YOU WERE AT YOUR MOST VULNERABLE.
YOU WOULD EACH DIE TO SAVE YOUR RESPECTIVE LOVED ONE.
THAT'S OF GREAT VALUE IN THE GAME.
WHAT GAME?
HOW DO I KNOW YOU CAN RETURN THE LADY DORMA TO MY SIDE?
BECAUSE, AVENGING SON, SINCE THE DAWN OF TIME, AN ELDER HAS NEVER BROKEN A TRUE PROMISE.
NOW, IT IS TIME TO MEET MY BROTHER --
THE COLLECTOR!
WELL PLAYED, BROTHER. YOU'VE PUT TOGETHER A FORMIDABLE GROUP --
-- TOO BAD I HAD THE SAME NOTION AND BEGAN WITH THE OTHER HULK TO COLLECT MY CHAMPIONS.
WHAT OTHER HULK?

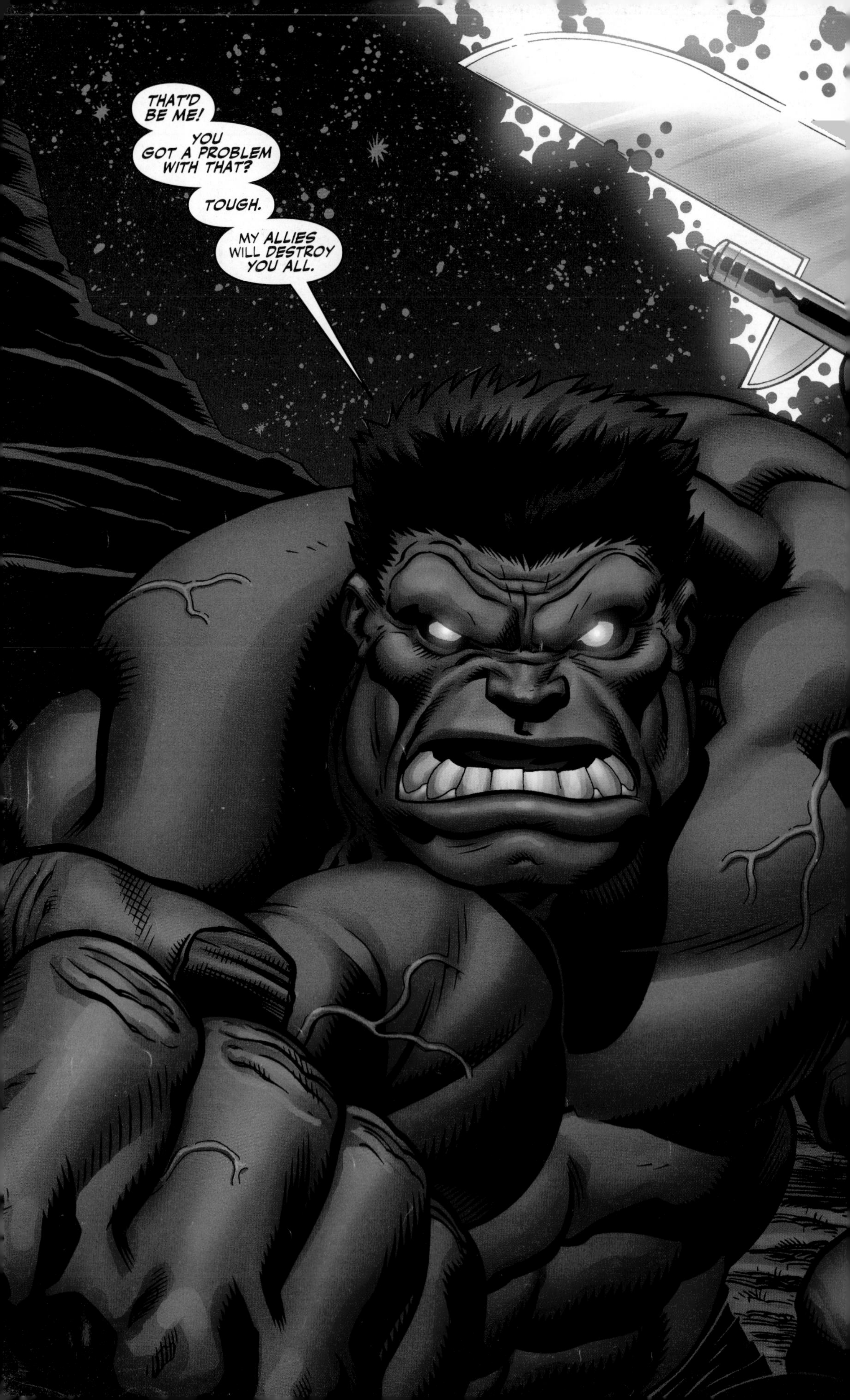
THAT'D BE ME!
YOU GOT A PROBLEM WITH THAT?
TOUGH.
MY ALLIES WILL DESTROY YOU ALL.

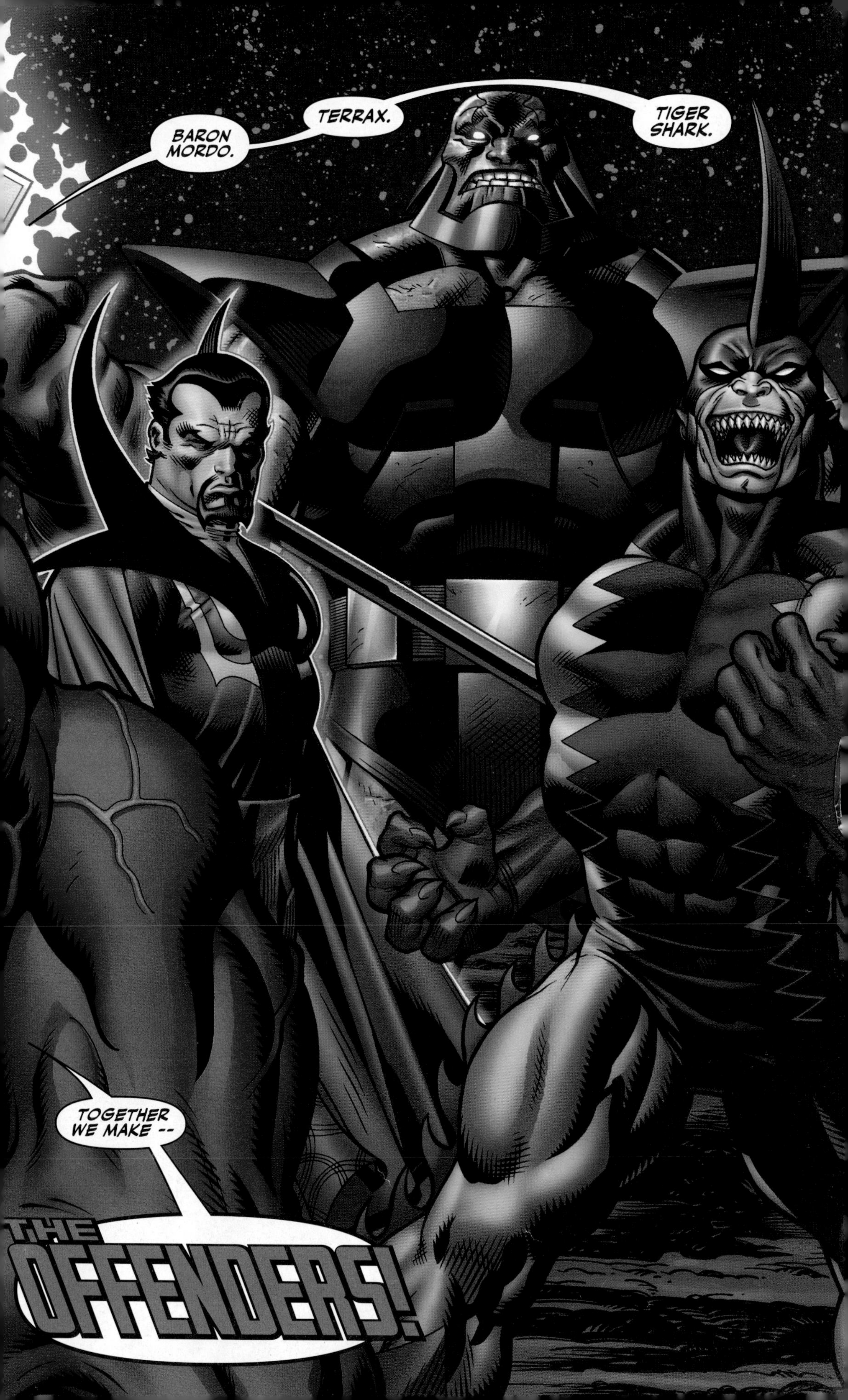
BARON MORDO.
TERRAX.
TIGER SHARK.
TOGETHER WE MAKE --
THE OFFENDERS!

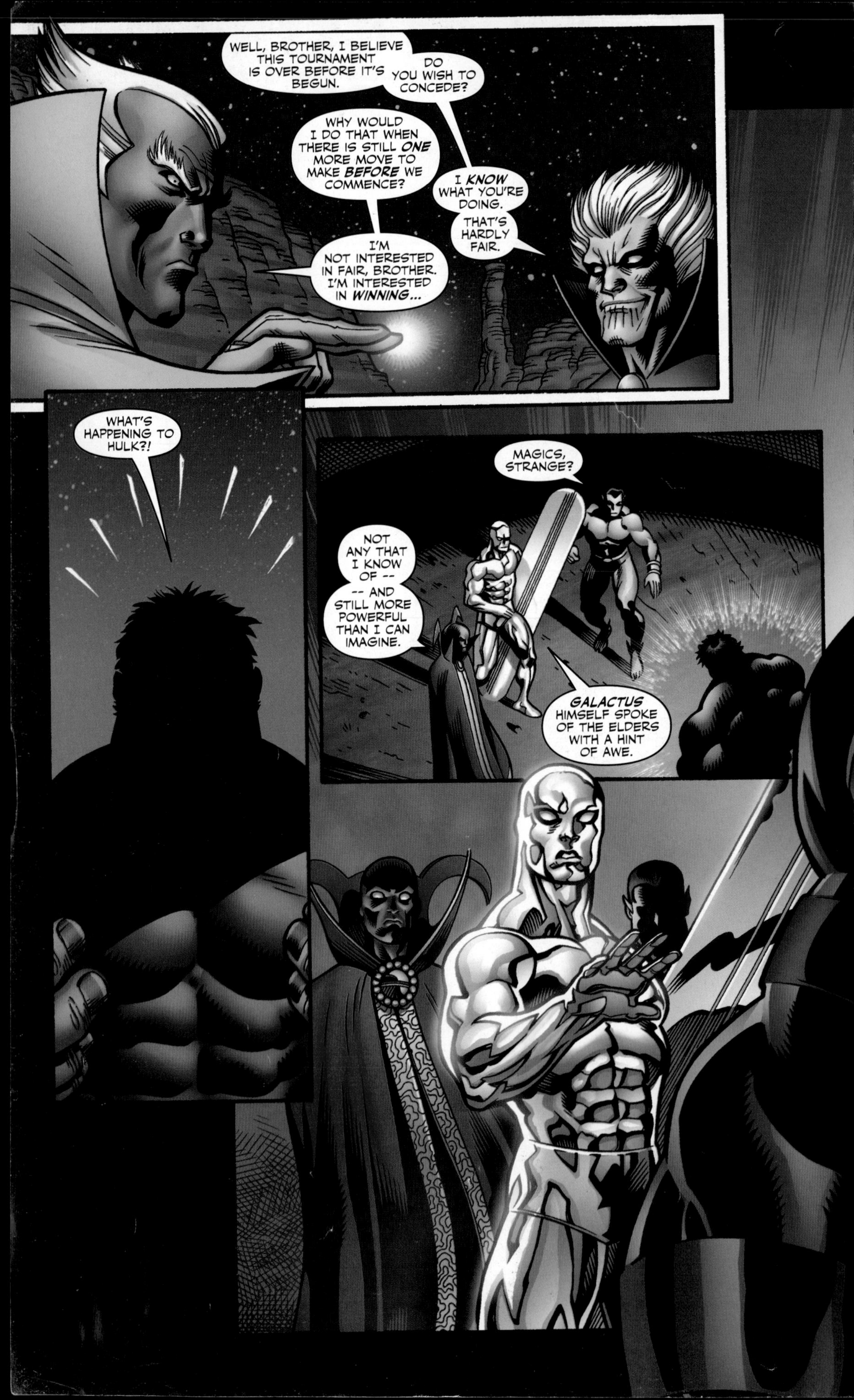

WELL, BROTHER, I BELIEVE THIS TOURNAMENT IS OVER BEFORE IT'S BEGUN.
DO YOU WISH TO CONCEDE?
WHY WOULD I DO THAT WHEN THERE IS STILL ONE MORE MOVE TO MAKE BEFORE WE COMMENCE?
I KNOW WHAT YOU'RE DOING.
THAT'S HARDLY FAIR.
I'M NOT INTERESTED IN FAIR, BROTHER. I'M INTERESTED IN WINNING...
WHAT'S HAPPENING TO HULK?!
MAGICS, STRANGE?
NOT ANY THAT I KNOW OF --
-- AND STILL MORE POWERFUL THAN I CAN IMAGINE.
GALACTUS HIMSELF SPOKE OF THE ELDERS WITH A HINT OF AWE.

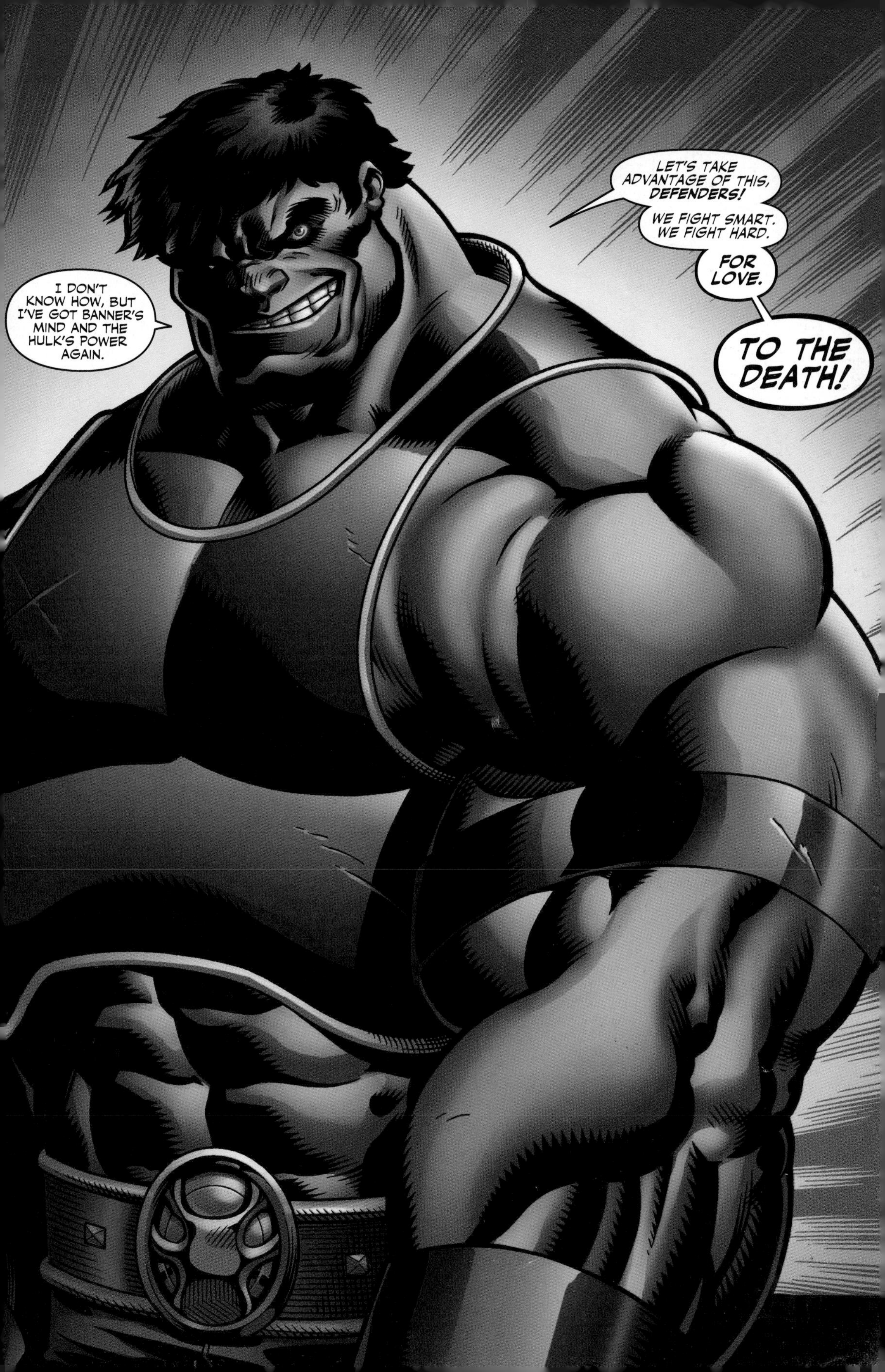
I DON'T KNOW HOW, BUT I'VE GOT BANNER'S MIND AND THE HULK'S POWER AGAIN.
LET'S TAKE ADVANTAGE OF THIS, DEFENDERS!
WE FIGHT SMART. WE FIGHT HARD.
FOR LOVE.
TO THE DEATH!

ROUND ★ TWO

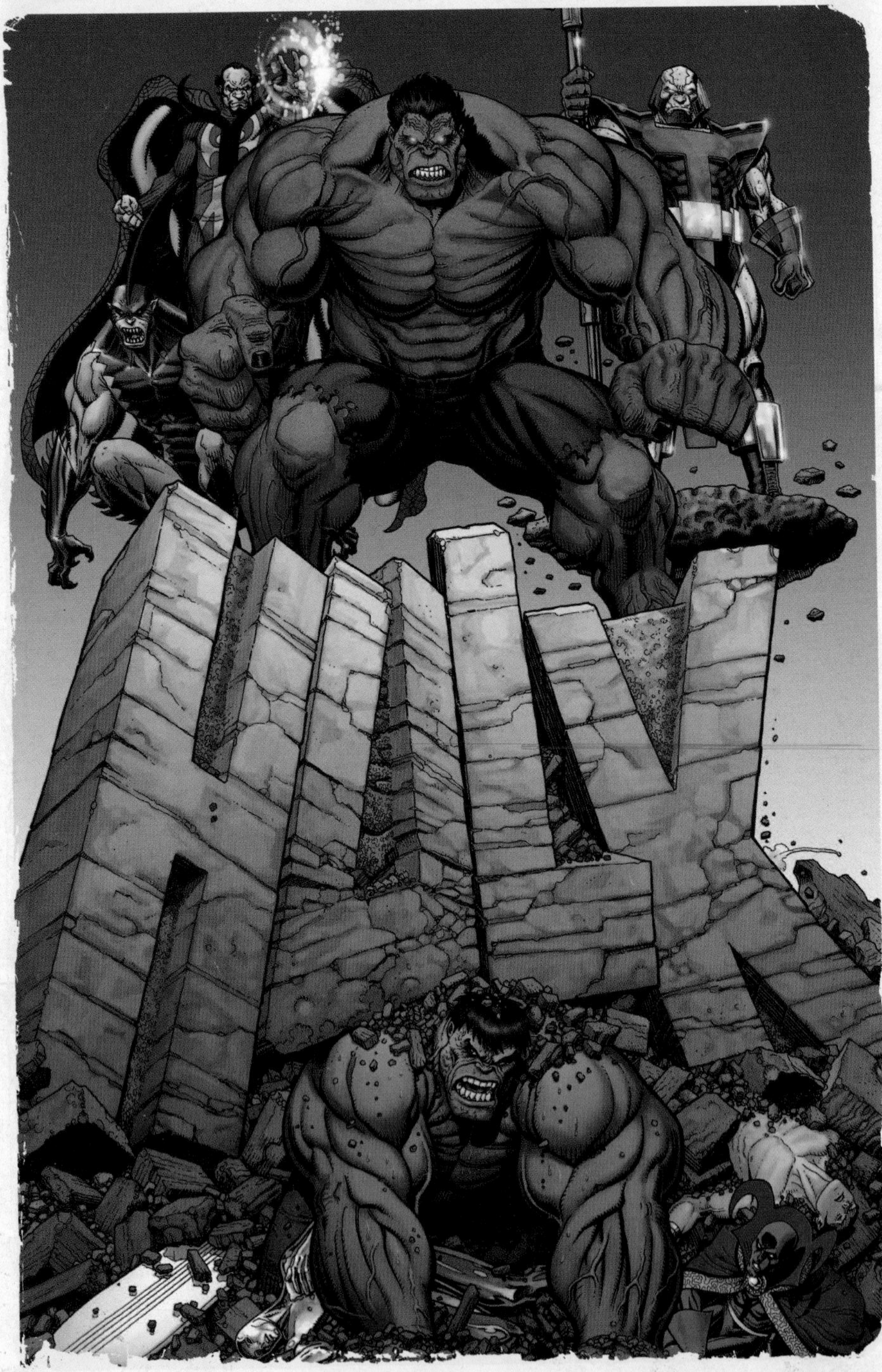

TRAPPED IN A WORLD THEY NEVER MADE

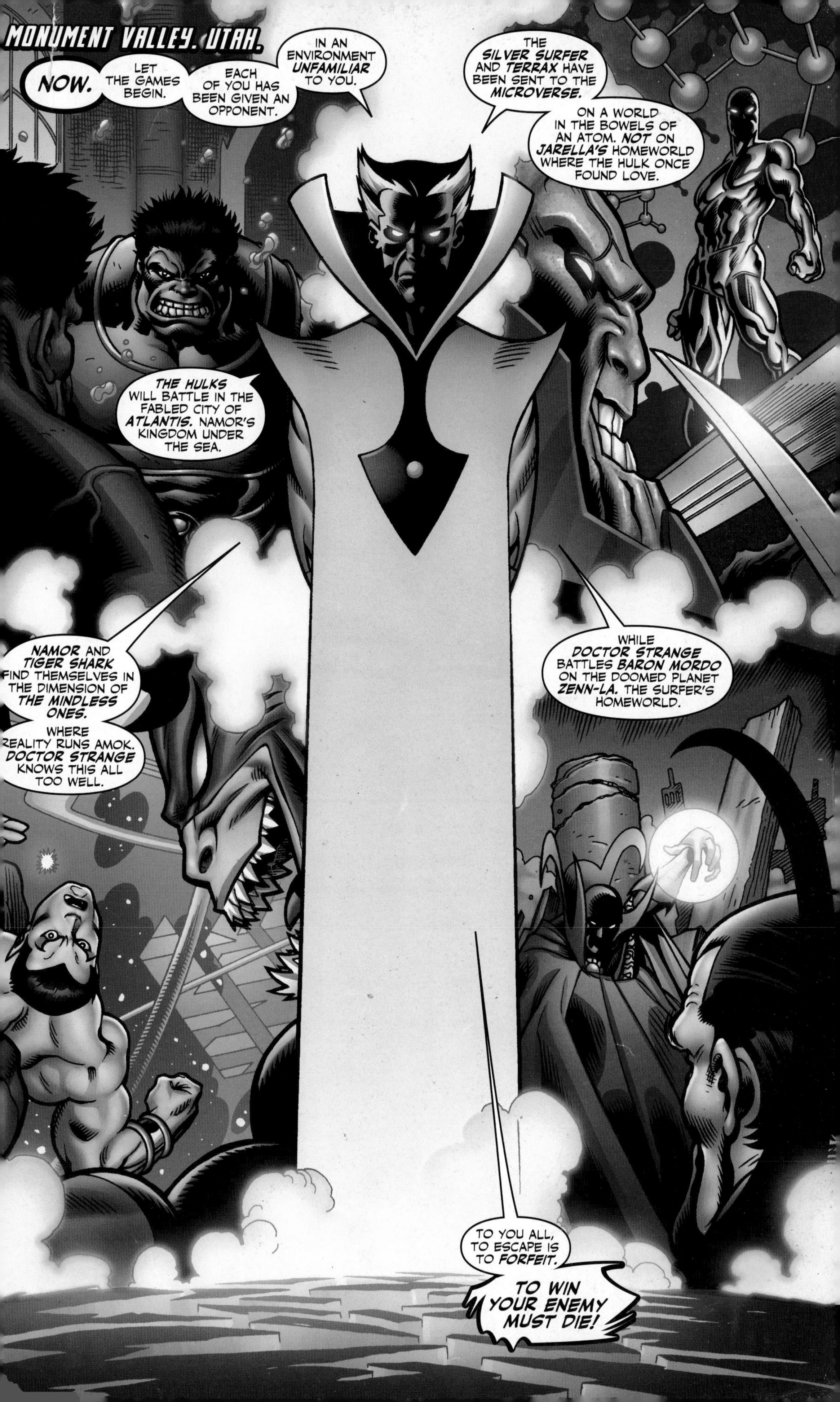
MONUMENT VALLEY. UTAH.
NOW.
LET THE GAMES BEGIN.
EACH OF YOU HAS BEEN GIVEN AN OPPONENT.
IN AN ENVIRONMENT UNFAMILIAR TO YOU.
THE SILVER SURFER AND TERRAX HAVE BEEN SENT TO THE MICROVERSE.
ON A WORLD IN THE BOWELS OF AN ATOM. NOT ON JARELLA'S HOMEWORLD WHERE THE HULK ONCE FOUND LOVE.
THE HULKS WILL BATTLE IN THE FABLED CITY OF ATLANTIS. NAMOR'S KINGDOM UNDER THE SEA.
NAMOR AND TIGER SHARK FIND THEMSELVES IN THE DIMENSION OF THE MINDLESS ONES.
WHERE REALITY RUNS AMOK. DOCTOR STRANGE KNOWS THIS ALL TOO WELL.
WHILE DOCTOR STRANGE BATTLES BARON MORDO ON THE DOOMED PLANET ZENN-LA. THE SURFER'S HOMEWORLD.
TO YOU ALL, TO ESCAPE IS TO FORFEIT.
TO WIN YOUR ENEMY MUST DIE!

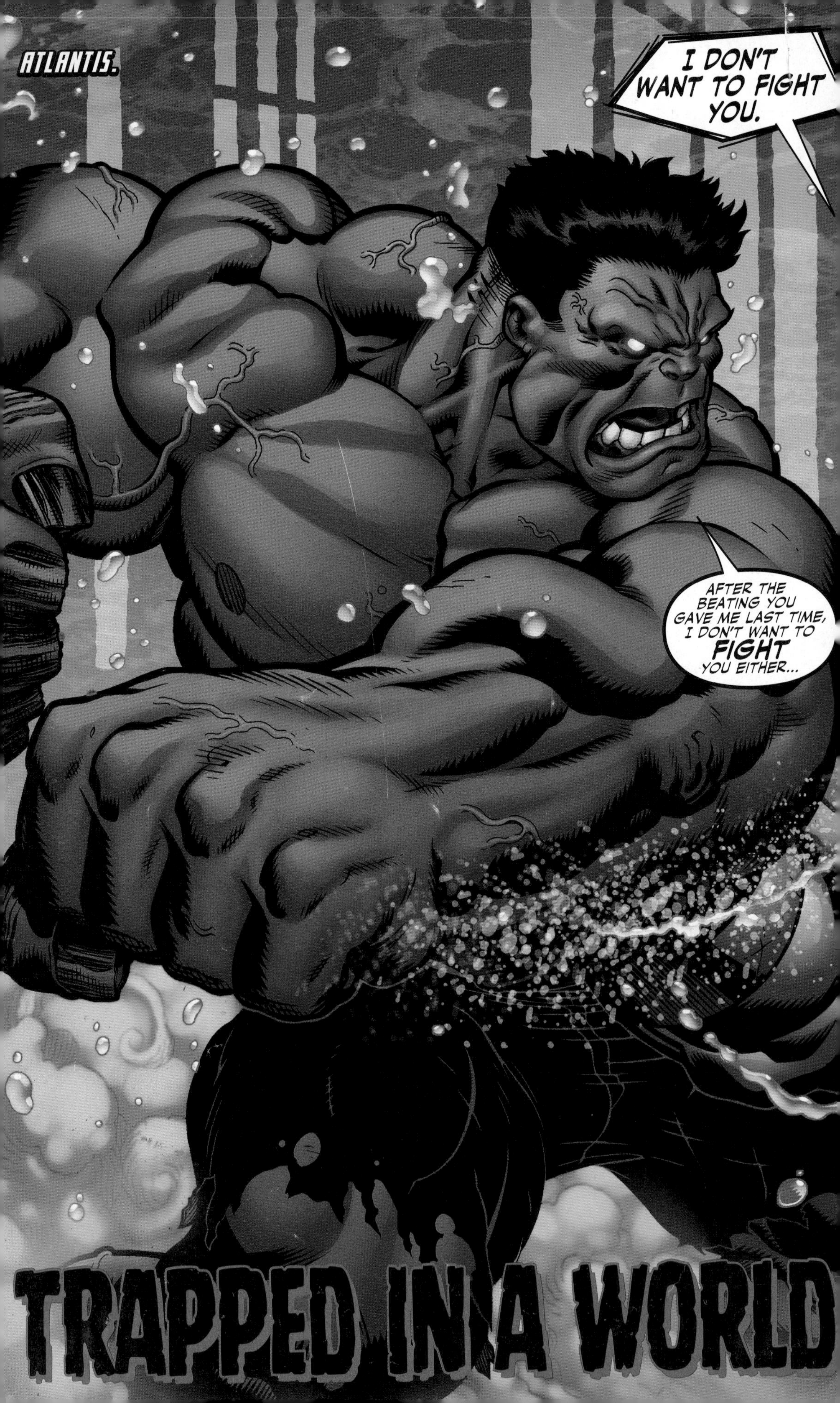

ATLANTIS.
I DON'T WANT TO FIGHT YOU.
AFTER THE BEATING YOU GAVE ME LAST TIME, I DON'T WANT TO FIGHT YOU EITHER...
TRAPPED IN A WORLD

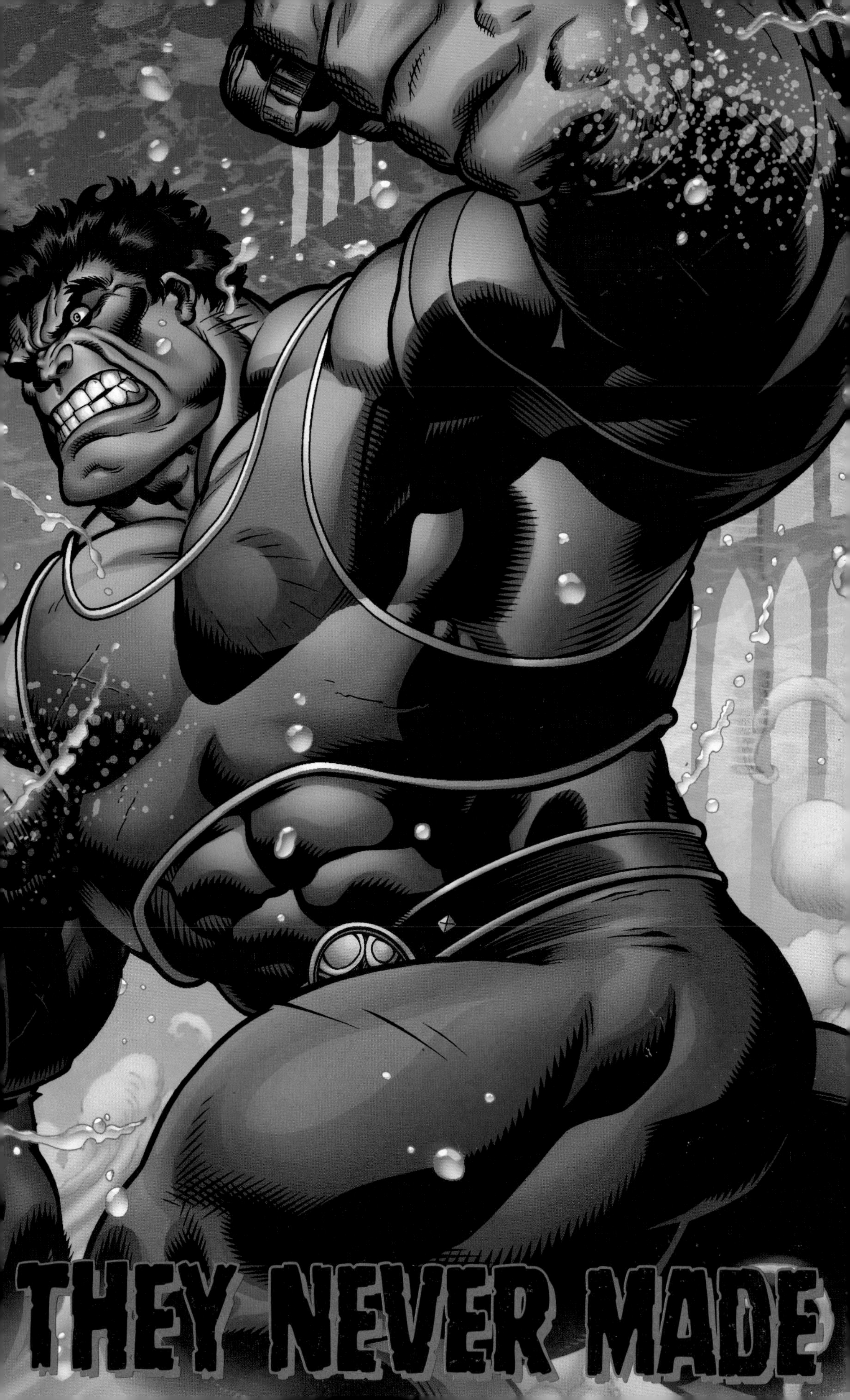
THEY NEVER MADE

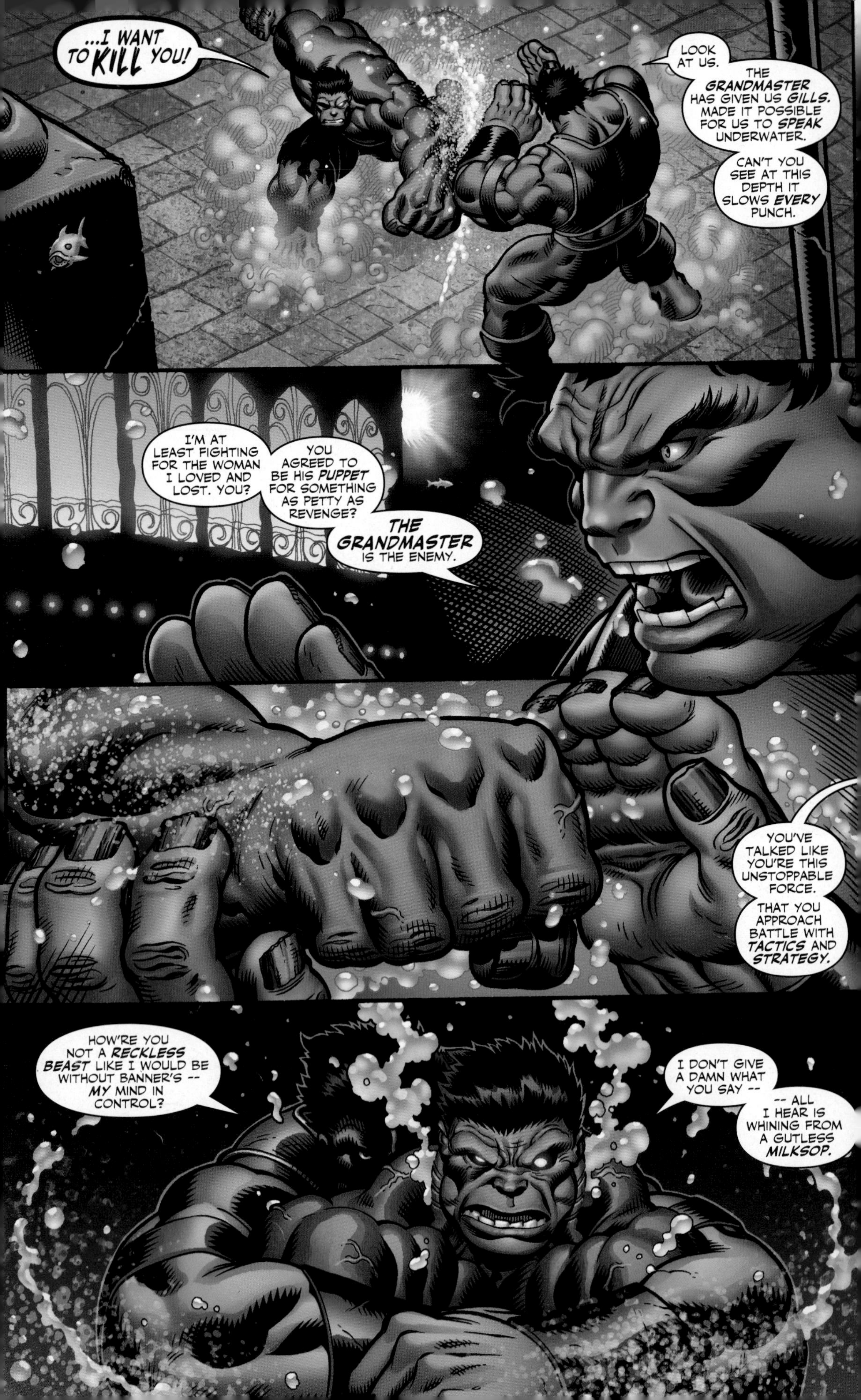
...I WANT TO KILL YOU!
LOOK AT US.
THE GRANDMASTER HAS GIVEN US GILLS. MADE IT POSSIBLE FOR US TO SPEAK UNDERWATER.
CAN'T YOU SEE AT THIS DEPTH IT SLOWS EVERY PUNCH.
I'M AT LEAST FIGHTING FOR THE WOMAN I LOVED AND LOST. YOU?
YOU AGREED TO BE HIS PUPPET FOR SOMETHING AS PETTY AS REVENGE?
THE GRANDMASTER IS THE ENEMY.
YOU'VE TALKED LIKE YOU'RE THIS UNSTOPPABLE FORCE.
THAT YOU APPROACH BATTLE WITH TACTICS AND STRATEGY.
HOW'RE YOU NOT A RECKLESS BEAST LIKE I WOULD BE WITHOUT BANNER'S -- MY MIND IN CONTROL?
I DON'T GIVE A DAMN WHAT YOU SAY --
-- ALL I HEAR IS WHINING FROM A GUTLESS MILKSOP.

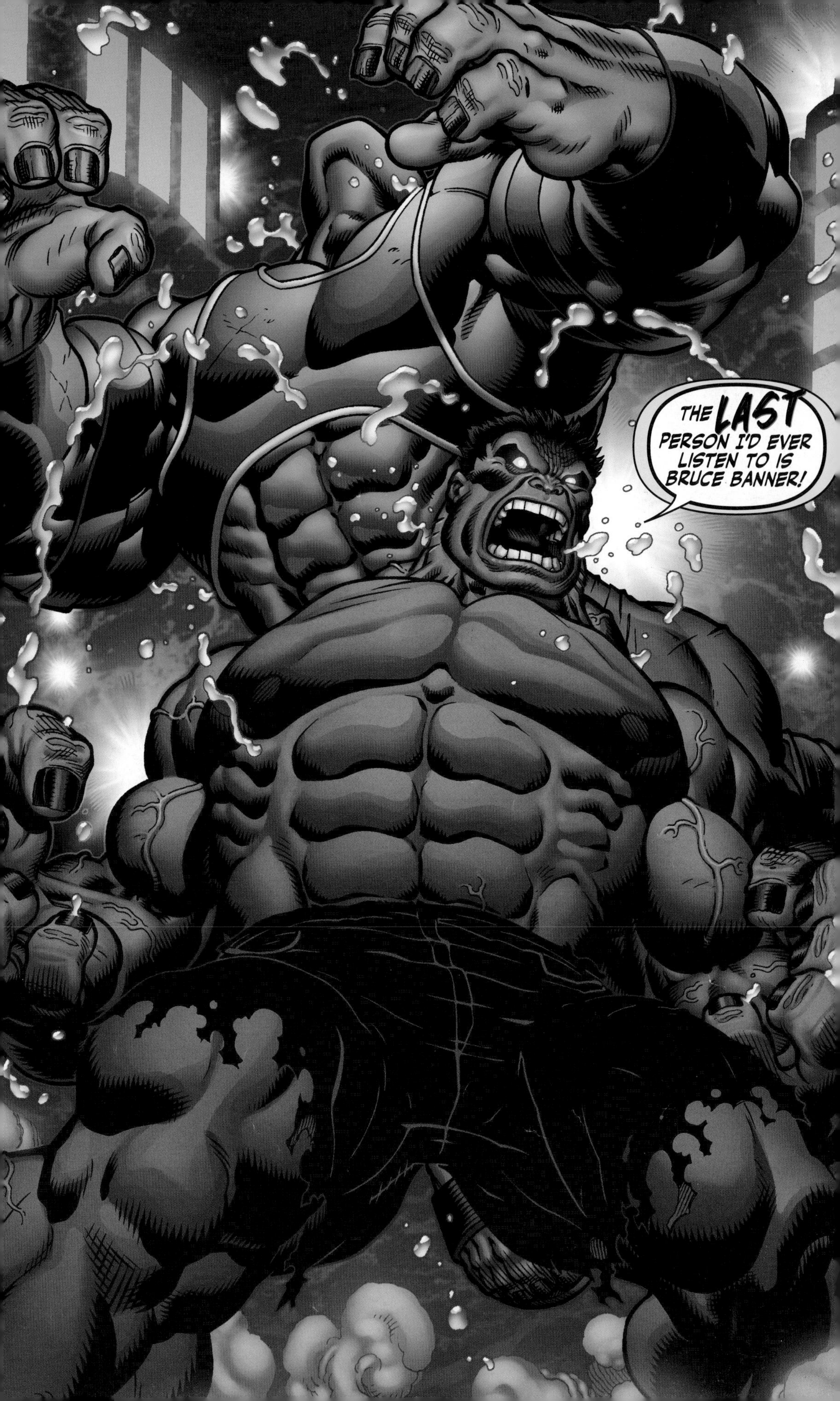
THE LAST PERSON I'D EVER LISTEN TO IS BRUCE BANNER!

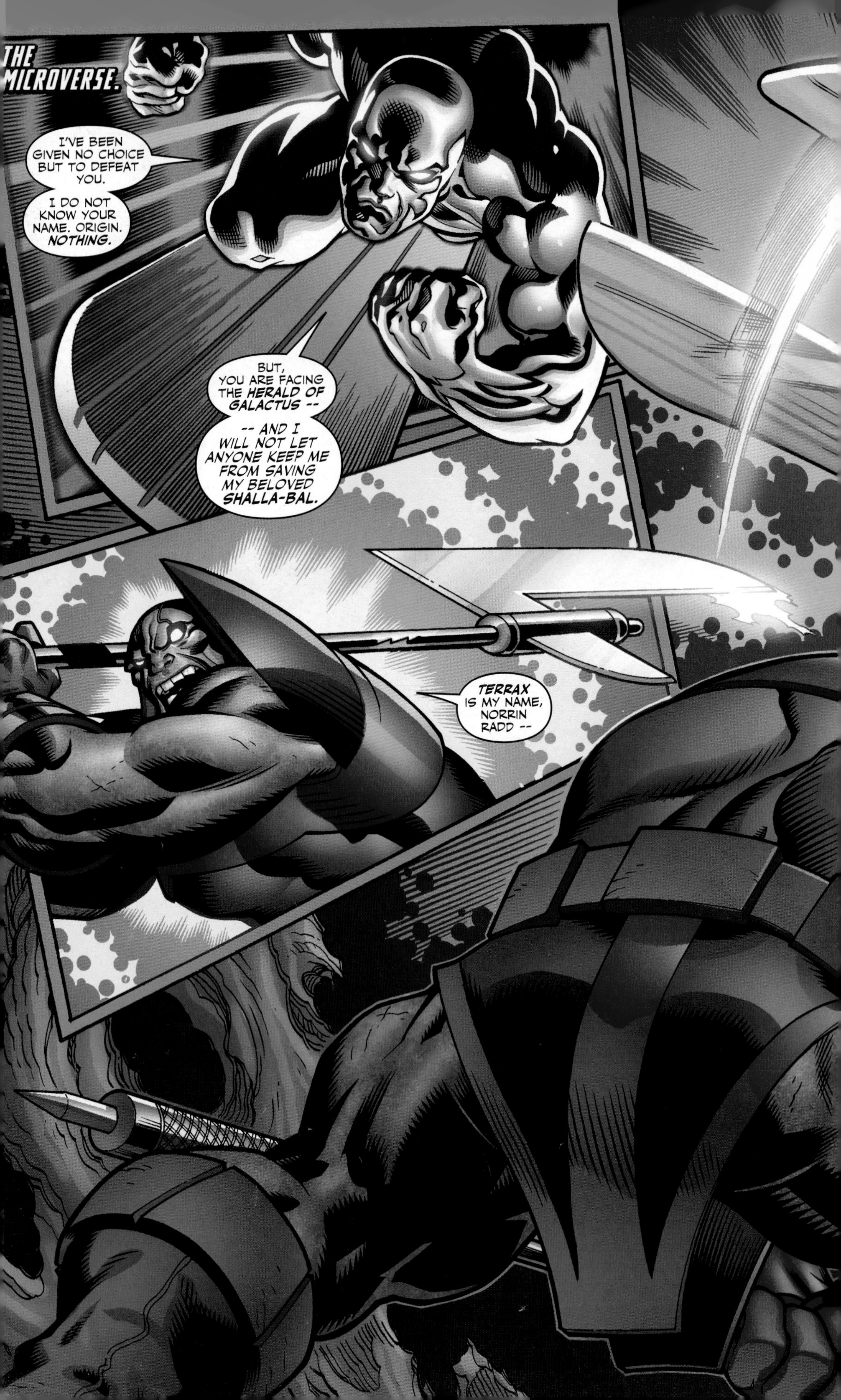
THE MICROVERSE.
I'VE BEEN GIVEN NO CHOICE BUT TO DEFEAT YOU.
I DO NOT KNOW YOUR NAME. ORIGIN. *NOTHING.*
BUT, YOU ARE FACING THE *HERALD OF GALACTUS* --
-- AND I WILL NOT LET ANYONE KEEP ME FROM SAVING MY BELOVED *SHALLA-BAL.*
TERRAX IS MY NAME, NORRIN RADD --

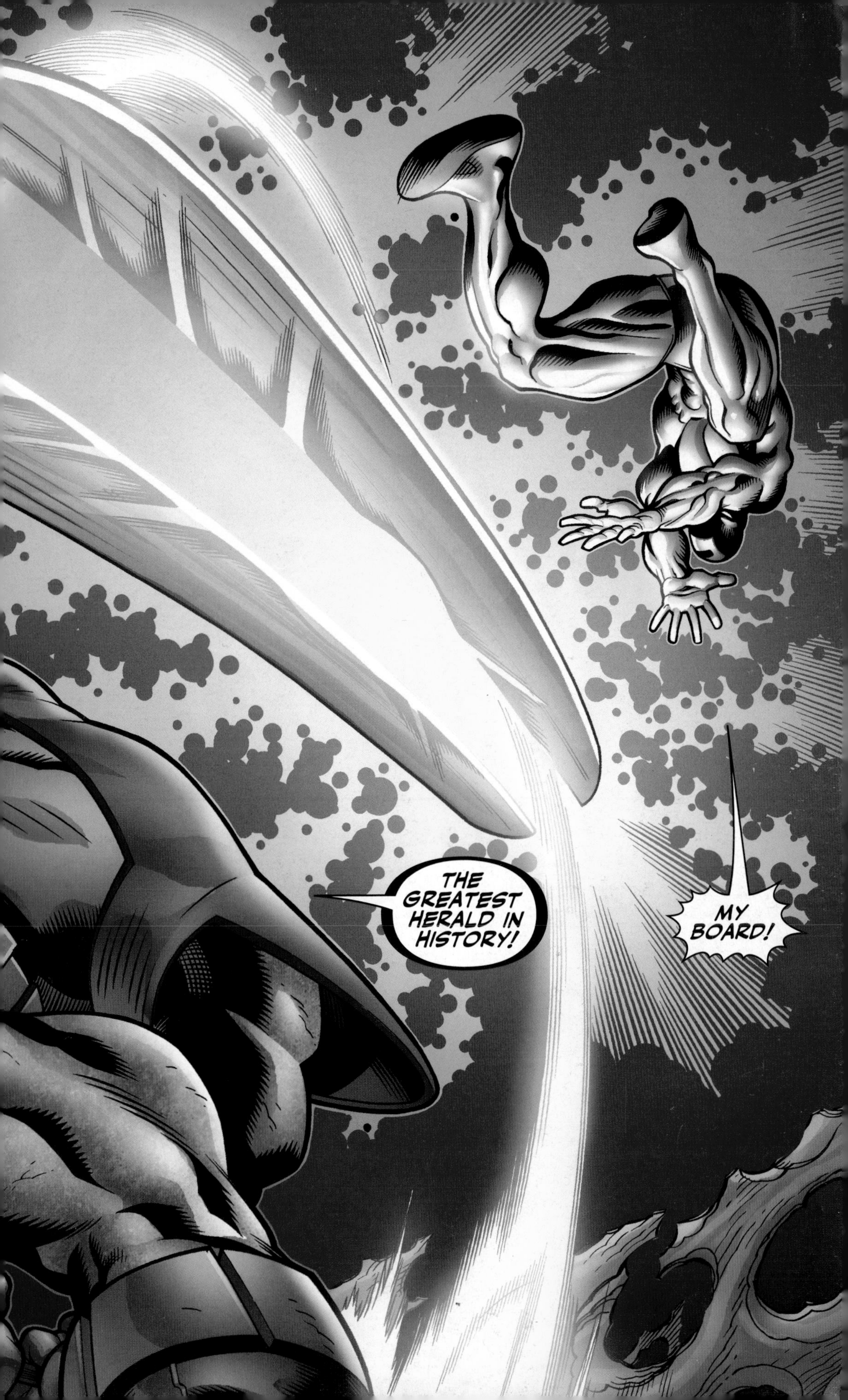
THE GREATEST HERALD IN HISTORY!
MY BOARD!

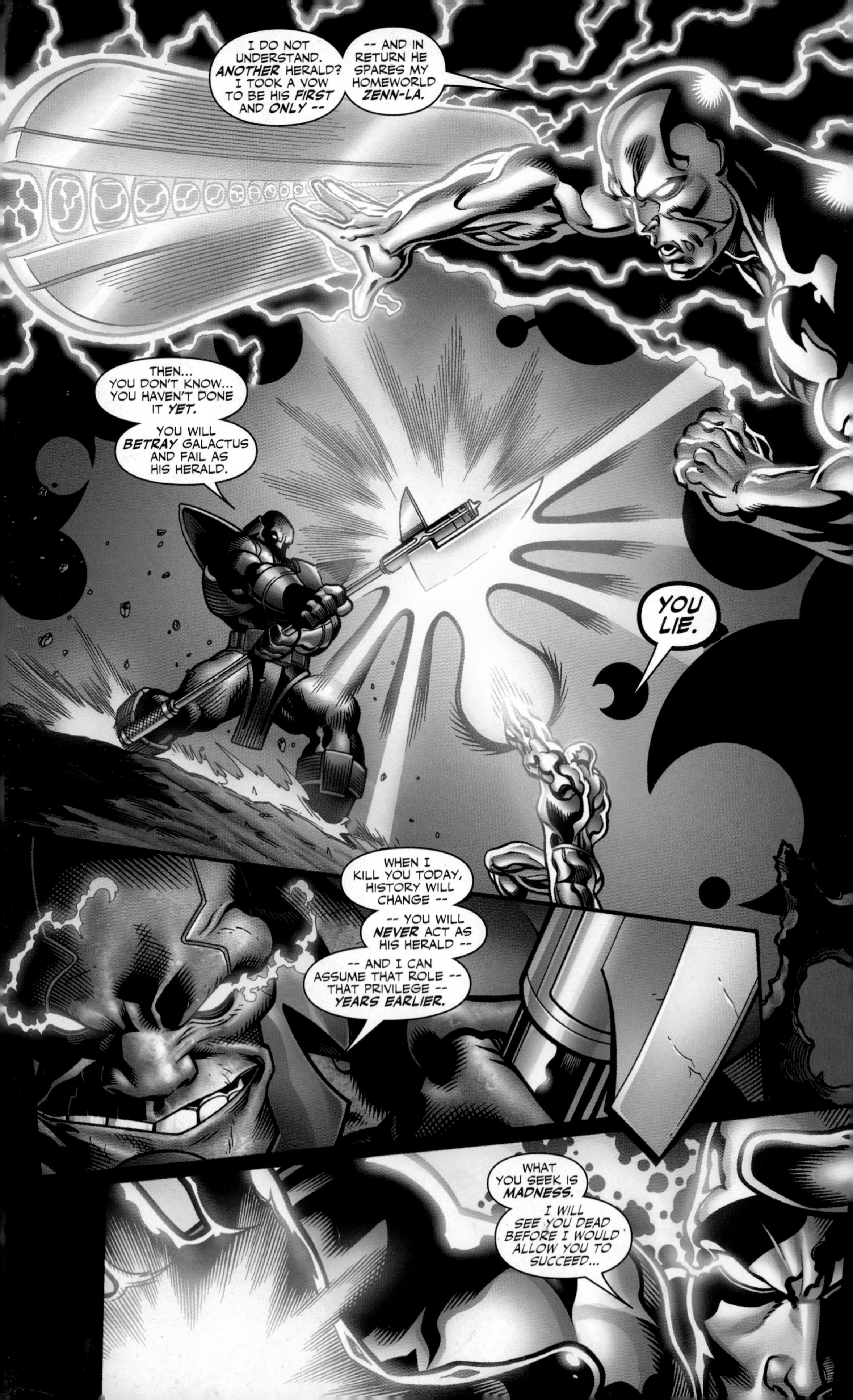

I DO NOT UNDERSTAND. ANOTHER HERALD? I TOOK A VOW TO BE HIS FIRST AND ONLY --
-- AND IN RETURN HE SPARES MY HOMEWORLD ZENN-LA.
THEN... YOU DON'T KNOW... YOU HAVEN'T DONE IT YET.
YOU WILL BETRAY GALACTUS AND FAIL AS HIS HERALD.
YOU LIE.
WHEN I KILL YOU TODAY, HISTORY WILL CHANGE --
-- YOU WILL NEVER ACT AS HIS HERALD --
-- AND I CAN ASSUME THAT ROLE -- THAT PRIVILEGE -- YEARS EARLIER.
WHAT YOU SEEK IS MADNESS.
I WILL SEE YOU DEAD BEFORE I WOULD ALLOW YOU TO SUCCEED...

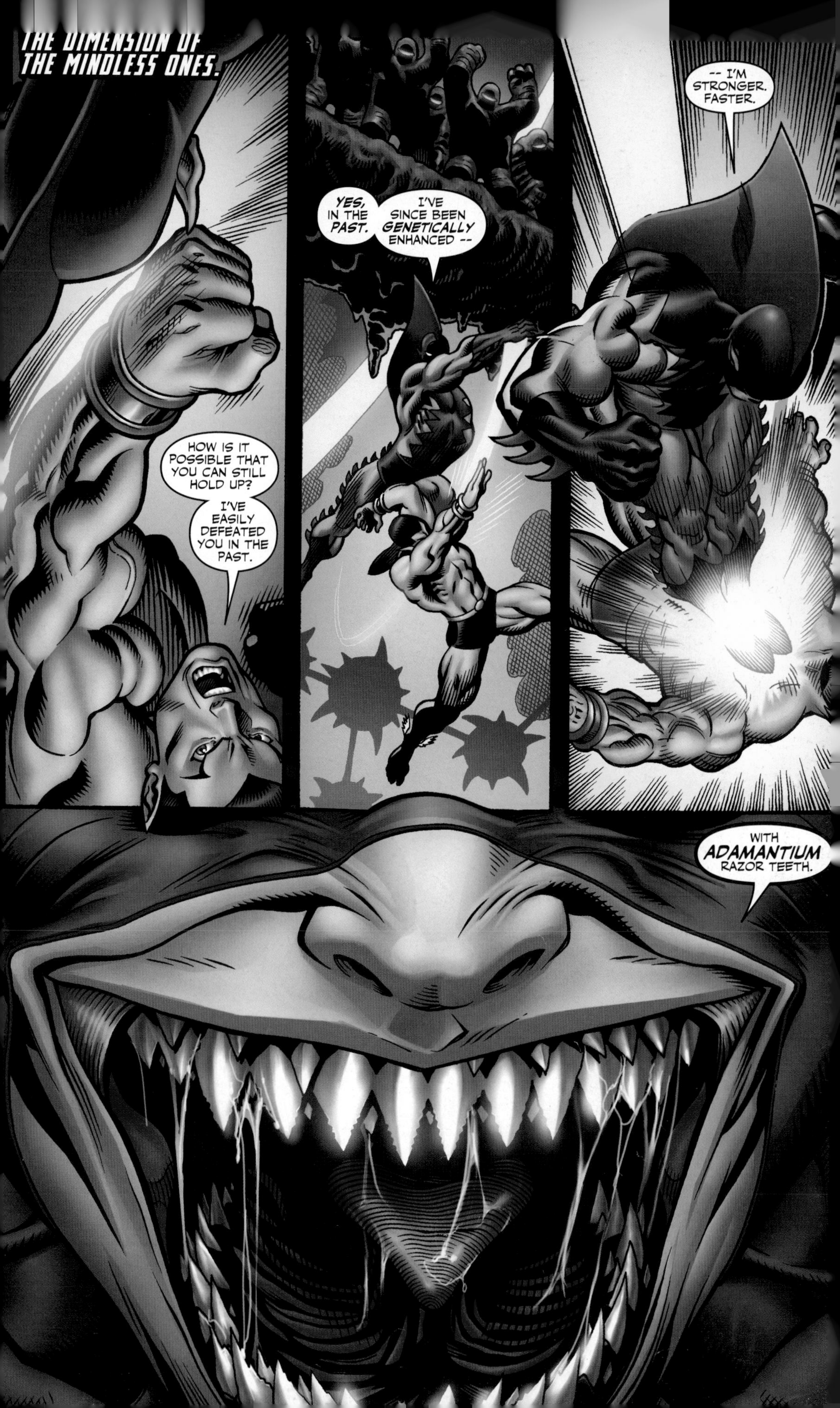
THE DIMENSION OF
THE MINDLESS ONES.
HOW IS IT POSSIBLE THAT YOU CAN STILL HOLD UP?
I'VE EASILY DEFEATED YOU IN THE PAST.
YES, IN THE PAST.
I'VE SINCE BEEN GENETICALLY ENHANCED --
-- I'M STRONGER. FASTER.
WITH ADAMANTIUM RAZOR TEETH.

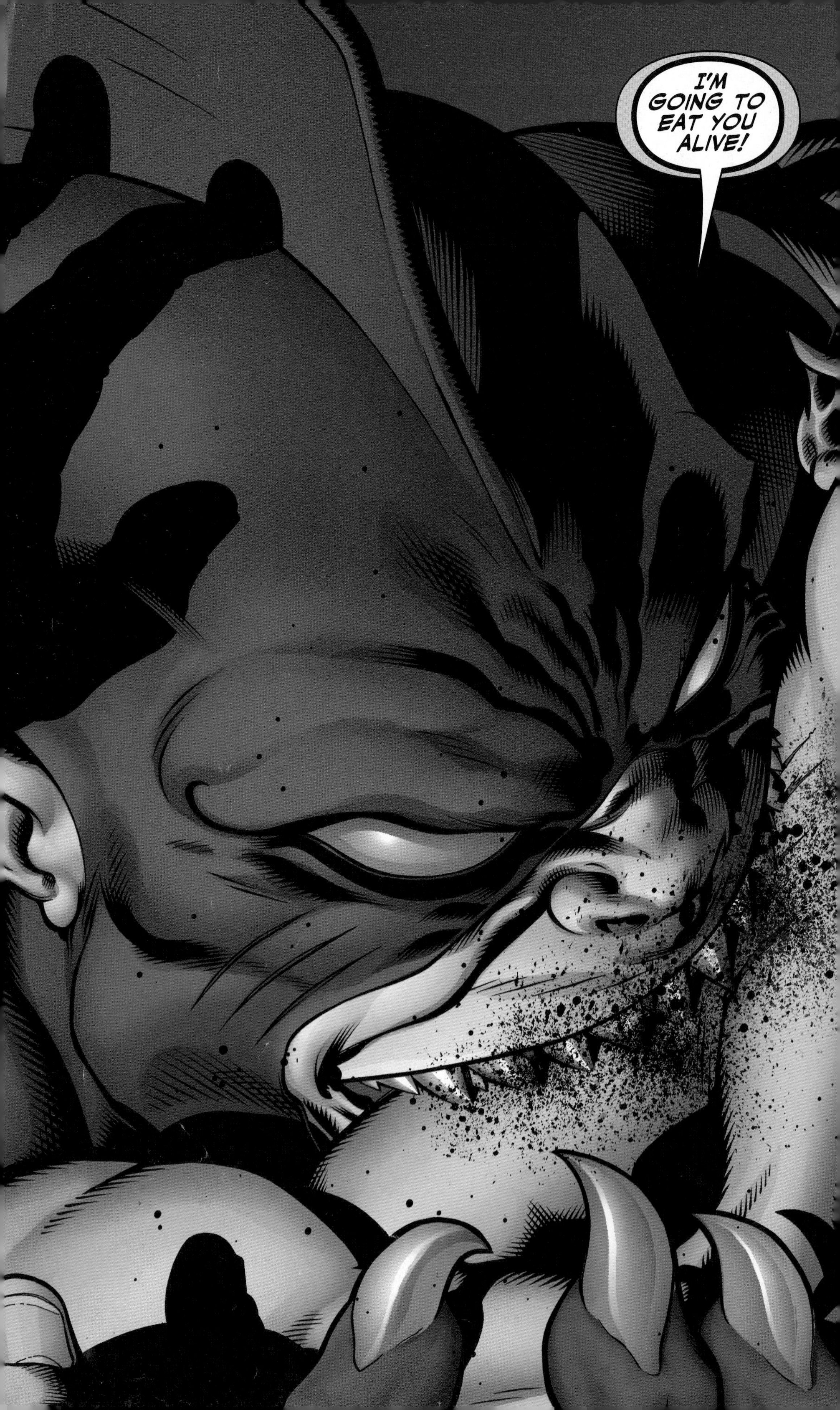
I'M GOING TO EAT YOU ALIVE!

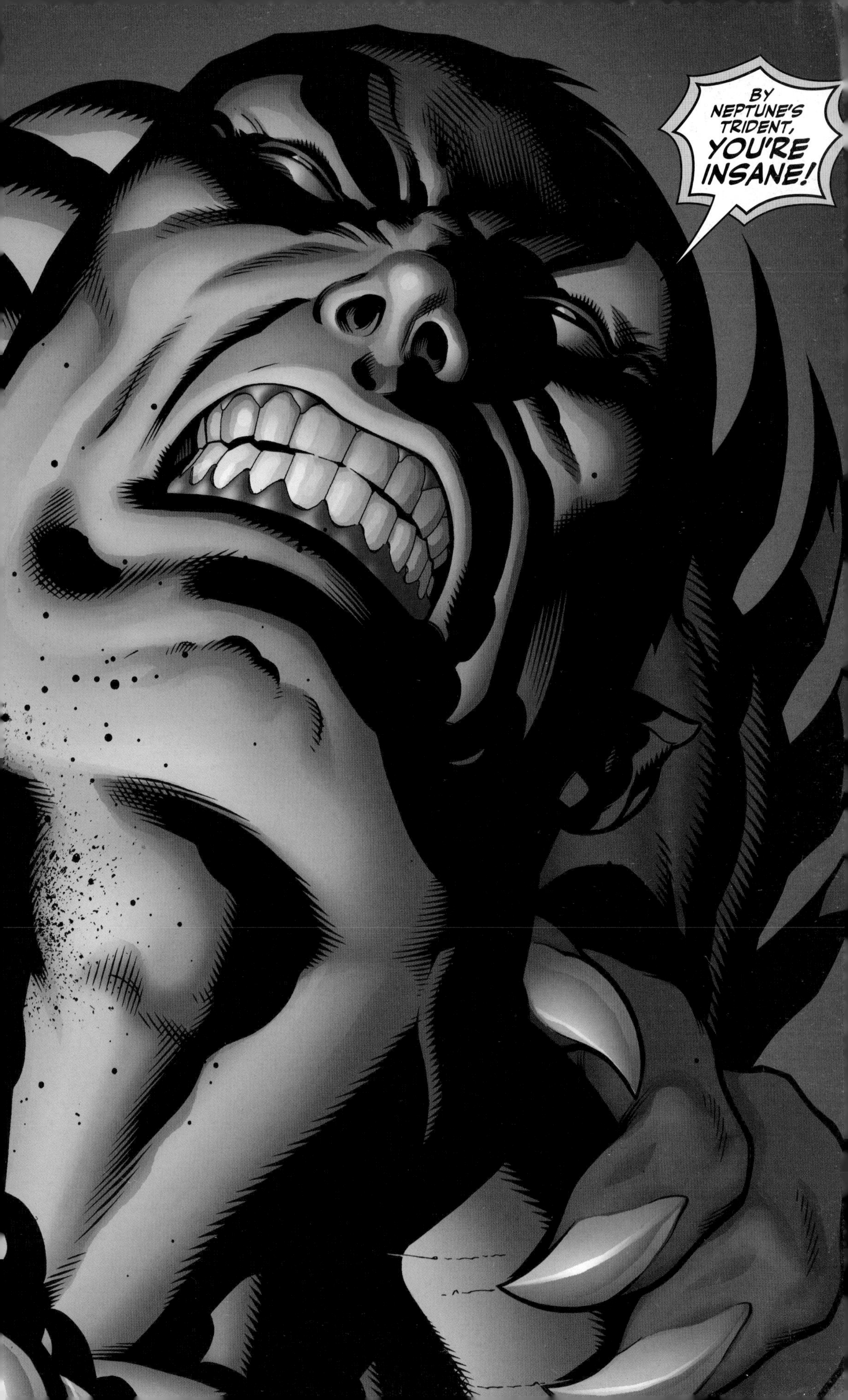
BY NEPTUNE'S TRIDENT, YOU'RE INSANE!

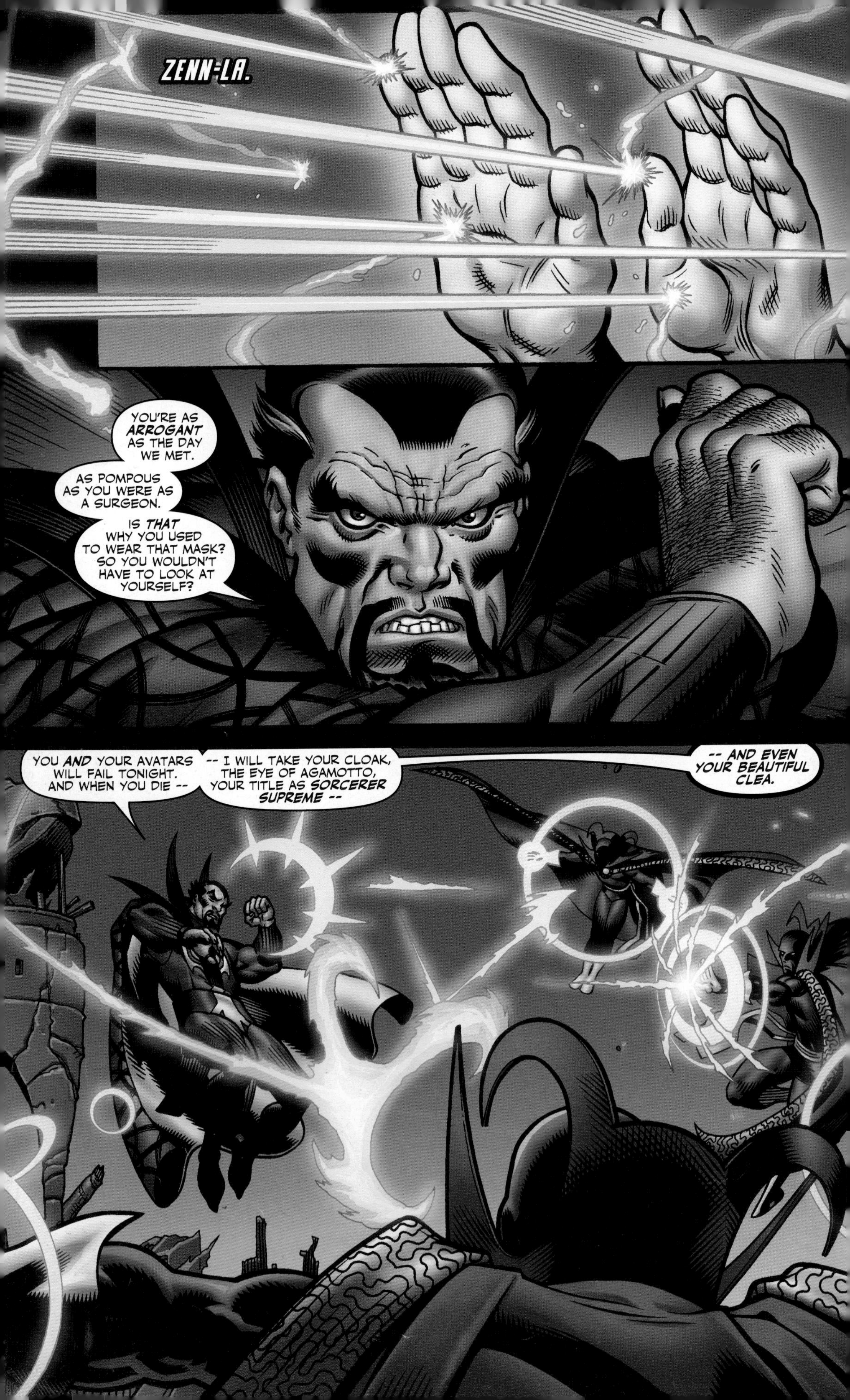
ZENN-LA.
YOU'RE AS ARROGANT AS THE DAY WE MET.
AS POMPOUS AS YOU WERE AS A SURGEON.
IS THAT WHY YOU USED TO WEAR THAT MASK? SO YOU WOULDN'T HAVE TO LOOK AT YOURSELF?
YOU AND YOUR AVATARS WILL FAIL TONIGHT. AND WHEN YOU DIE --
-- I WILL TAKE YOUR CLOAK, THE EYE OF AGAMOTTO, YOUR TITLE AS SORCERER SUPREME --
-- AND EVEN YOUR BEAUTIFUL CLEA.

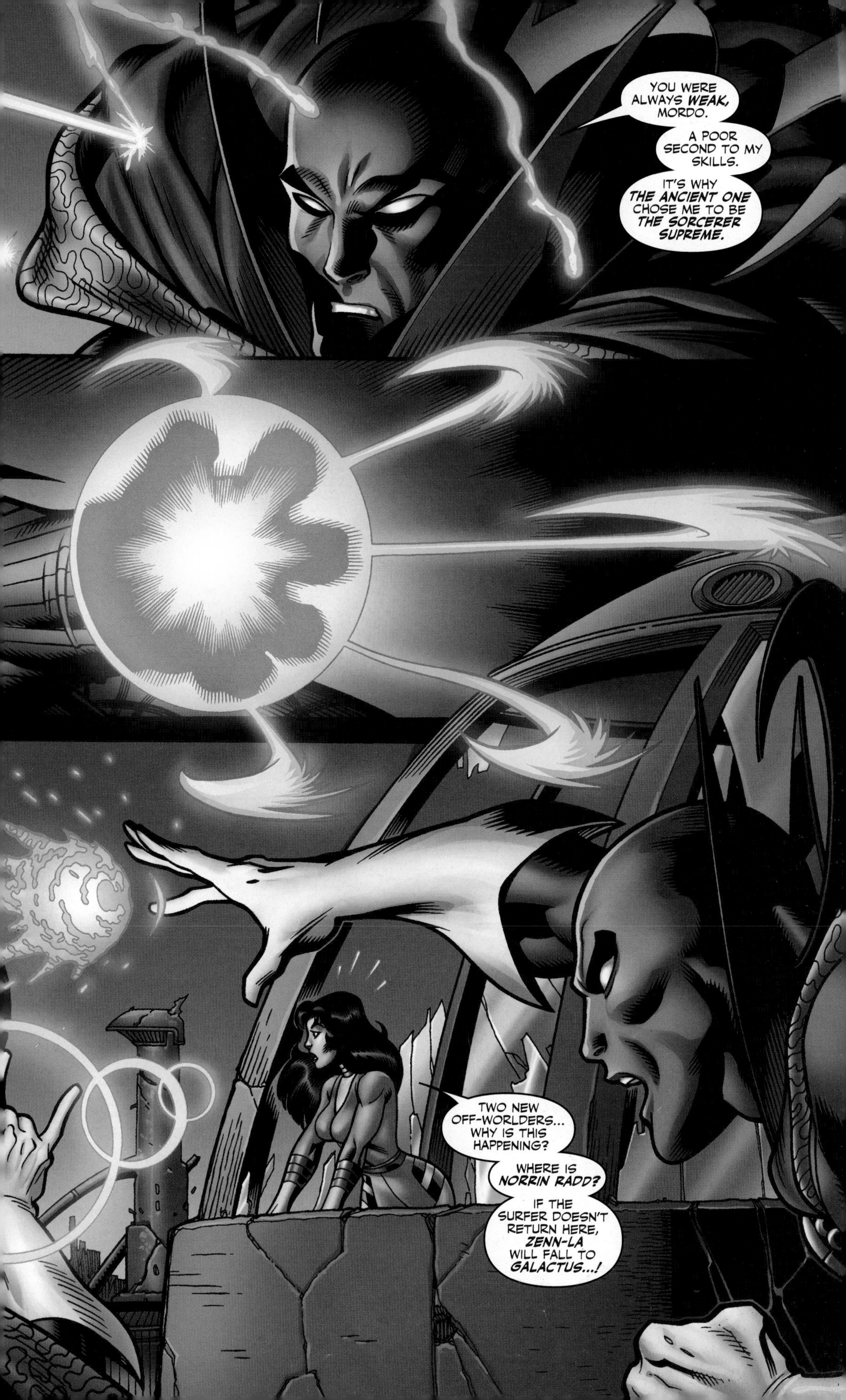
YOU WERE ALWAYS WEAK, MORDO.
A POOR SECOND TO MY SKILLS.
IT'S WHY THE ANCIENT ONE CHOSE ME TO BE THE SORCERER SUPREME.
TWO NEW OFF-WORLDERS... WHY IS THIS HAPPENING?
WHERE IS NORRIN RADD?
IF THE SURFER DOESN'T RETURN HERE, ZENN-LA WILL FALL TO GALACTUS...!

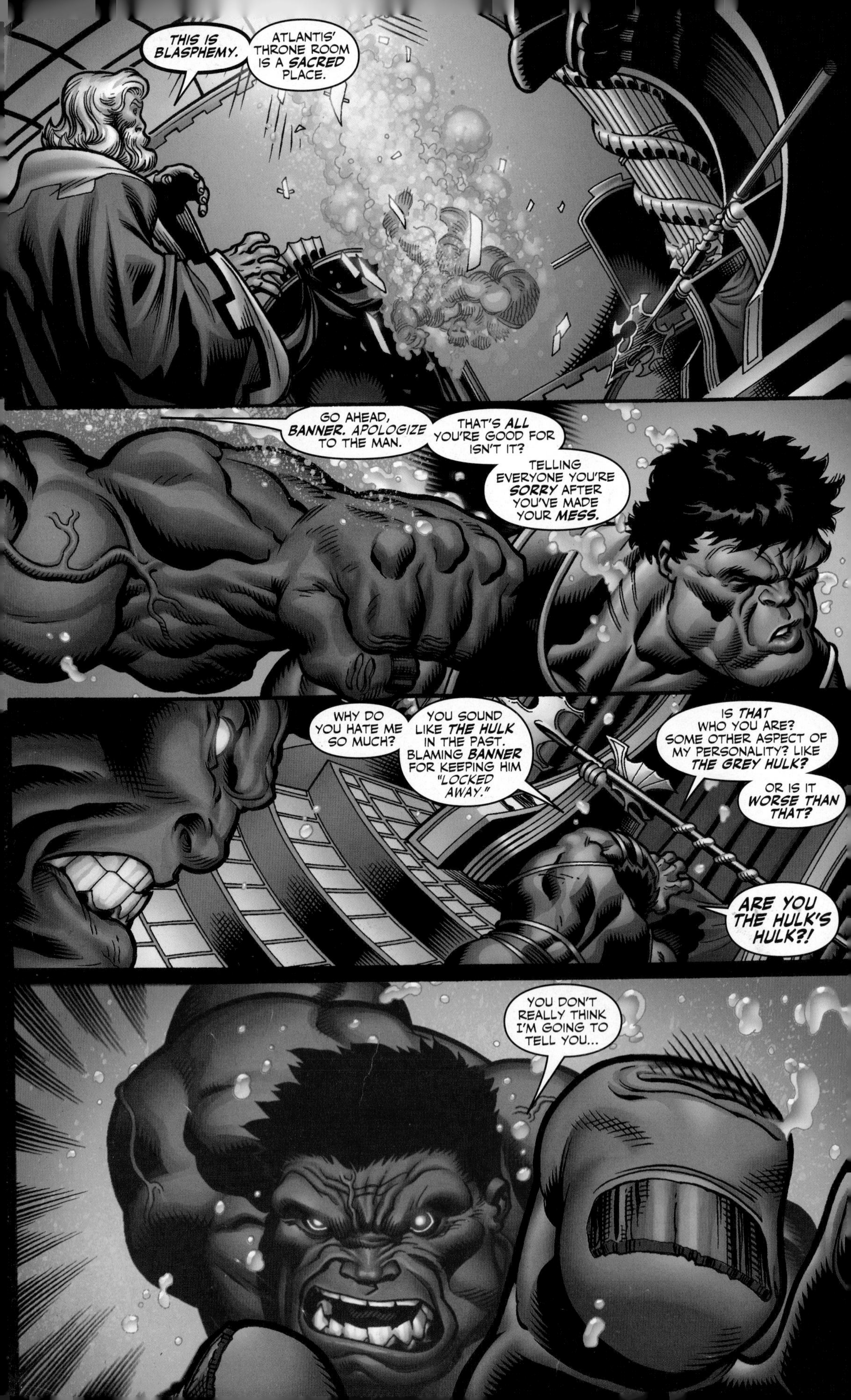
THIS IS BLASPHEMY.
ATLANTIS' THRONE ROOM IS A SACRED PLACE.
GO AHEAD, BANNER. APOLOGIZE TO THE MAN.
THAT'S ALL YOU'RE GOOD FOR ISN'T IT?
TELLING EVERYONE YOU'RE SORRY AFTER YOU'VE MADE YOUR MESS.
WHY DO YOU HATE ME SO MUCH?
YOU SOUND LIKE THE HULK IN THE PAST. BLAMING BANNER FOR KEEPING HIM "LOCKED AWAY."
IS THAT WHO YOU ARE? SOME OTHER ASPECT OF MY PERSONALITY? LIKE THE GREY HULK?
OR IS IT WORSE THAN THAT?
ARE YOU THE HULK'S HULK?!
YOU DON'T REALLY THINK I'M GOING TO TELL YOU...

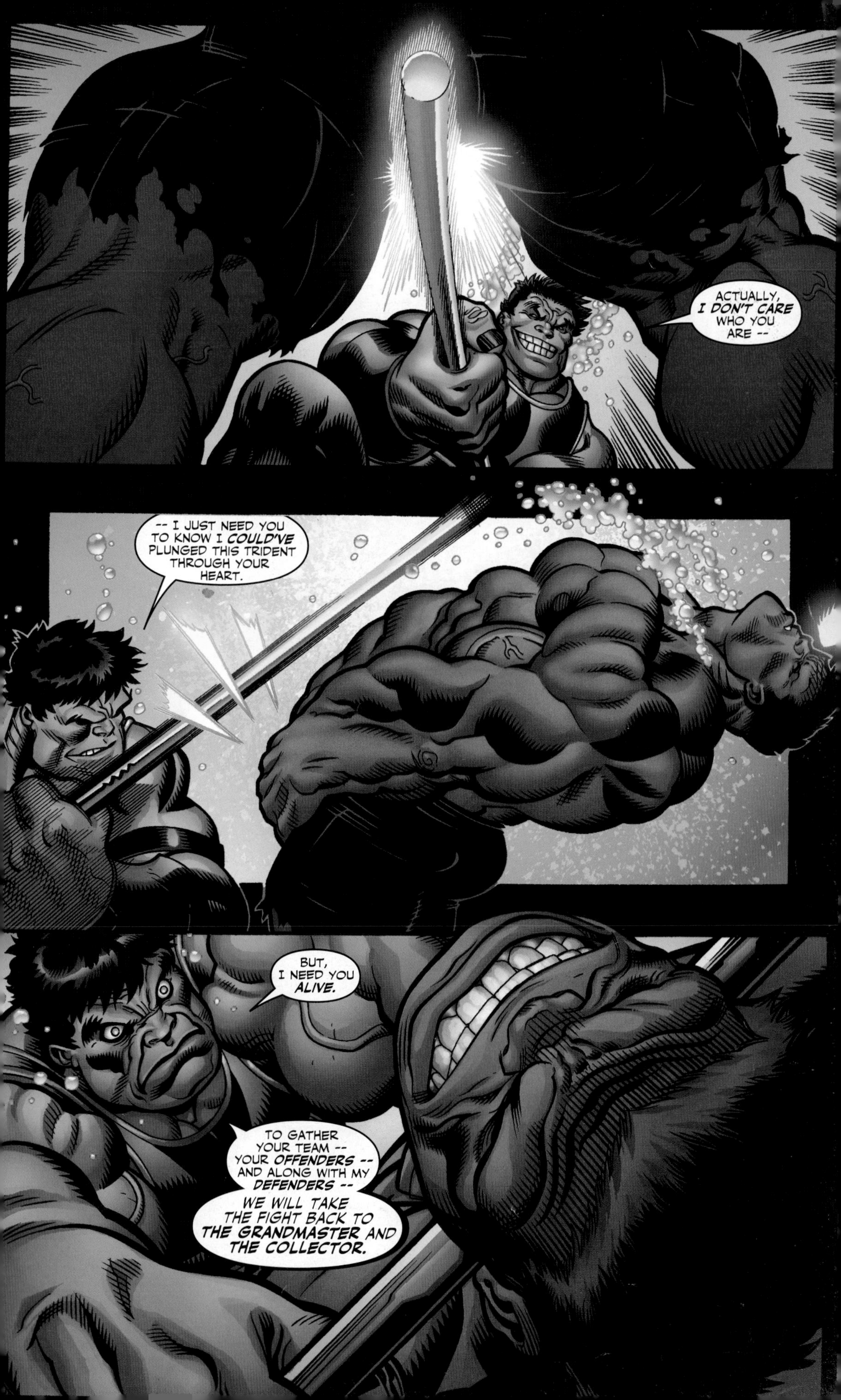
ACTUALLY, I DON'T CARE WHO YOU ARE --
-- I JUST NEED YOU TO KNOW I COULD'VE PLUNGED THIS TRIDENT THROUGH YOUR HEART.
BUT, I NEED YOU ALIVE.
TO GATHER YOUR TEAM -- YOUR OFFENDERS -- AND ALONG WITH MY DEFENDERS --
WE WILL TAKE THE FIGHT BACK TO THE GRANDMASTER AND THE COLLECTOR.

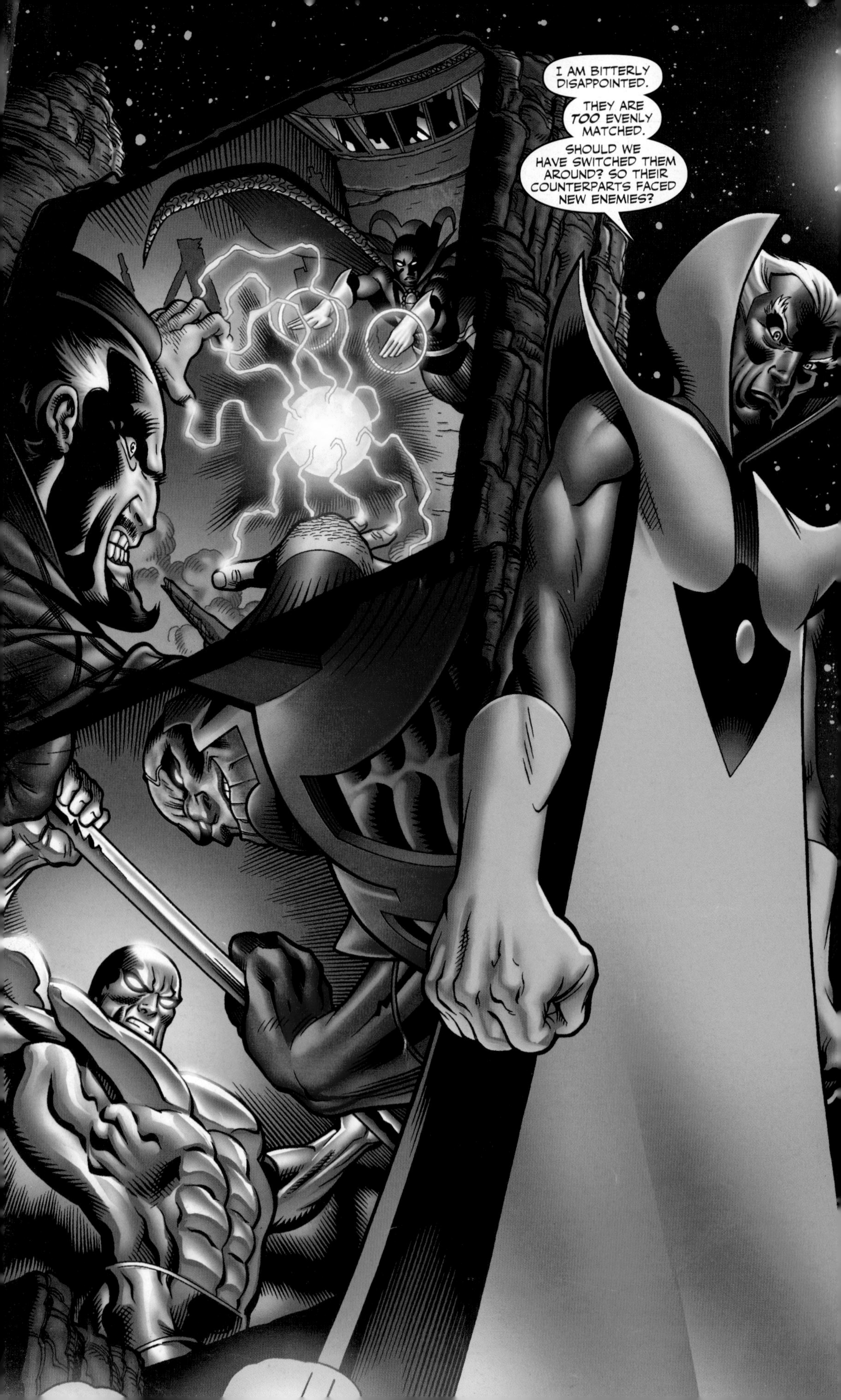
I AM BITTERLY DISAPPOINTED.
THEY ARE TOO EVENLY MATCHED.
SHOULD WE HAVE SWITCHED THEM AROUND? SO THEIR COUNTERPARTS FACED NEW ENEMIES?

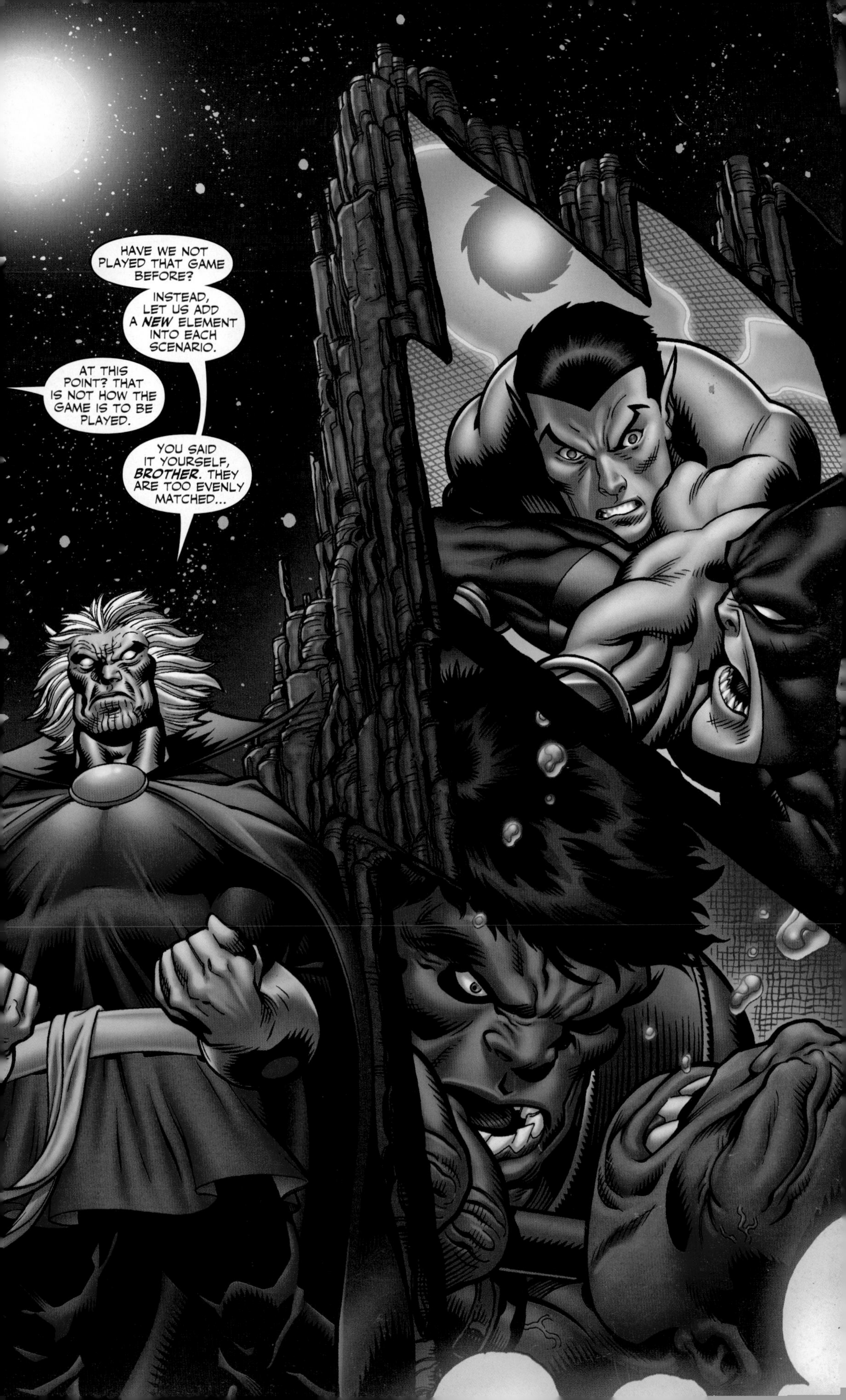
HAVE WE NOT PLAYED THAT GAME BEFORE?
INSTEAD, LET US ADD A NEW ELEMENT INTO EACH SCENARIO.
AT THIS POINT? THAT IS NOT HOW THE GAME IS TO BE PLAYED.
YOU SAID IT YOURSELF, BROTHER. THEY ARE TOO EVENLY MATCHED...

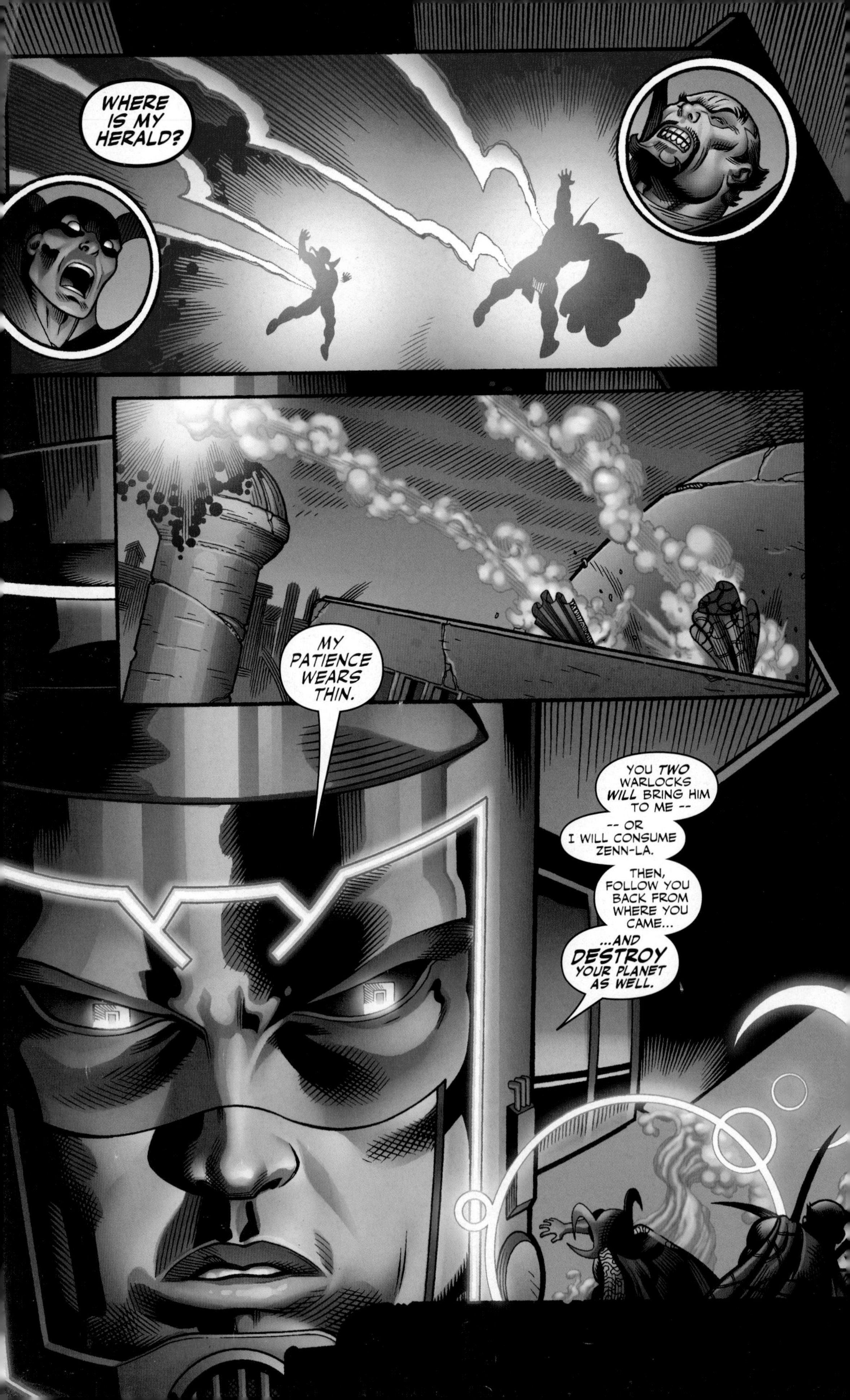
WHERE IS MY HERALD?
MY PATIENCE WEARS THIN.
YOU TWO WARLOCKS WILL BRING HIM TO ME --
-- OR I WILL CONSUME ZENN-LA.
THEN, FOLLOW YOU BACK FROM WHERE YOU CAME...
...AND DESTROY YOUR PLANET AS WELL.

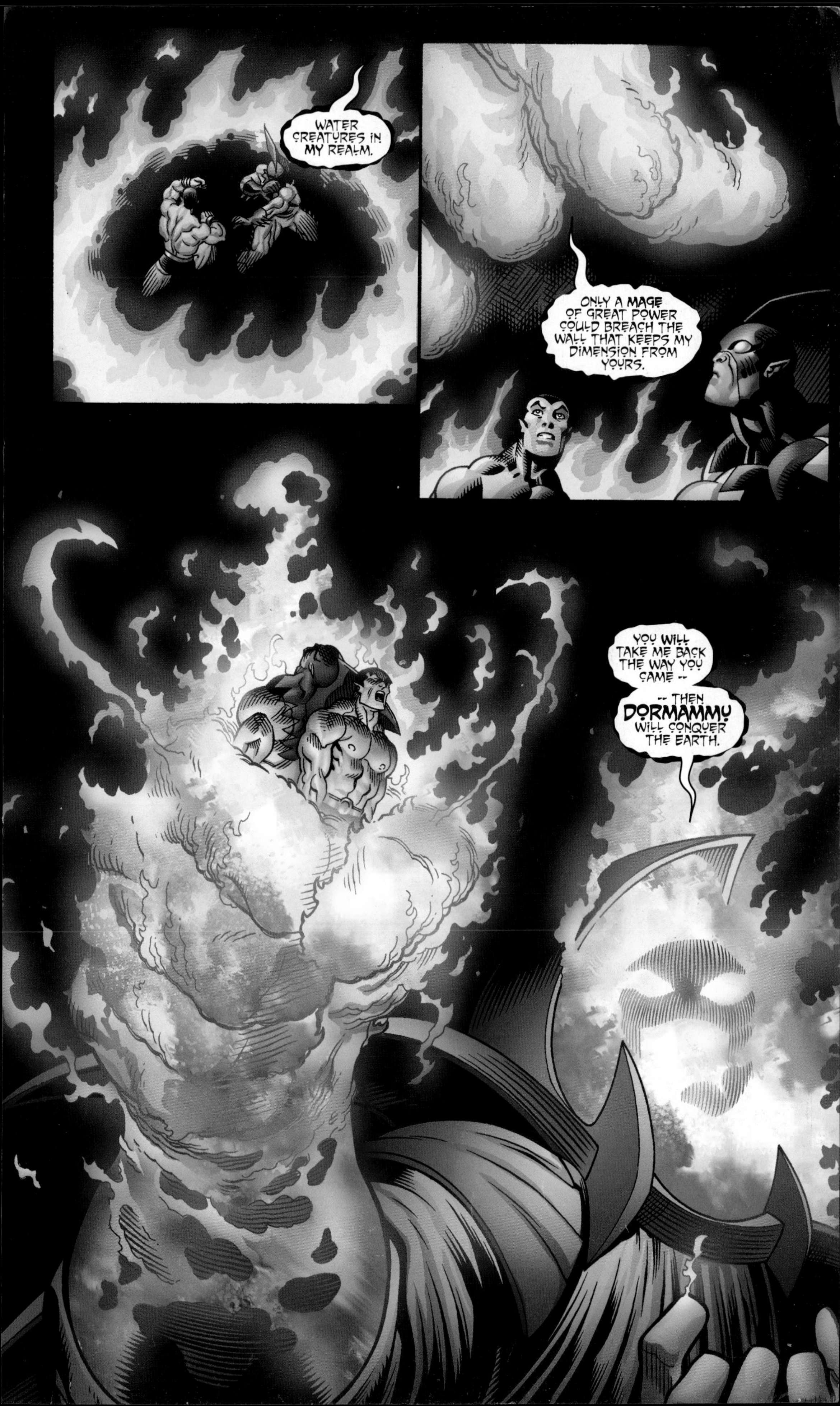
WATER CREATURES IN MY REALM.
ONLY A MAGE OF GREAT POWER COULD BREACH THE WALL THAT KEEPS MY DIMENSION FROM YOURS.
YOU WILL TAKE ME BACK THE WAY YOU CAME --
-- THEN DORMAMMU WILL CONQUER THE EARTH.

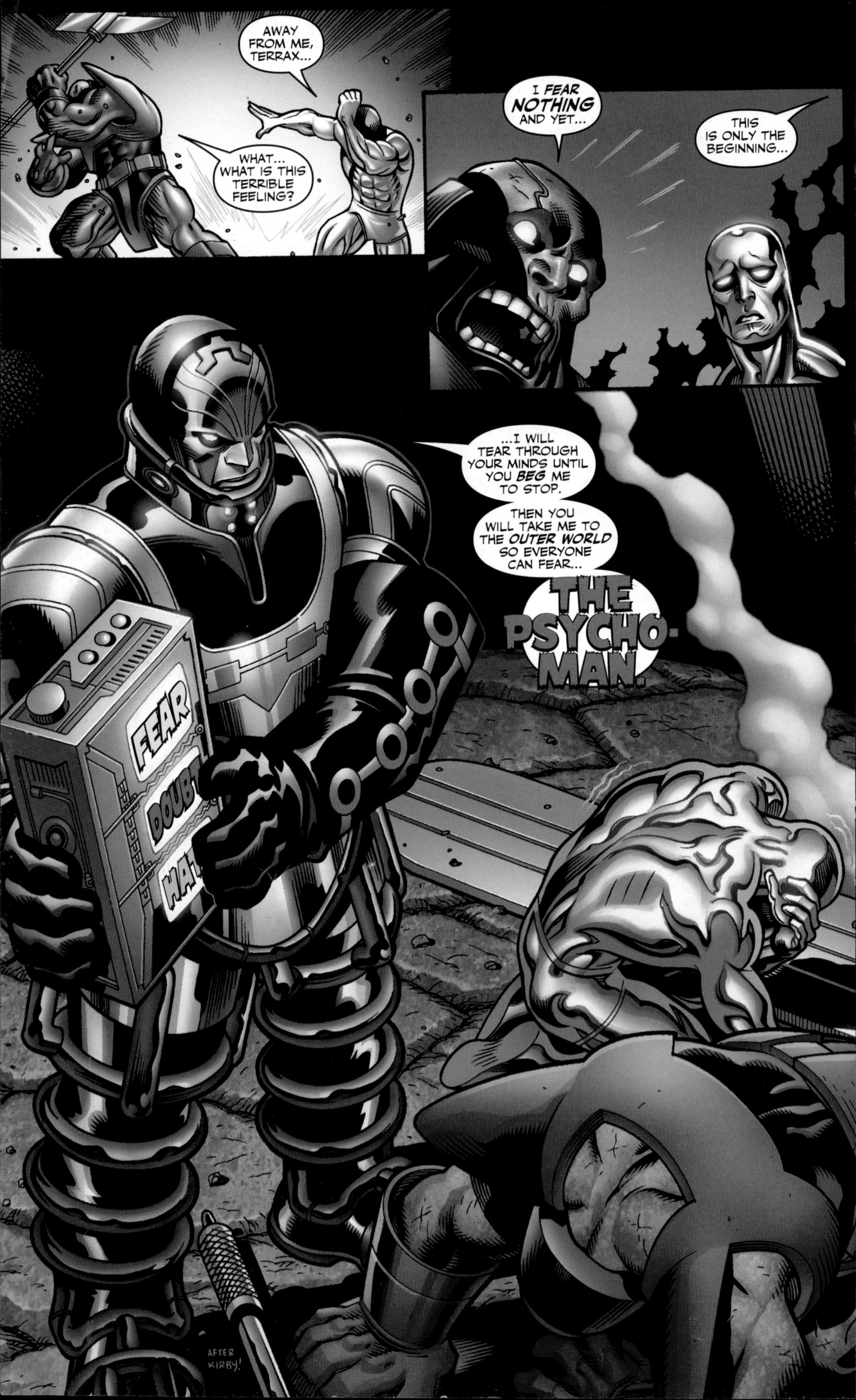
AWAY FROM ME, TERRAX...
WHAT... WHAT IS THIS TERRIBLE FEELING?
I FEAR NOTHING AND YET...
THIS IS ONLY THE BEGINNING...
...I WILL TEAR THROUGH YOUR MINDS UNTIL YOU BEG ME TO STOP.
THEN YOU WILL TAKE ME TO THE OUTER WORLD SO EVERYONE CAN FEAR...
THE PSYCHO-MAN.
FEAR
DOUBT
AFTER KIRBY!

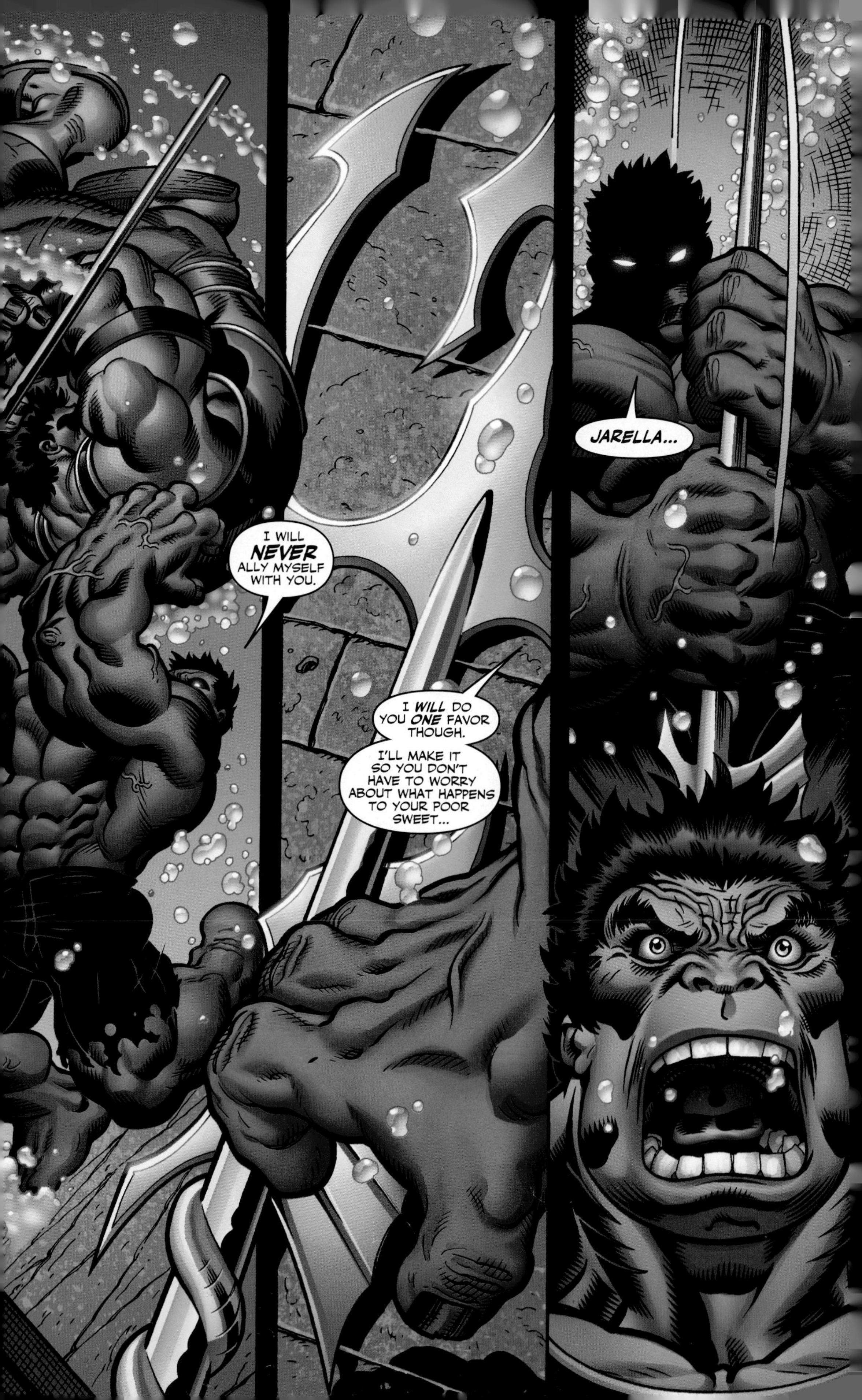
I WILL NEVER ALLY MYSELF WITH YOU.
I WILL DO YOU ONE FAVOR THOUGH.
I'LL MAKE IT SO YOU DON'T HAVE TO WORRY ABOUT WHAT HAPPENS TO YOUR POOR SWEET...
JARELLA...

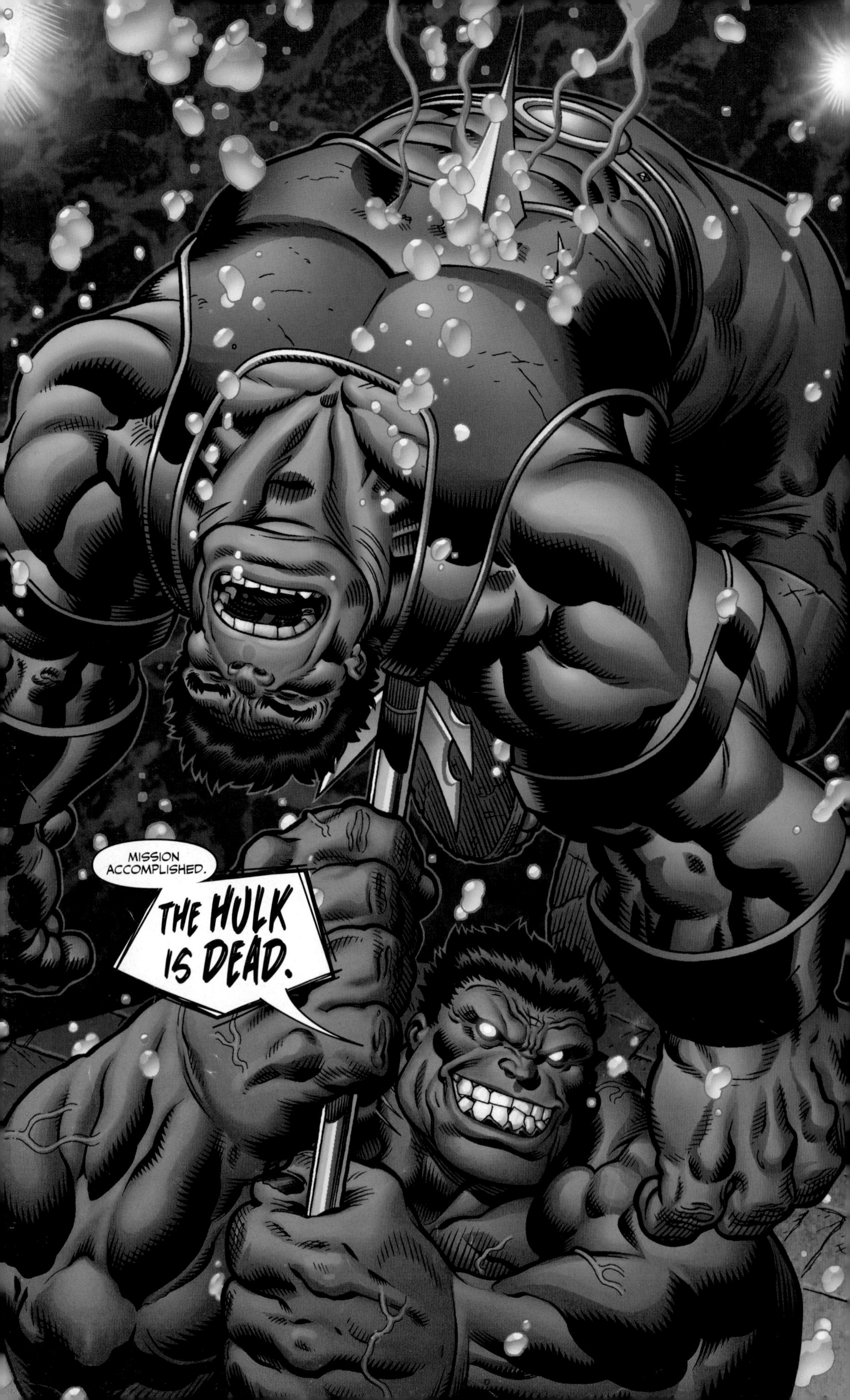
MISSION ACCOMPLISHED.
THE HULK IS DEAD.

ROUND ★ THREE

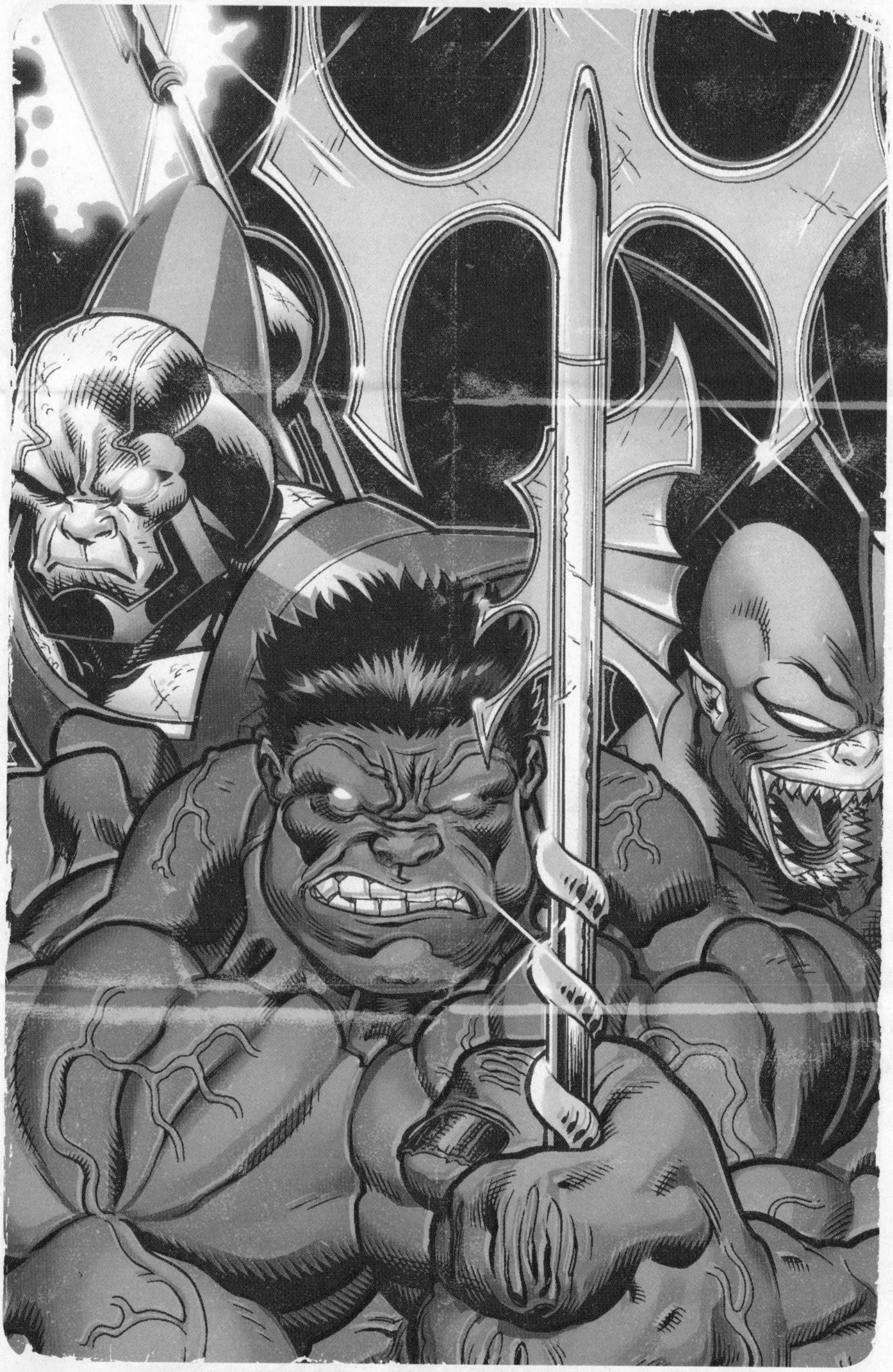

WINNER TAKES ALL

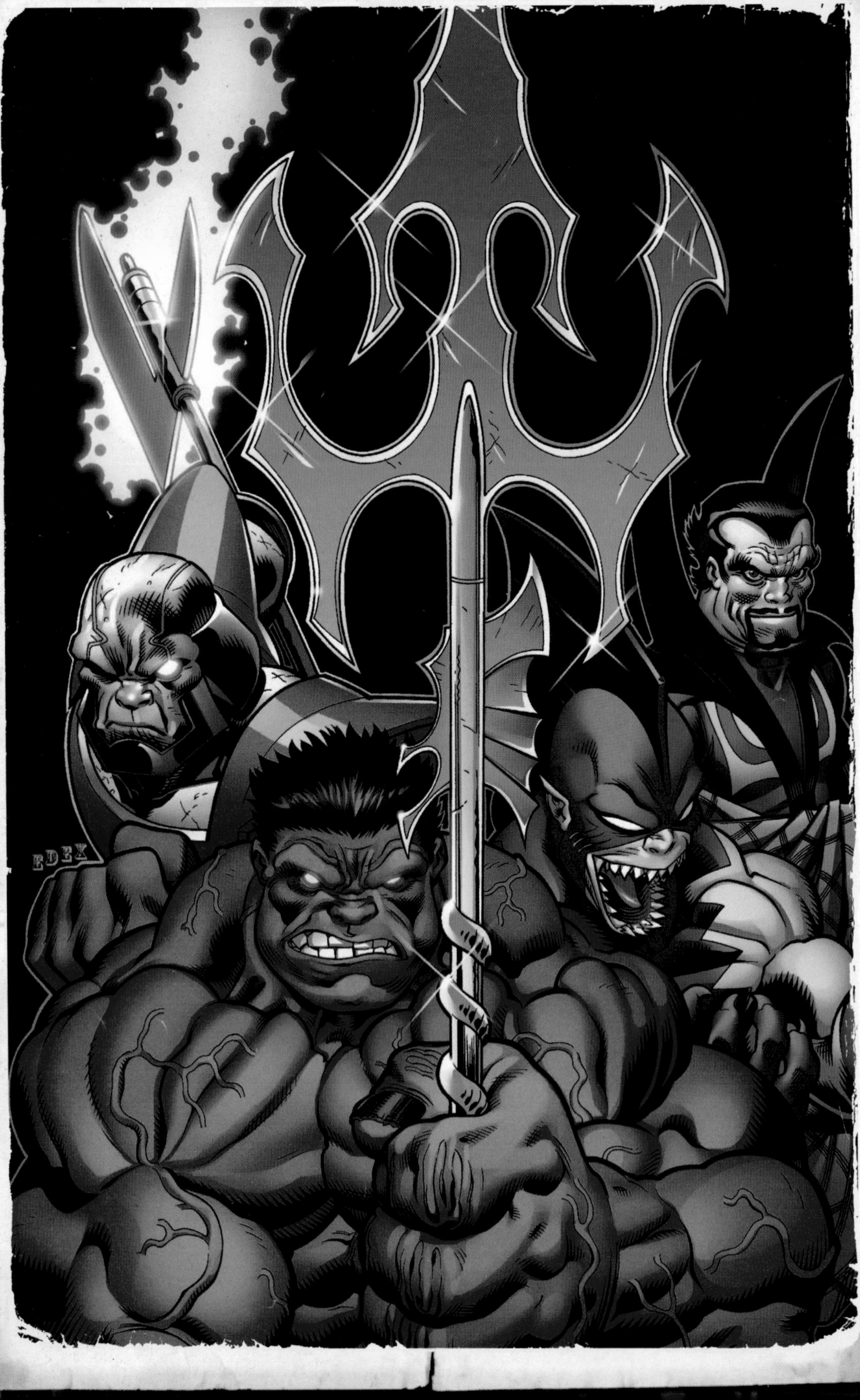

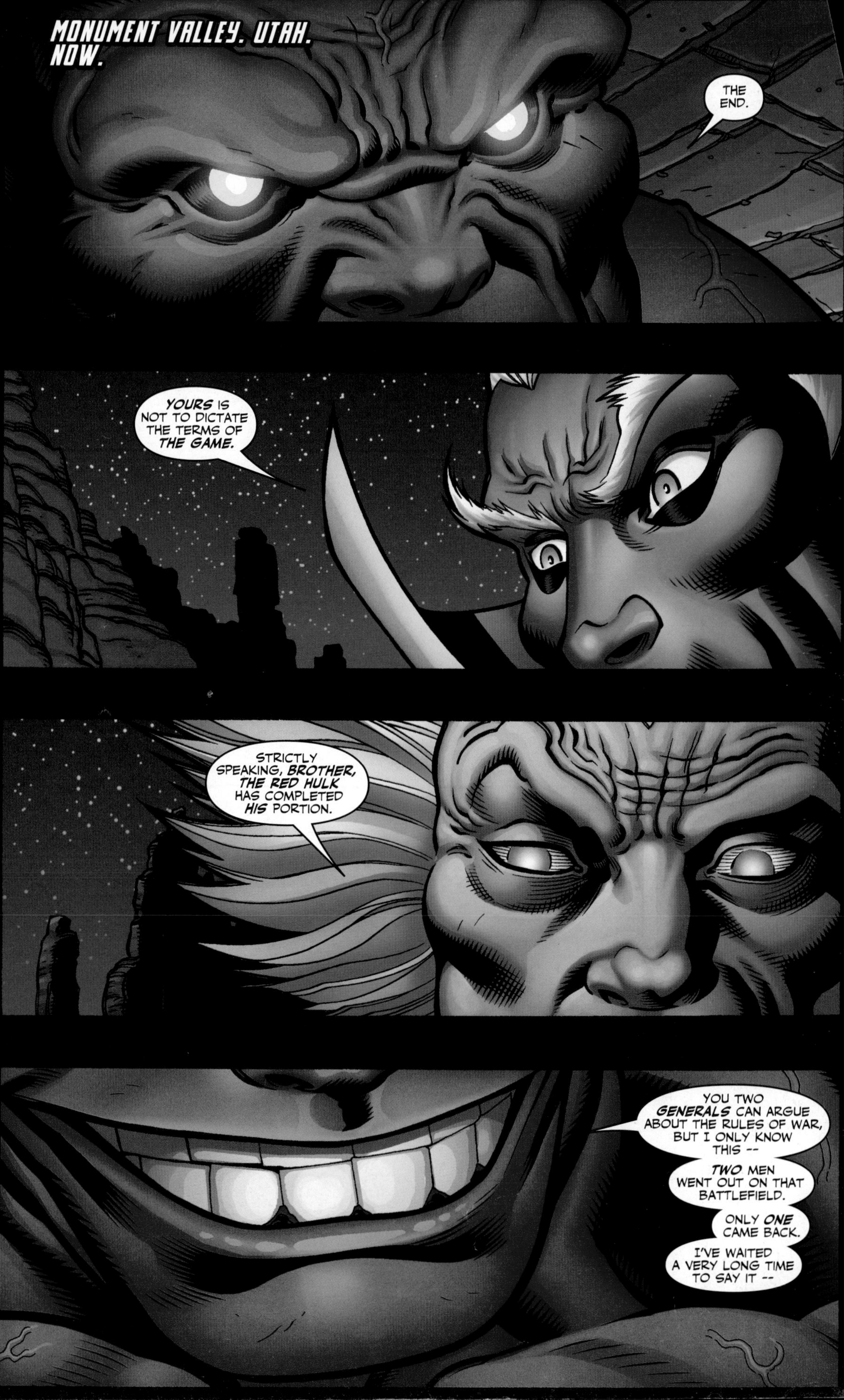
MONUMENT VALLEY. UTAH.
NOW.
THE END.
YOURS IS NOT TO DICTATE THE TERMS OF THE GAME.
STRICTLY SPEAKING, BROTHER, THE RED HULK HAS COMPLETED HIS PORTION.
YOU TWO GENERALS CAN ARGUE ABOUT THE RULES OF WAR, BUT I ONLY KNOW THIS --
TWO MEN WENT OUT ON THAT BATTLEFIELD.
ONLY ONE CAME BACK.
I'VE WAITED A VERY LONG TIME TO SAY IT --

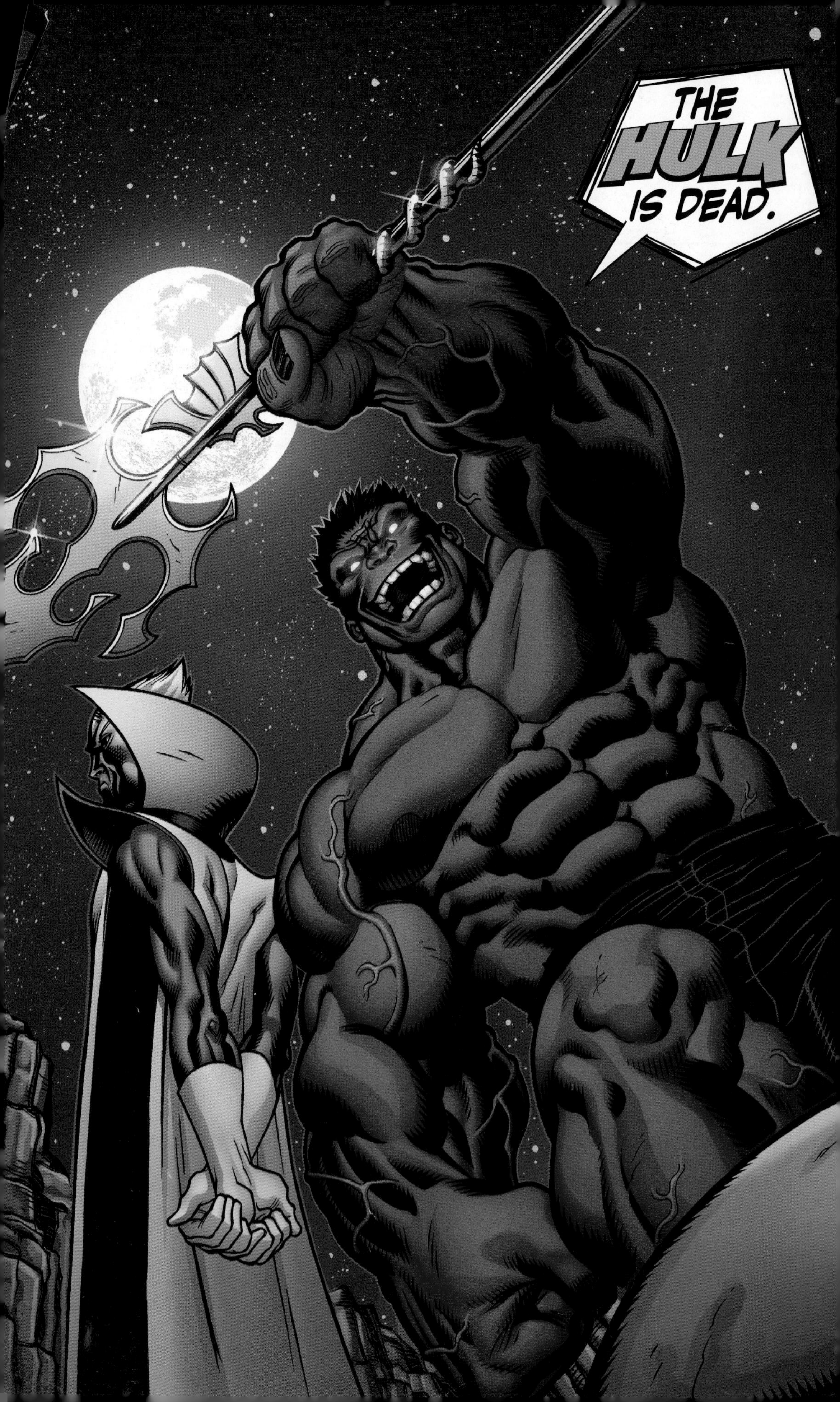
THE HULK IS DEAD.

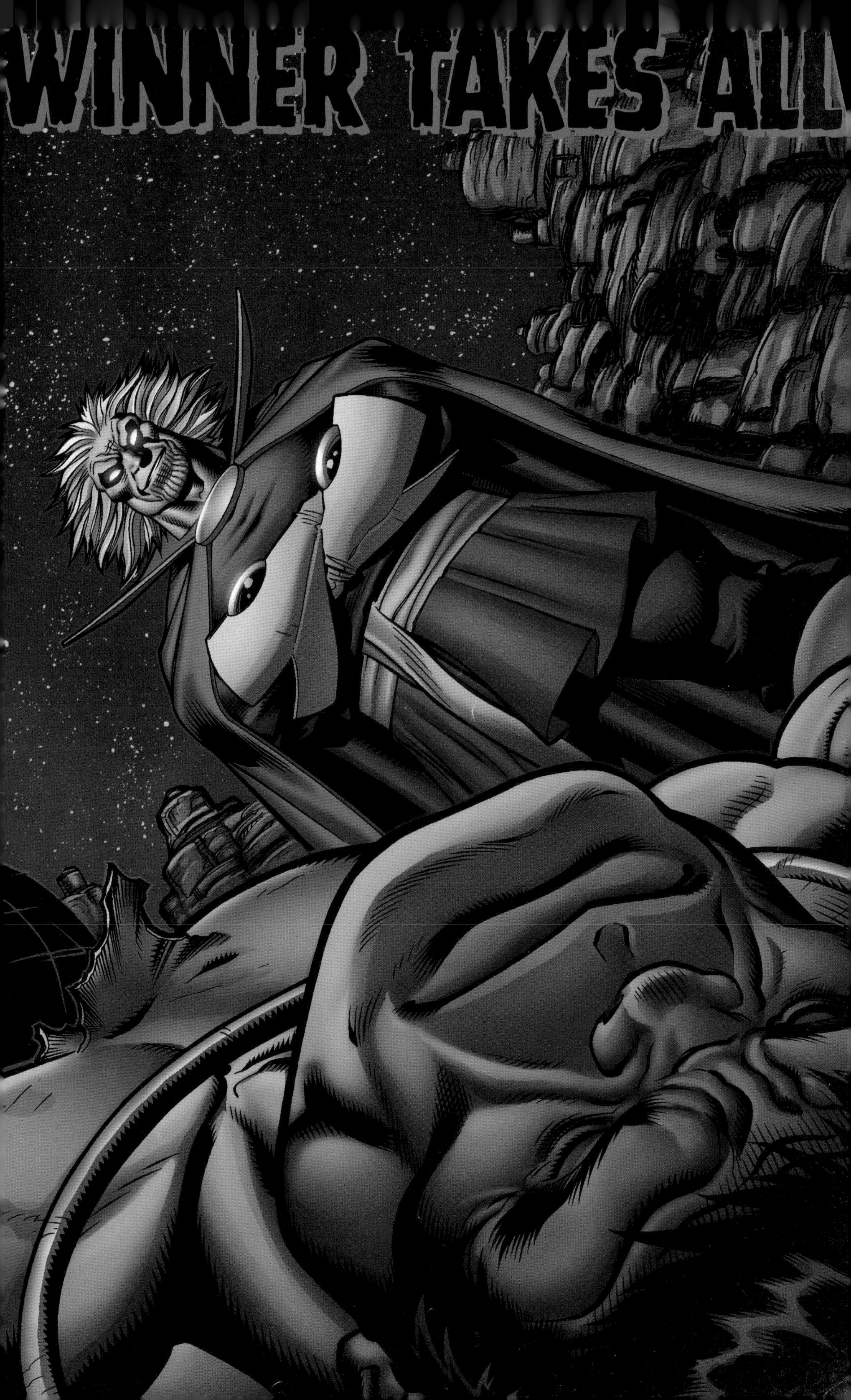
WINNER TAKES ALL

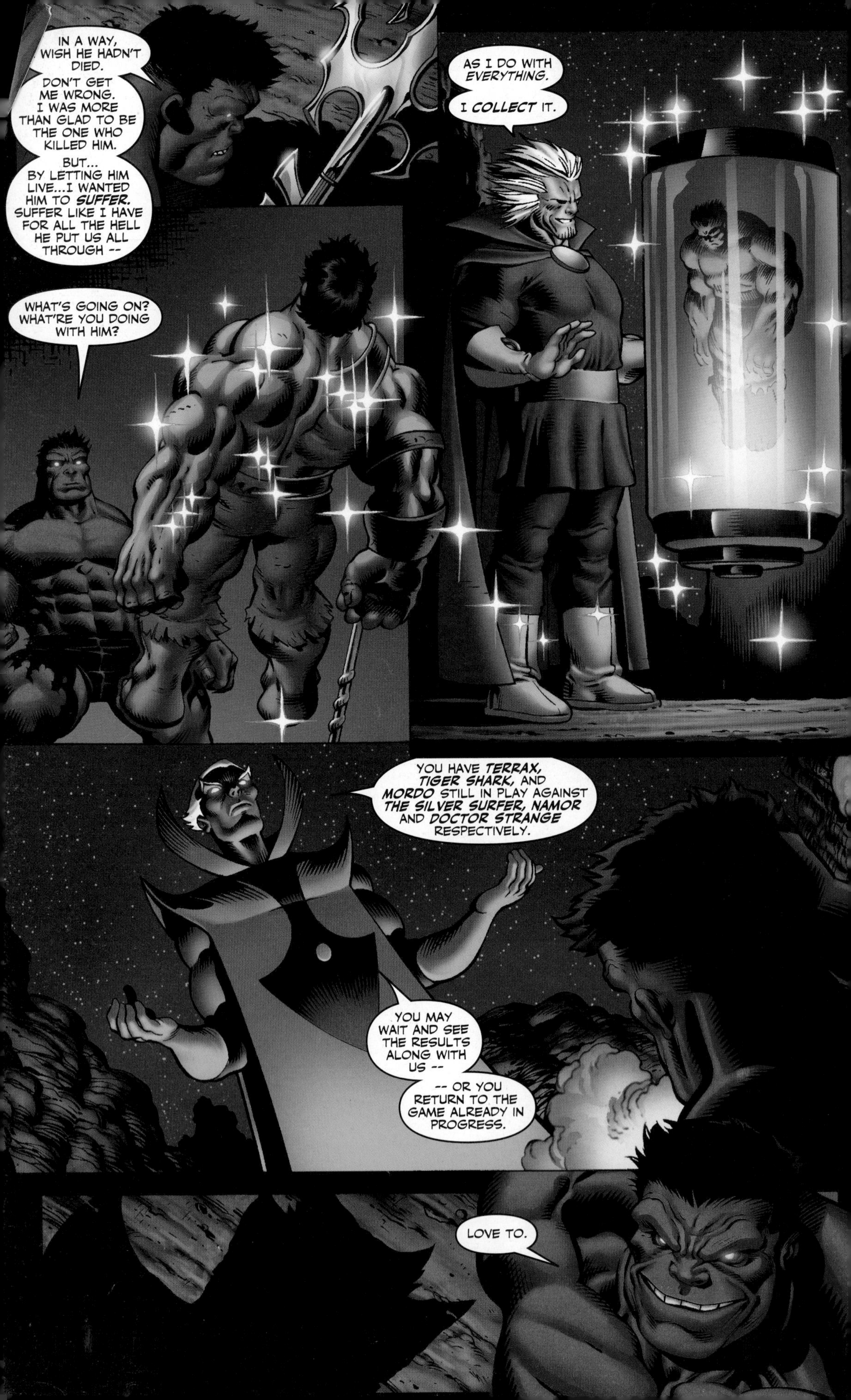
IN A WAY, WISH HE HADN'T DIED.
DON'T GET ME WRONG. I WAS MORE THAN GLAD TO BE THE ONE WHO KILLED HIM.
BUT... BY LETTING HIM LIVE...I WANTED HIM TO SUFFER. SUFFER LIKE I HAVE FOR ALL THE HELL HE PUT US ALL THROUGH --
AS I DO WITH EVERYTHING.
I COLLECT IT.
WHAT'S GOING ON? WHAT'RE YOU DOING WITH HIM?
YOU HAVE TERRAX, TIGER SHARK, AND MORDO STILL IN PLAY AGAINST THE SILVER SURFER, NAMOR AND DOCTOR STRANGE RESPECTIVELY.
YOU MAY WAIT AND SEE THE RESULTS ALONG WITH US --
-- OR YOU RETURN TO THE GAME ALREADY IN PROGRESS.
LOVE TO.

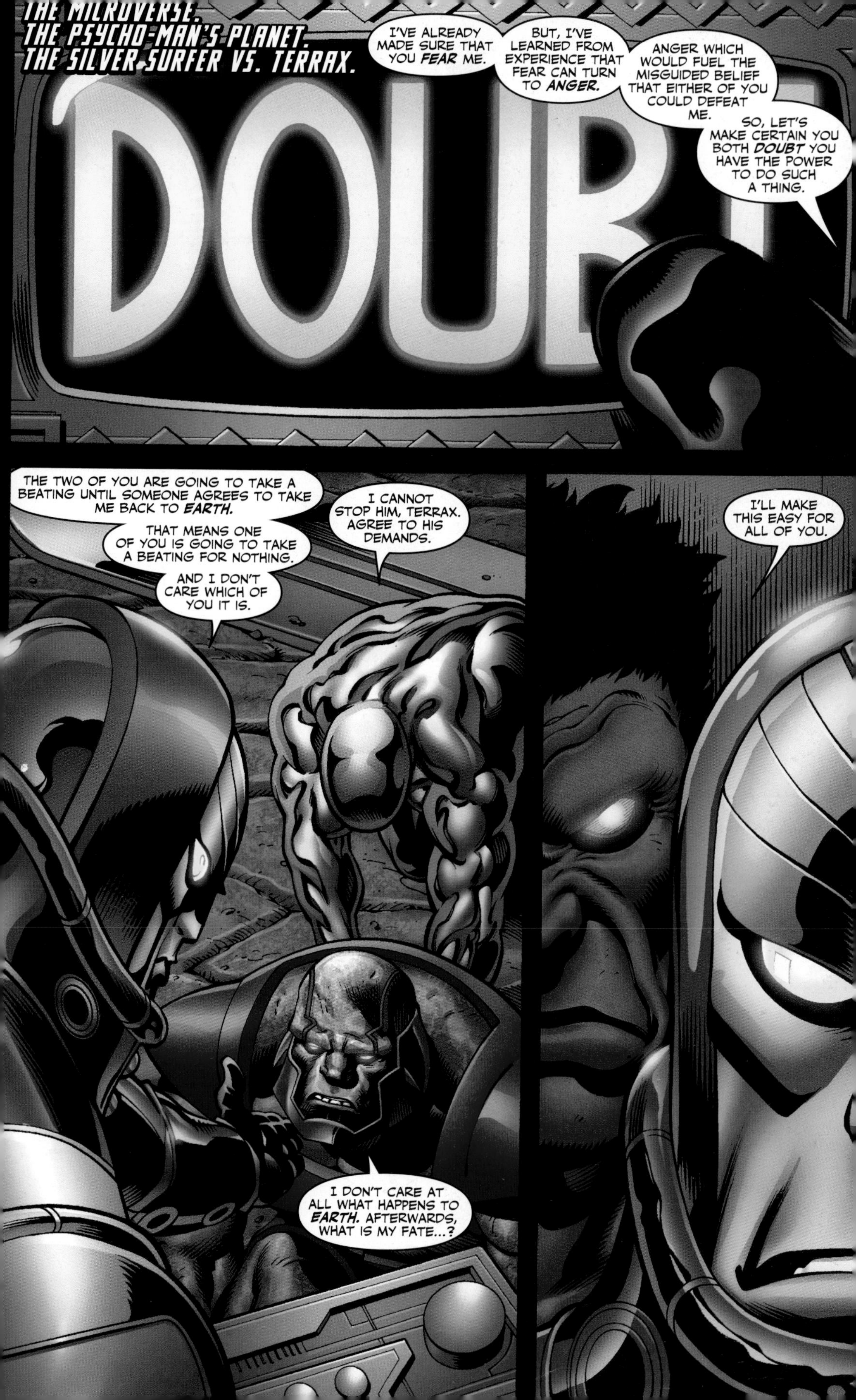
THE MICROVERSE.
THE PSYCHO-MAN'S PLANET.
THE SILVER SURFER VS. TERRAX.
I'VE ALREADY MADE SURE THAT YOU FEAR ME.
BUT, I'VE LEARNED FROM EXPERIENCE THAT FEAR CAN TURN TO ANGER.
ANGER WHICH WOULD FUEL THE MISGUIDED BELIEF THAT EITHER OF YOU COULD DEFEAT ME.
SO, LET'S MAKE CERTAIN YOU BOTH DOUBT YOU HAVE THE POWER TO DO SUCH A THING.
DOUBT
THE TWO OF YOU ARE GOING TO TAKE A BEATING UNTIL SOMEONE AGREES TO TAKE ME BACK TO EARTH.
THAT MEANS ONE OF YOU IS GOING TO TAKE A BEATING FOR NOTHING.
AND I DON'T CARE WHICH OF YOU IT IS.
I CANNOT STOP HIM, TERRAX. AGREE TO HIS DEMANDS.
I DON'T CARE AT ALL WHAT HAPPENS TO EARTH. AFTERWARDS, WHAT IS MY FATE...?
I'LL MAKE THIS EASY FOR ALL OF YOU.

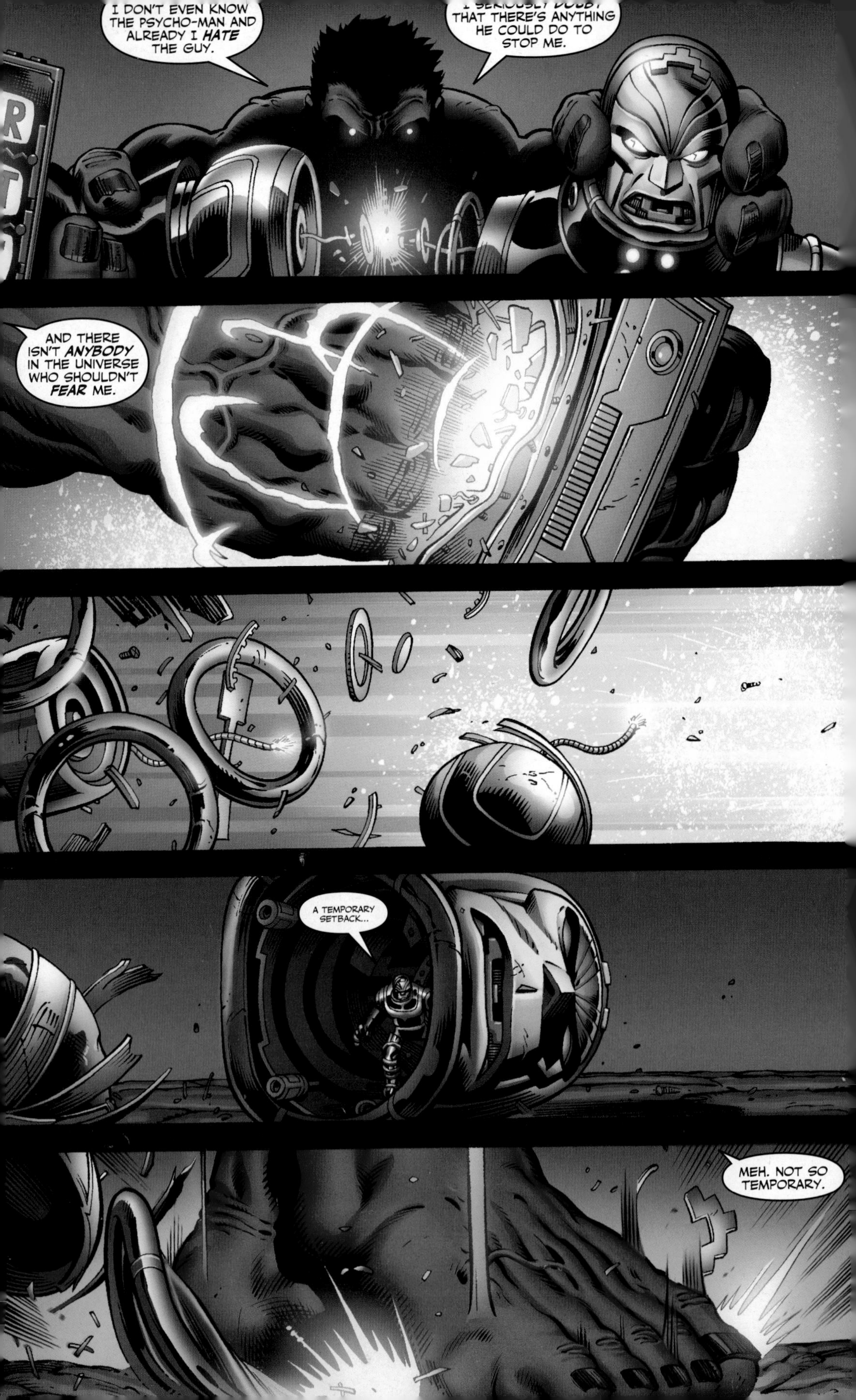
I DON'T EVEN KNOW THE PSYCHO-MAN AND ALREADY I *HATE* THE GUY.
THAT THERE'S ANYTHING HE COULD DO TO STOP ME.
AND THERE ISN'T *ANYBODY* IN THE UNIVERSE WHO SHOULDN'T *FEAR* ME.
A TEMPORARY SETBACK...
MEH. NOT SO TEMPORARY.

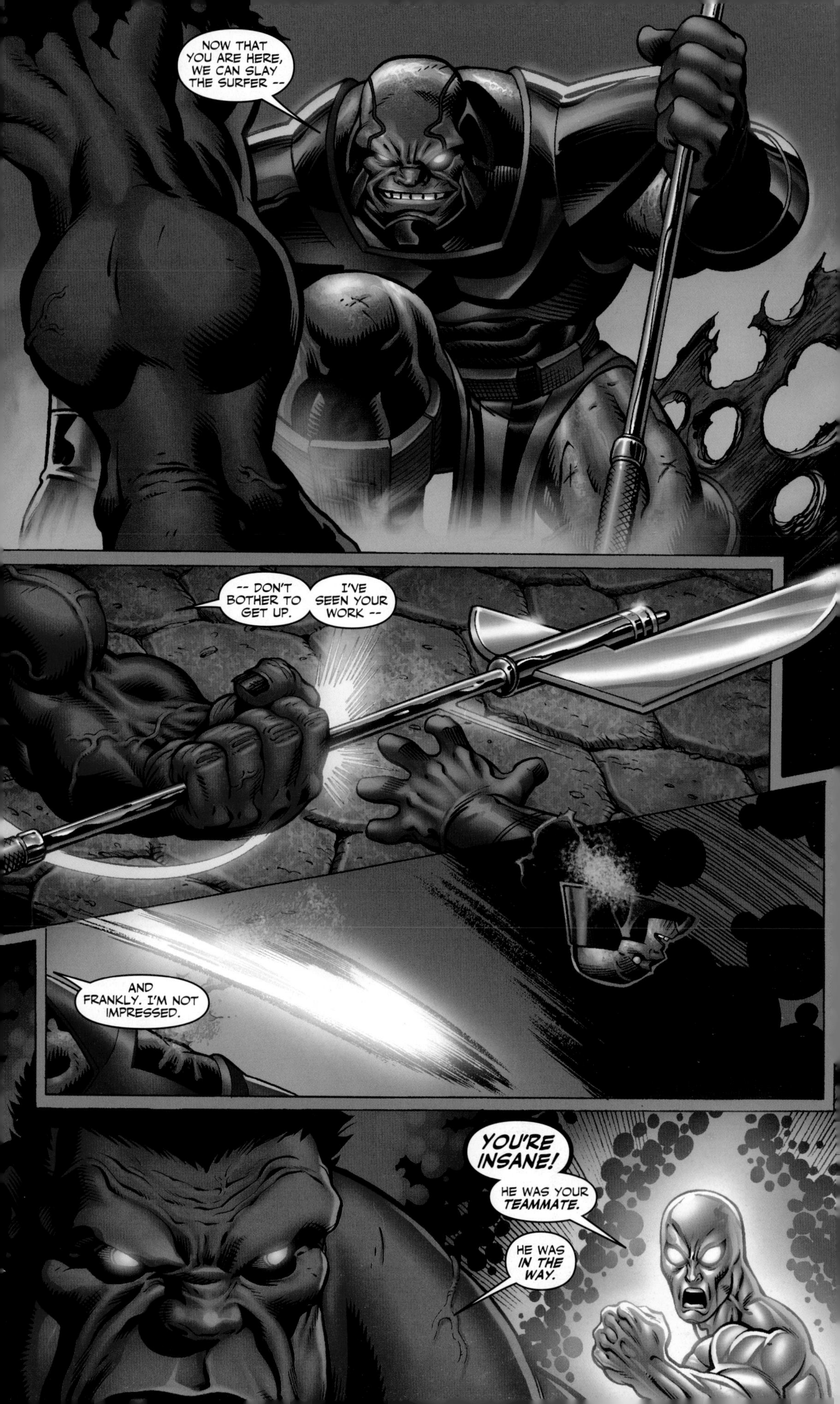
NOW THAT YOU ARE HERE, WE CAN SLAY THE SURFER --
-- DON'T BOTHER TO GET UP.
I'VE SEEN YOUR WORK --
AND FRANKLY. I'M NOT IMPRESSED.
YOU'RE INSANE!
HE WAS YOUR TEAMMATE.
HE WAS IN THE WAY.

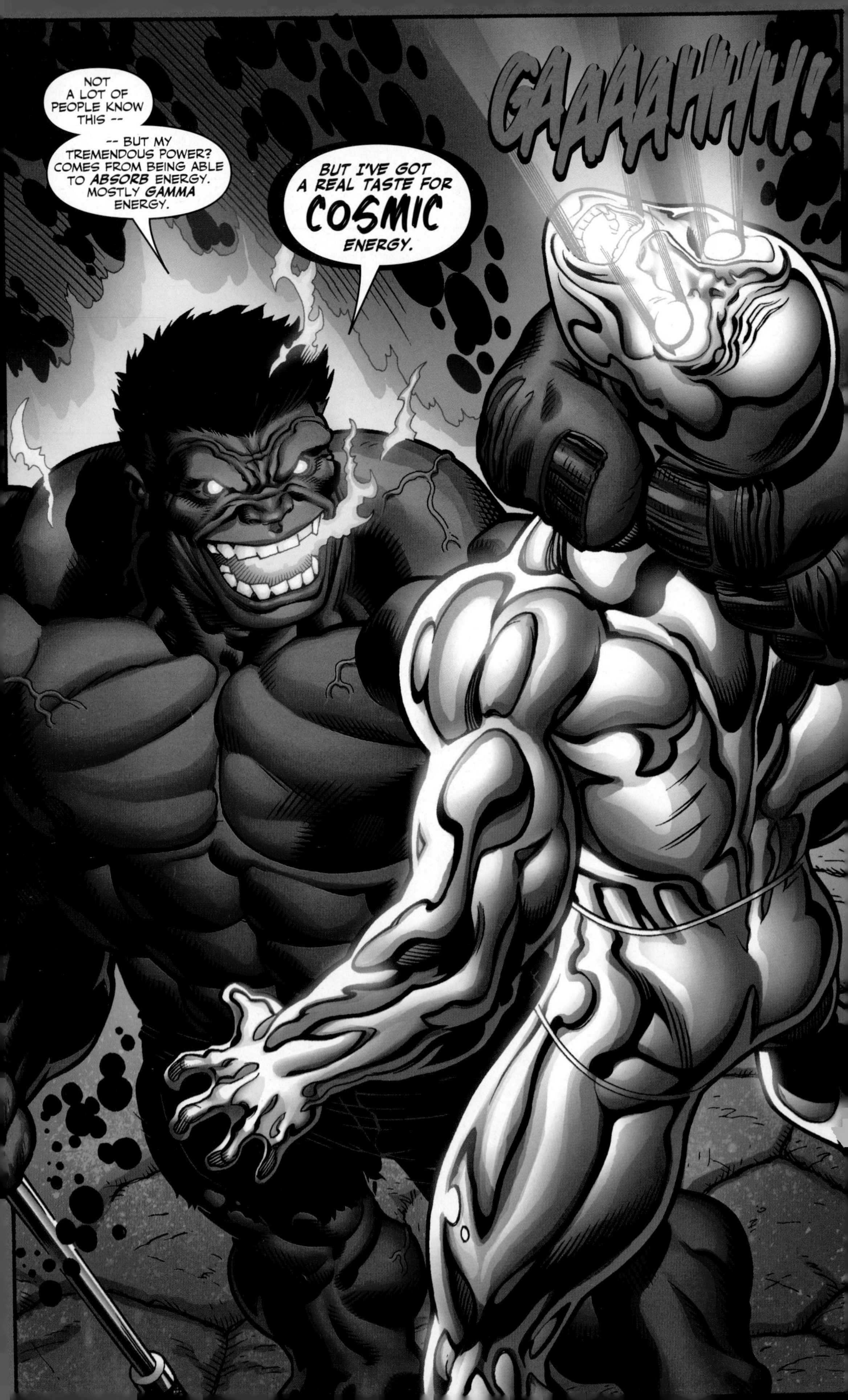
NOT A LOT OF PEOPLE KNOW THIS --
-- BUT MY TREMENDOUS POWER? COMES FROM BEING ABLE TO ABSORB ENERGY. MOSTLY GAMMA ENERGY.
BUT I'VE GOT A REAL TASTE FOR COSMIC ENERGY.
GAAAAHHH!

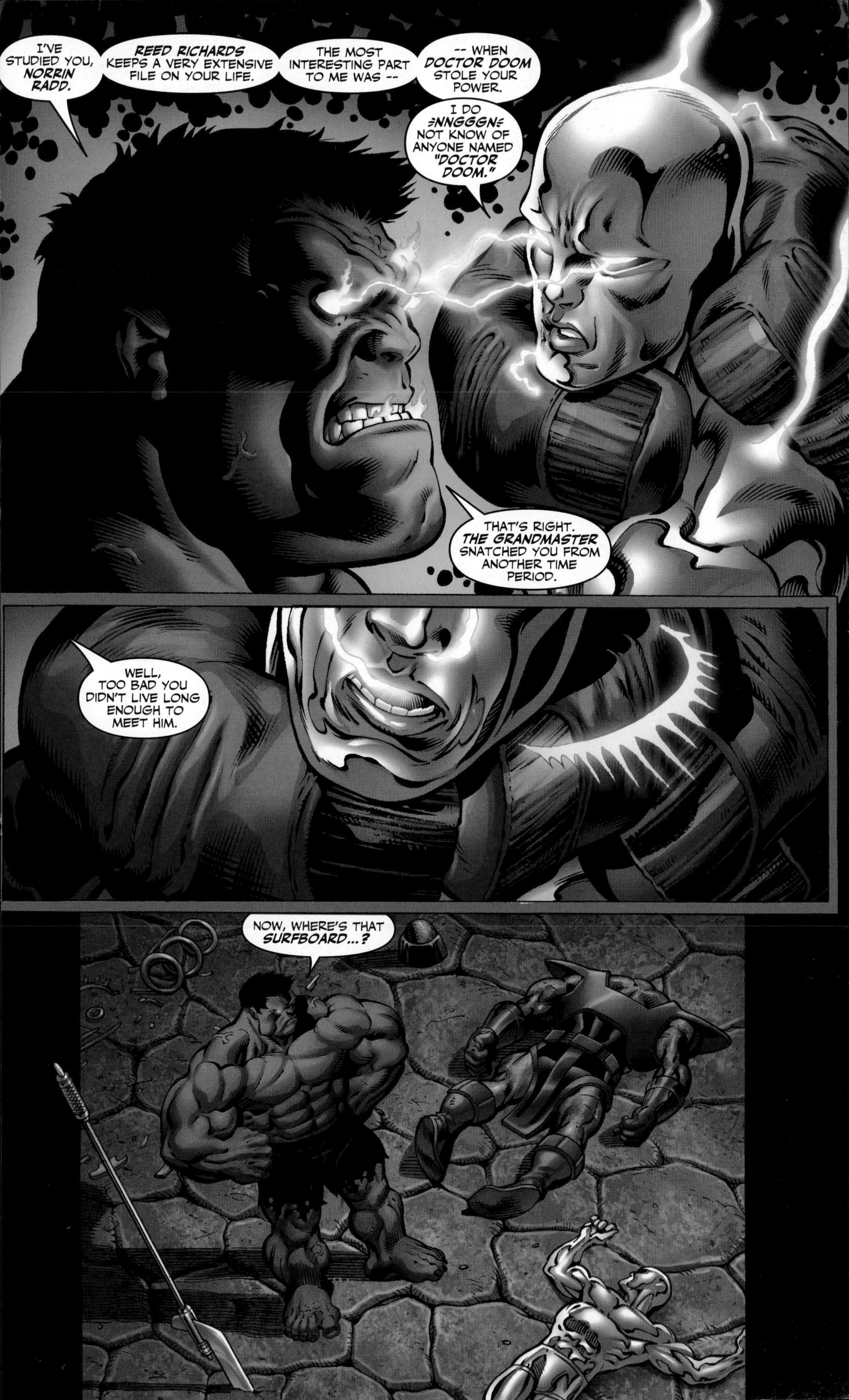
I'VE STUDIED YOU, NORRIN RADD.
REED RICHARDS KEEPS A VERY EXTENSIVE FILE ON YOUR LIFE.
THE MOST INTERESTING PART TO ME WAS --
-- WHEN DOCTOR DOOM STOLE YOUR POWER.
I DO NNGGGN NOT KNOW OF ANYONE NAMED "DOCTOR DOOM."
THAT'S RIGHT. THE GRANDMASTER SNATCHED YOU FROM ANOTHER TIME PERIOD.
WELL, TOO BAD YOU DIDN'T LIVE LONG ENOUGH TO MEET HIM.
NOW, WHERE'S THAT SURFBOARD...?

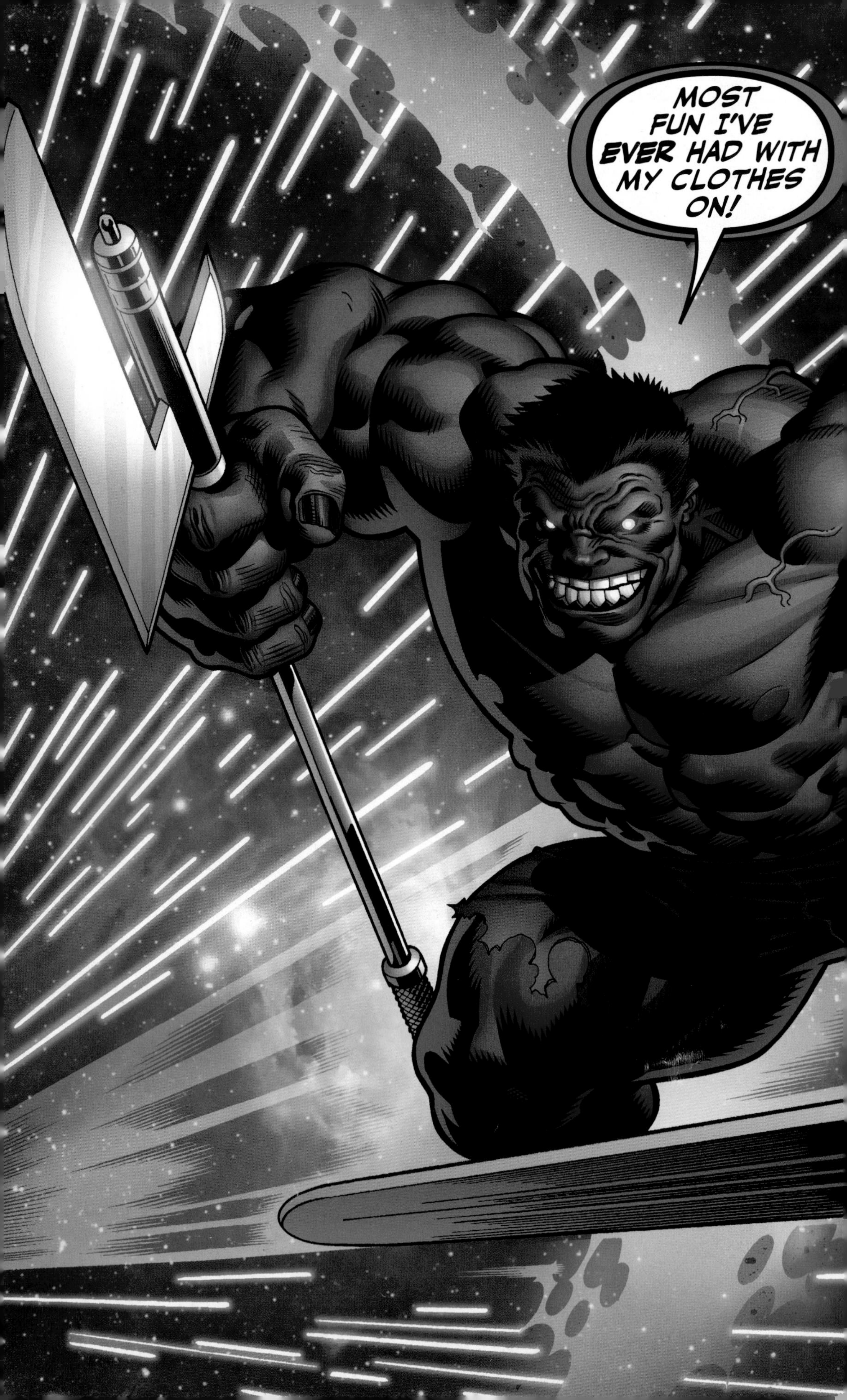
MOST FUN I'VE EVER HAD WITH MY CLOTHES ON!

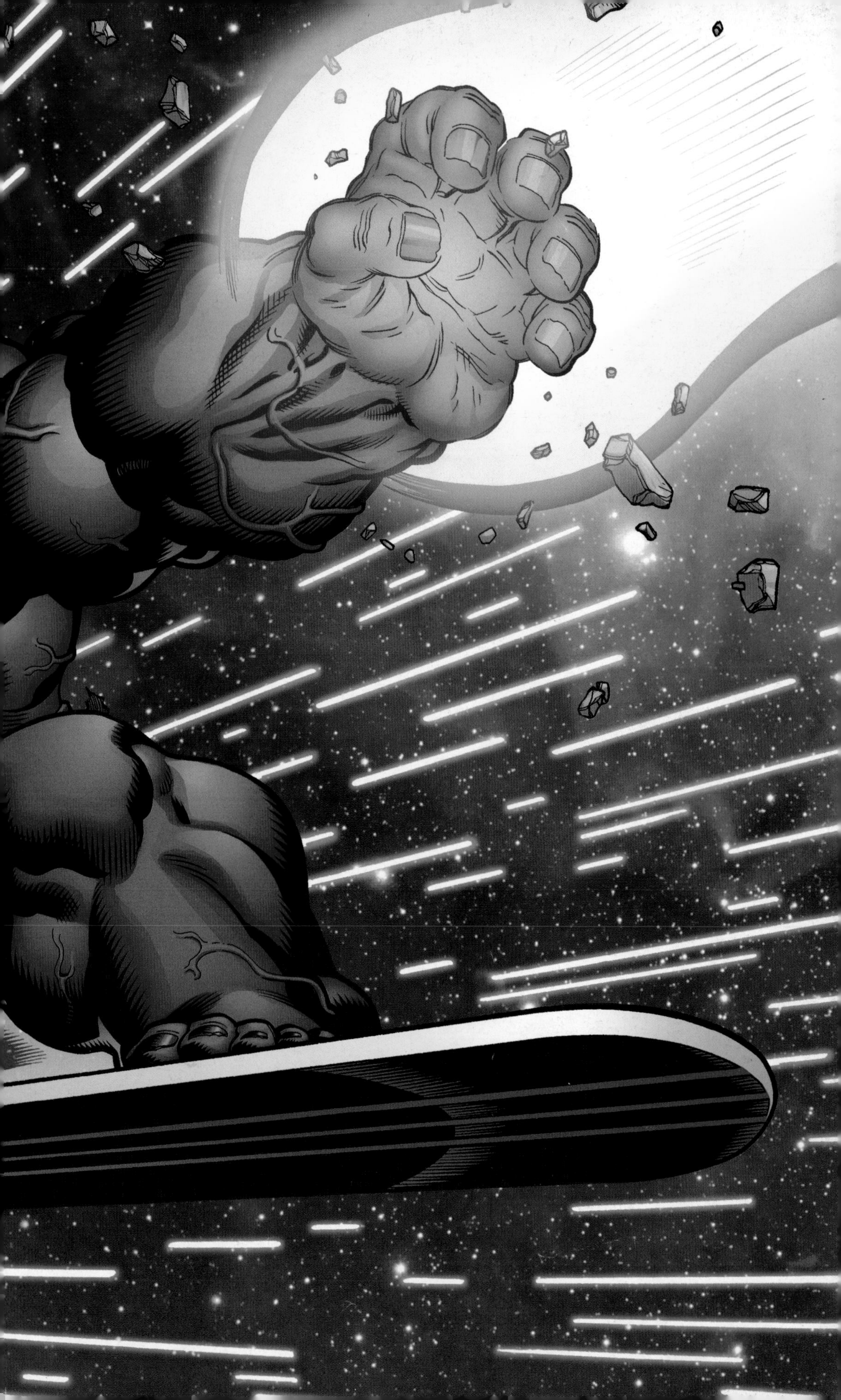

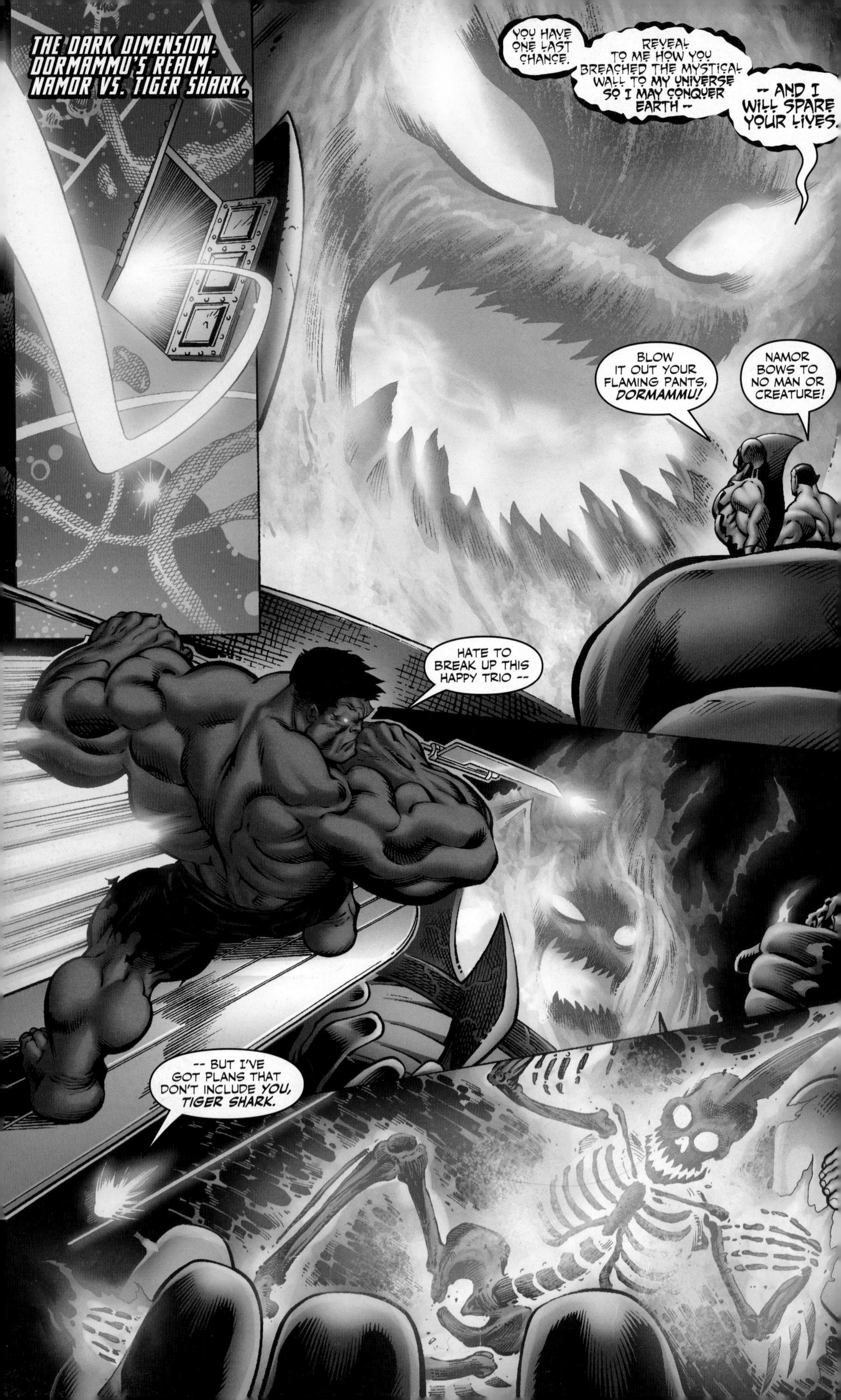
THE DARK DIMENSION. DORMAMMU'S REALM. NAMOR VS. TIGER SHARK.
YOU HAVE ONE LAST CHANCE.
REVEAL TO ME HOW YOU BREACHED THE MYSTICAL WALL TO MY UNIVERSE SO I MAY CONQUER EARTH --
-- AND I WILL SPARE YOUR LIVES.
BLOW IT OUT YOUR FLAMING PANTS, DORMAMMU!
NAMOR BOWS TO NO MAN OR CREATURE!
HATE TO BREAK UP THIS HAPPY TRIO --
-- BUT I'VE GOT PLANS THAT DON'T INCLUDE YOU, TIGER SHARK.

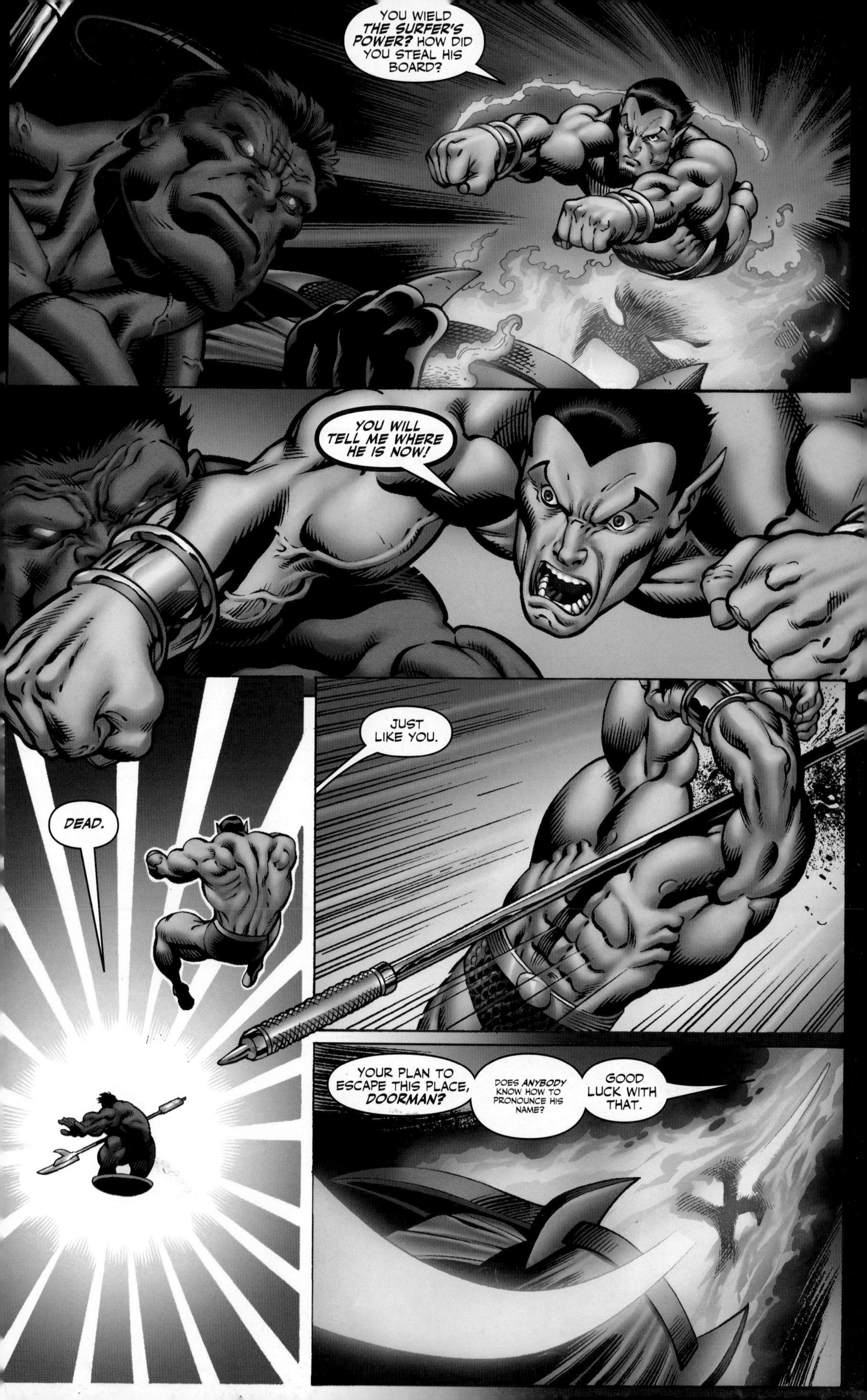
YOU WIELD THE SURFER'S POWER? HOW DID YOU STEAL HIS BOARD?
YOU WILL TELL ME WHERE HE IS NOW!
DEAD.
JUST LIKE YOU.
YOUR PLAN TO ESCAPE THIS PLACE, DOORMAN?
DOES ANYBODY KNOW HOW TO PRONOUNCE HIS NAME?
GOOD LUCK WITH THAT.

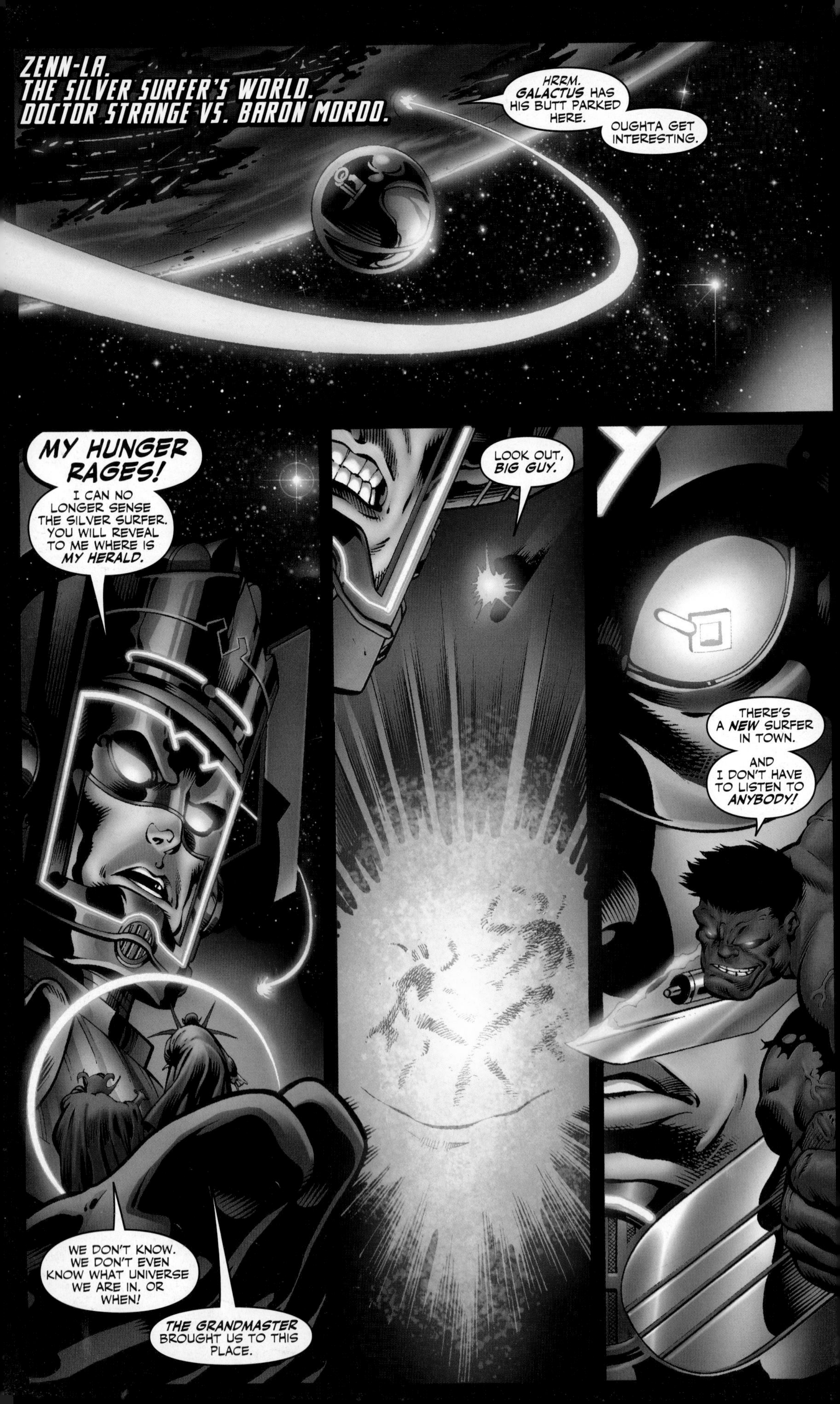

ZENN-LA.
THE SILVER SURFER'S WORLD.
DOCTOR STRANGE VS. BARON MORDO.
HRRM. GALACTUS HAS HIS BUTT PARKED HERE.
OUGHTA GET INTERESTING.
MY HUNGER RAGES!
I CAN NO LONGER SENSE THE SILVER SURFER. YOU WILL REVEAL TO ME WHERE IS MY HERALD.
WE DON'T KNOW. WE DON'T EVEN KNOW WHAT UNIVERSE WE ARE IN. OR WHEN!
THE GRANDMASTER BROUGHT US TO THIS PLACE.
LOOK OUT, BIG GUY.
THERE'S A NEW SURFER IN TOWN.
AND I DON'T HAVE TO LISTEN TO ANYBODY!

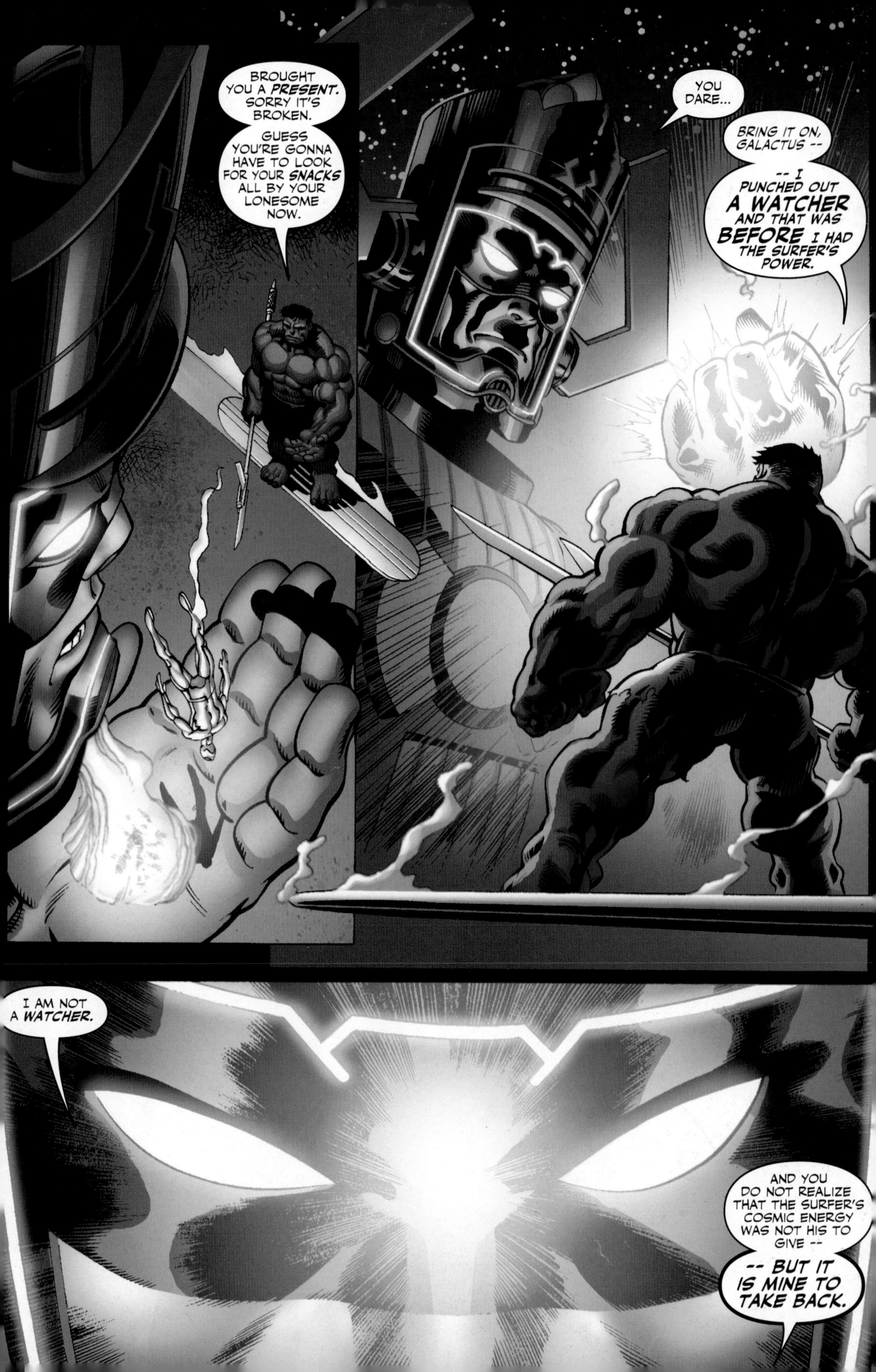
BROUGHT YOU A PRESENT. SORRY IT'S BROKEN.
GUESS YOU'RE GONNA HAVE TO LOOK FOR YOUR SNACKS ALL BY YOUR LONESOME NOW.
YOU DARE...
BRING IT ON, GALACTUS --
-- I PUNCHED OUT A WATCHER AND THAT WAS BEFORE I HAD THE SURFER'S POWER.
I AM NOT A WATCHER.
AND YOU DO NOT REALIZE THAT THE SURFER'S COSMIC ENERGY WAS NOT HIS TO GIVE --
-- BUT IT IS MINE TO TAKE BACK.

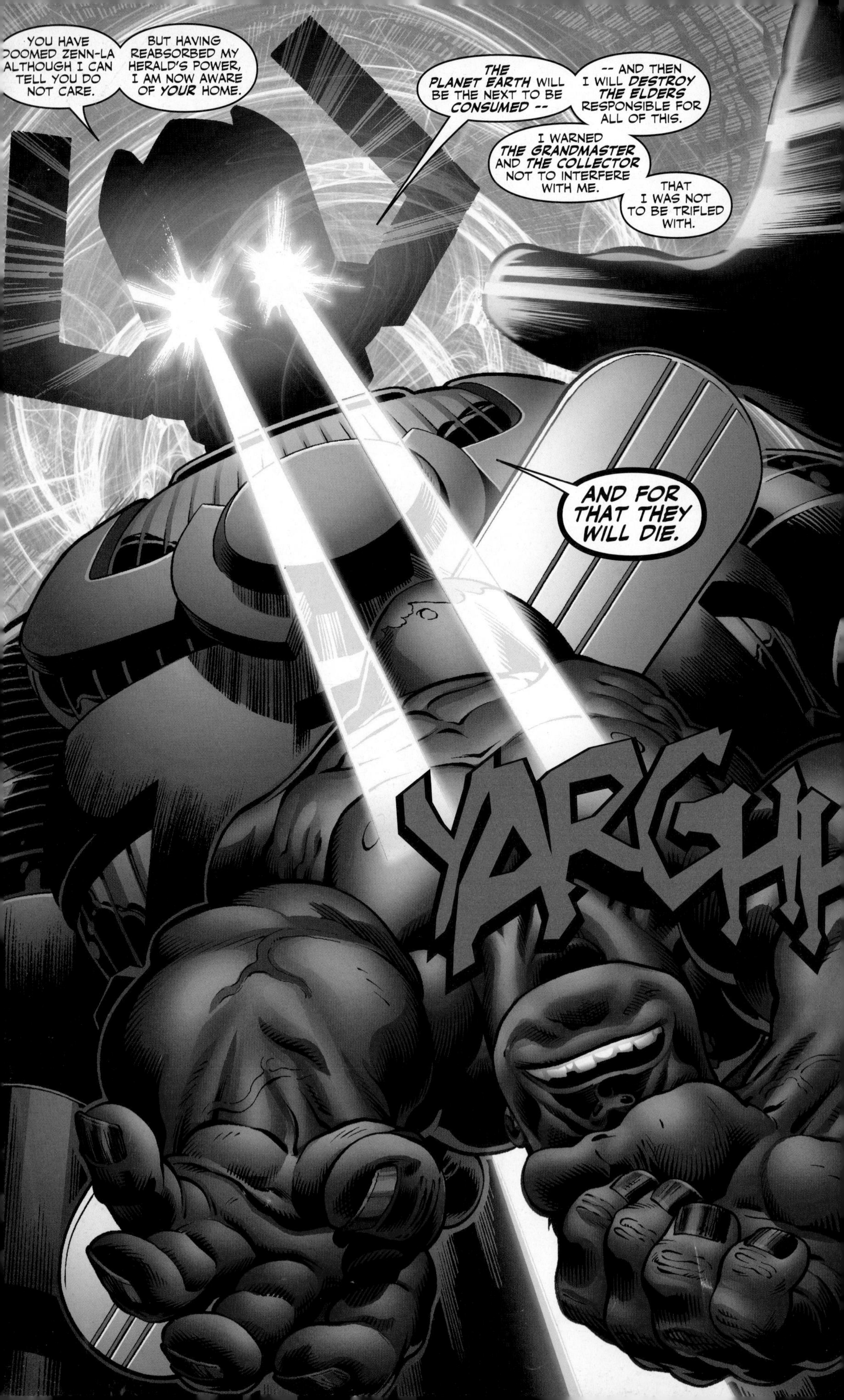
YOU HAVE DOOMED ZENN-LA ALTHOUGH I CAN TELL YOU DO NOT CARE.
BUT HAVING REABSORBED MY HERALD'S POWER, I AM NOW AWARE OF YOUR HOME.
THE PLANET EARTH WILL BE THE NEXT TO BE CONSUMED --
-- AND THEN I WILL DESTROY THE ELDERS RESPONSIBLE FOR ALL OF THIS.
I WARNED THE GRANDMASTER AND THE COLLECTOR NOT TO INTERFERE WITH ME.
THAT I WAS NOT TO BE TRIFLED WITH.
AND FOR THAT THEY WILL DIE.
YARGH!

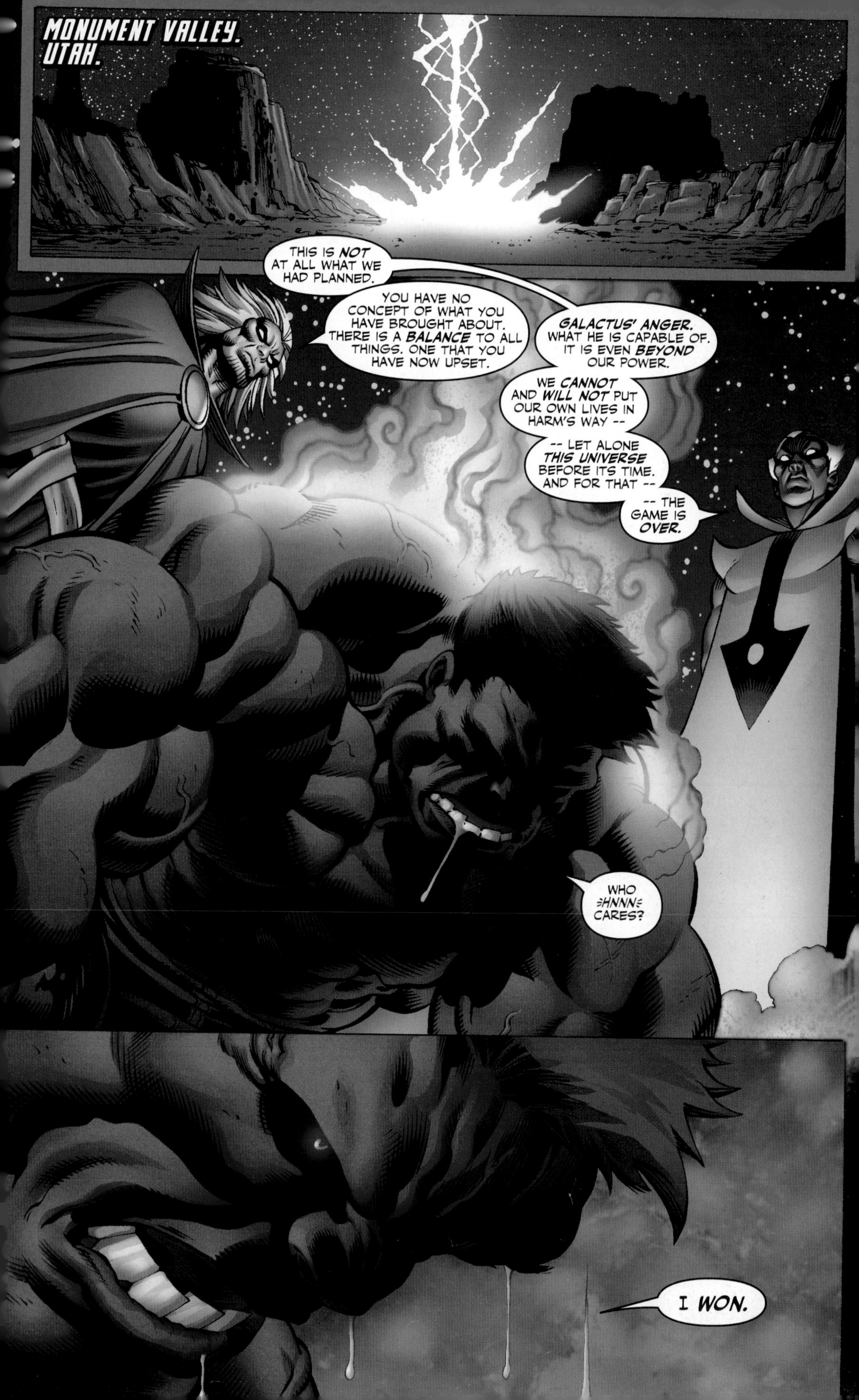
MONUMENT VALLEY. UTAH.
THIS IS NOT AT ALL WHAT WE HAD PLANNED.
YOU HAVE NO CONCEPT OF WHAT YOU HAVE BROUGHT ABOUT. THERE IS A BALANCE TO ALL THINGS. ONE THAT YOU HAVE NOW UPSET.
GALACTUS' ANGER. WHAT HE IS CAPABLE OF. IT IS EVEN BEYOND OUR POWER.
WE CANNOT AND WILL NOT PUT OUR OWN LIVES IN HARM'S WAY --
-- LET ALONE THIS UNIVERSE BEFORE ITS TIME. AND FOR THAT --
-- THE GAME IS OVER.
WHO =HNNN= CARES?
I WON.

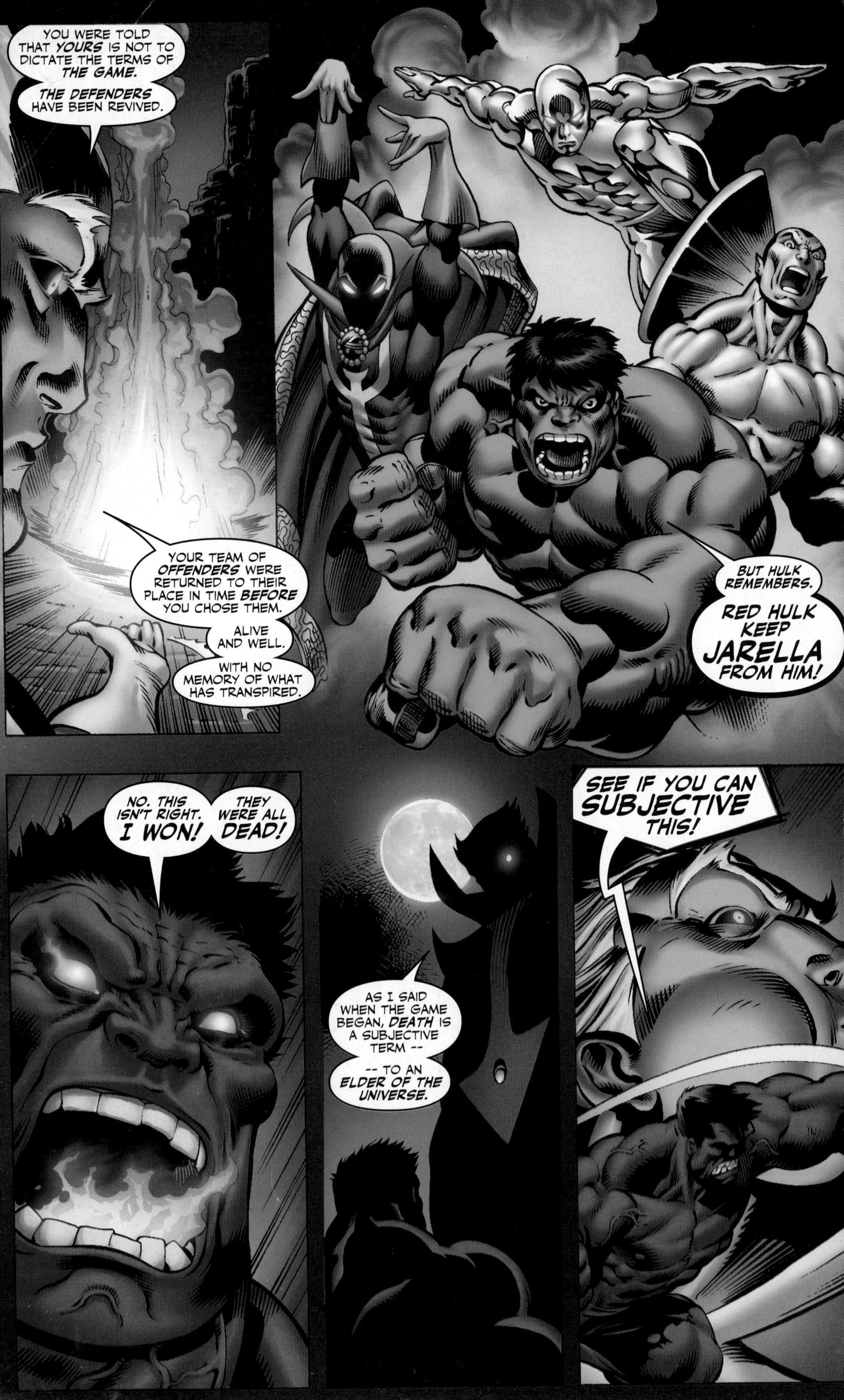
YOU WERE TOLD THAT YOURS IS NOT TO DICTATE THE TERMS OF THE GAME.
THE DEFENDERS HAVE BEEN REVIVED.
YOUR TEAM OF OFFENDERS WERE RETURNED TO THEIR PLACE IN TIME BEFORE YOU CHOSE THEM.
ALIVE AND WELL.
WITH NO MEMORY OF WHAT HAS TRANSPIRED.
BUT HULK REMEMBERS.
RED HULK KEEP JARELLA FROM HIM!
NO. THIS ISN'T RIGHT. I WON!
THEY WERE ALL DEAD!
AS I SAID WHEN THE GAME BEGAN, DEATH IS A SUBJECTIVE TERM --
-- TO AN ELDER OF THE UNIVERSE.
SEE IF YOU CAN SUBJECTIVE THIS!

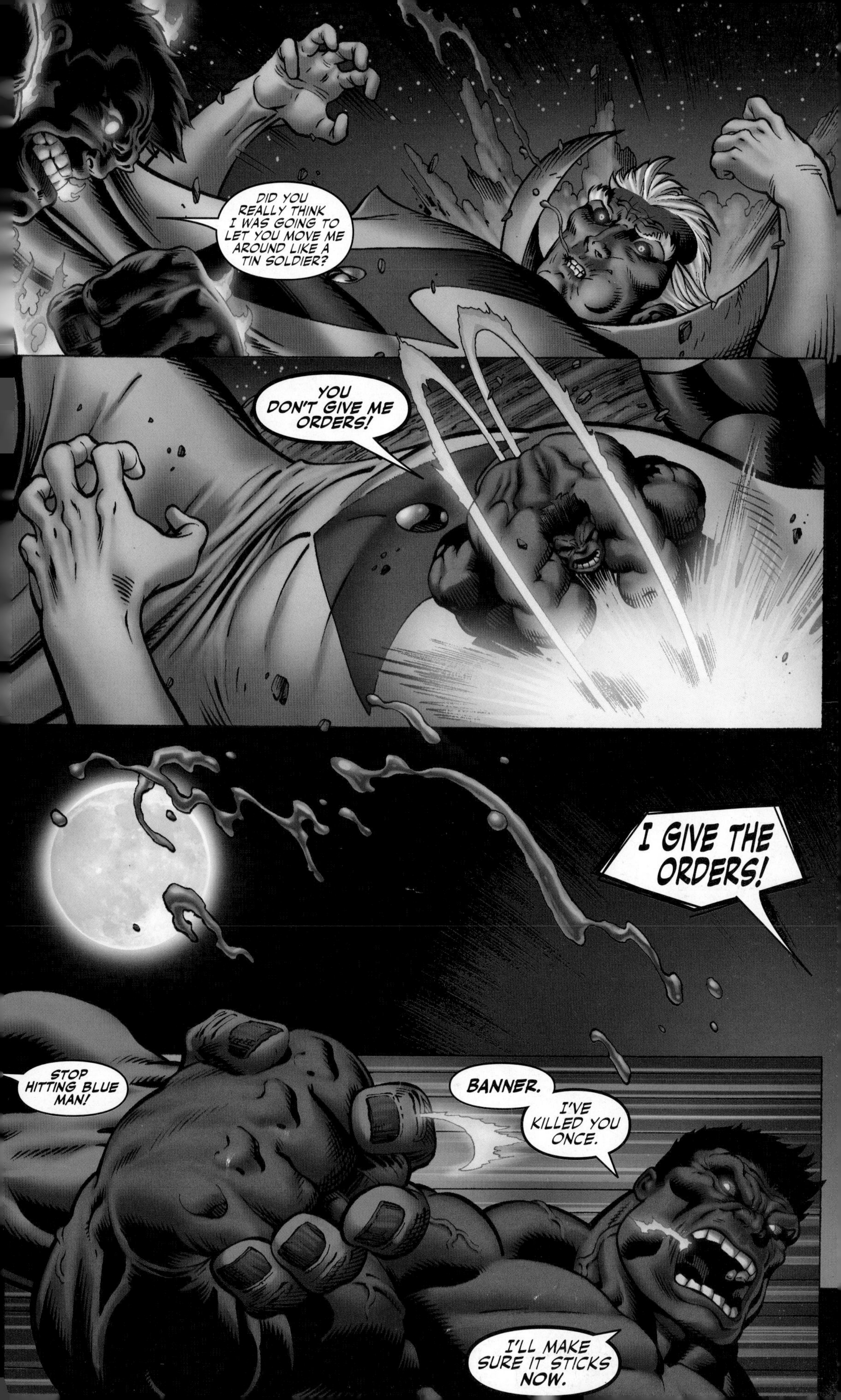
DID YOU REALLY THINK I WAS GOING TO LET YOU MOVE ME AROUND LIKE A TIN SOLDIER?
YOU DON'T GIVE ME ORDERS!
I GIVE THE ORDERS!
STOP HITTING BLUE MAN!
BANNER.
I'VE KILLED YOU ONCE.
I'LL MAKE SURE IT STICKS NOW.

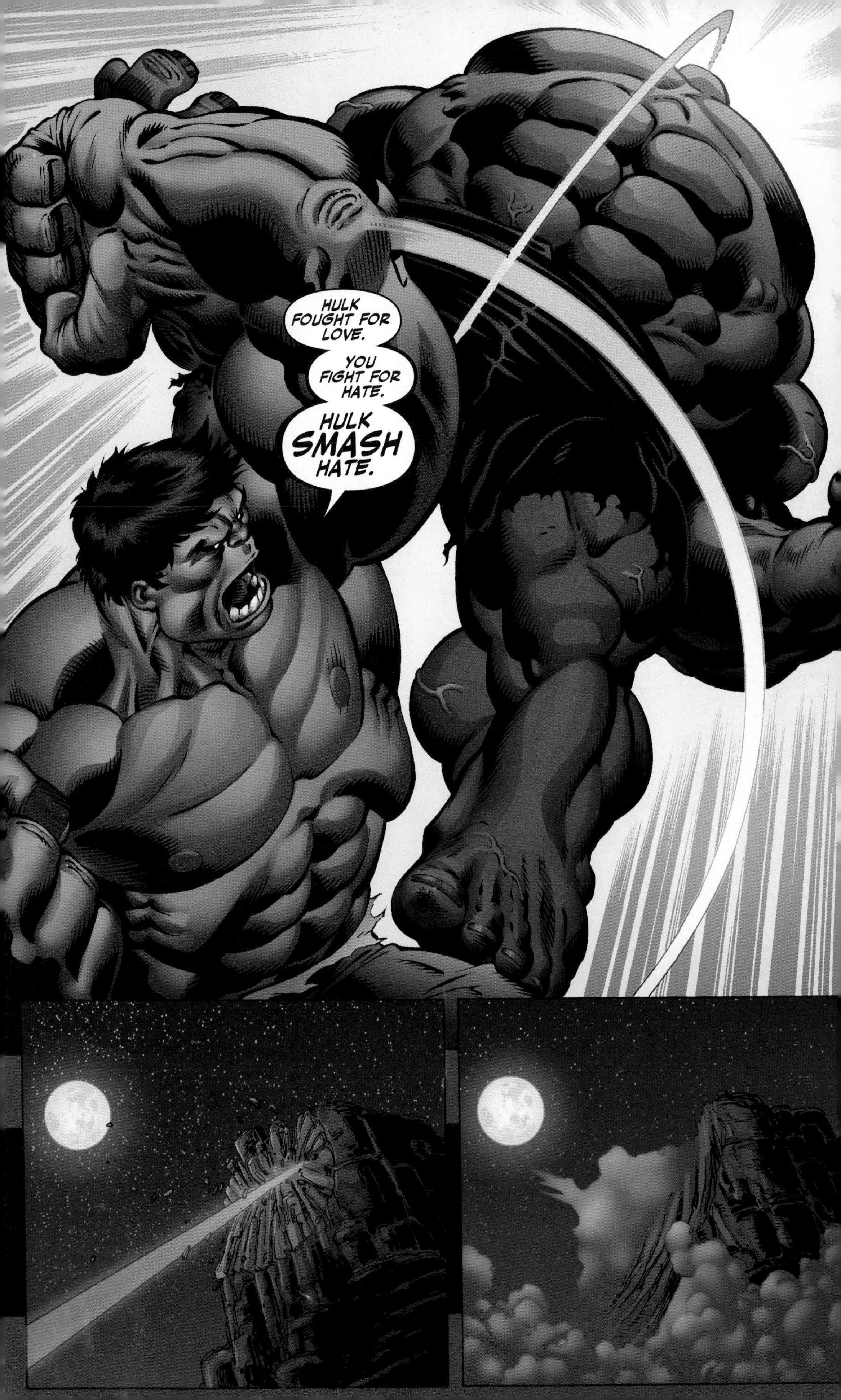

HULK FOUGHT FOR LOVE.
YOU FIGHT FOR HATE.
HULK SMASH HATE.

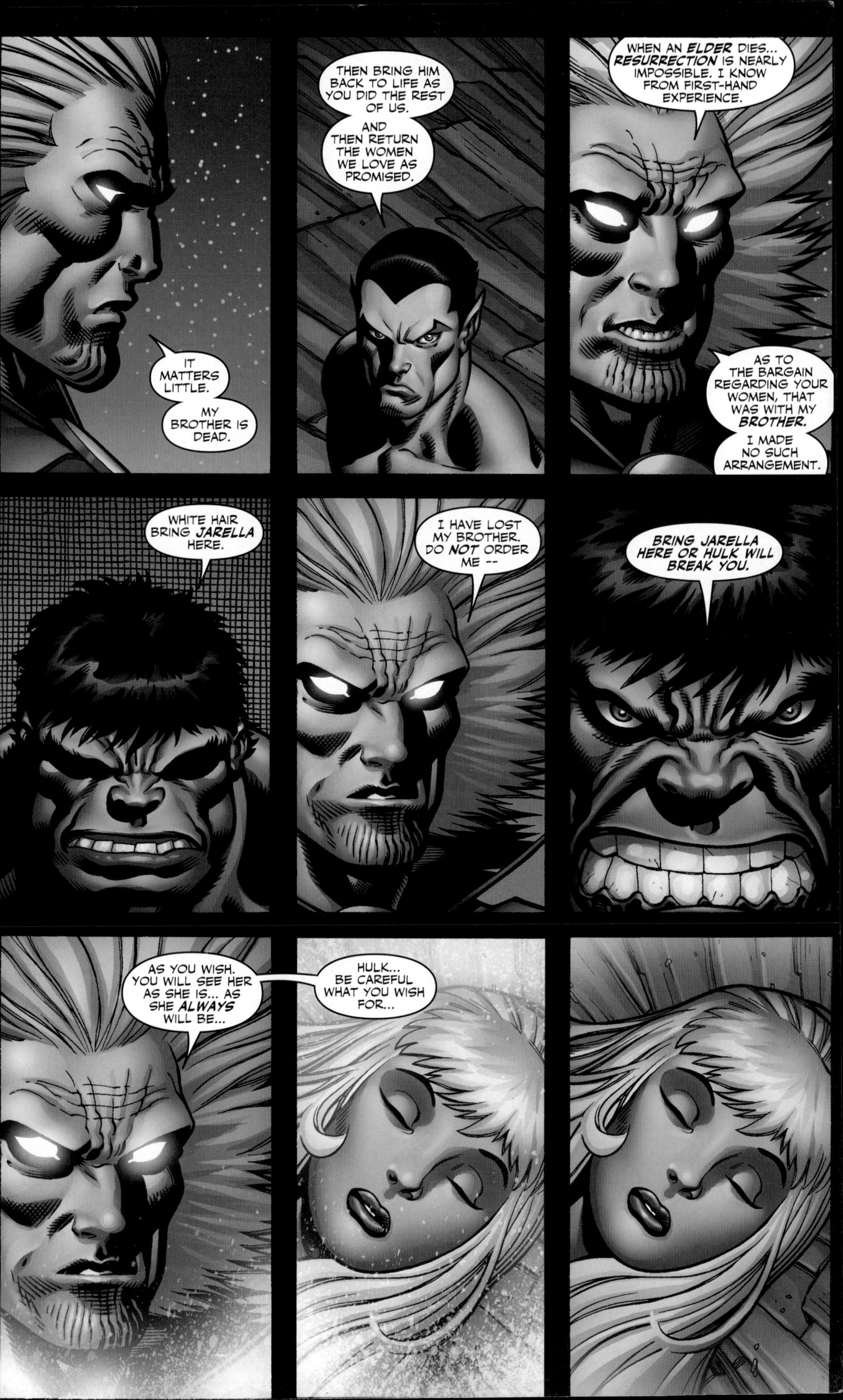
IT MATTERS LITTLE.
MY BROTHER IS DEAD.
THEN BRING HIM BACK TO LIFE AS YOU DID THE REST OF US.
AND THEN RETURN THE WOMEN WE LOVE AS PROMISED.
WHEN AN *ELDER* DIES... *RESURRECTION* IS NEARLY IMPOSSIBLE. I KNOW FROM FIRST-HAND EXPERIENCE.
AS TO THE BARGAIN REGARDING YOUR WOMEN, THAT WAS WITH MY *BROTHER.*
I MADE NO SUCH ARRANGEMENT.
WHITE HAIR BRING *JARELLA* HERE.
I HAVE LOST MY BROTHER. DO *NOT* ORDER ME --
BRING JARELLA HERE OR HULK WILL BREAK YOU.
AS YOU WISH. YOU WILL SEE HER AS SHE IS... AS SHE *ALWAYS* WILL BE...
HULK... BE CAREFUL WHAT YOU WISH FOR...

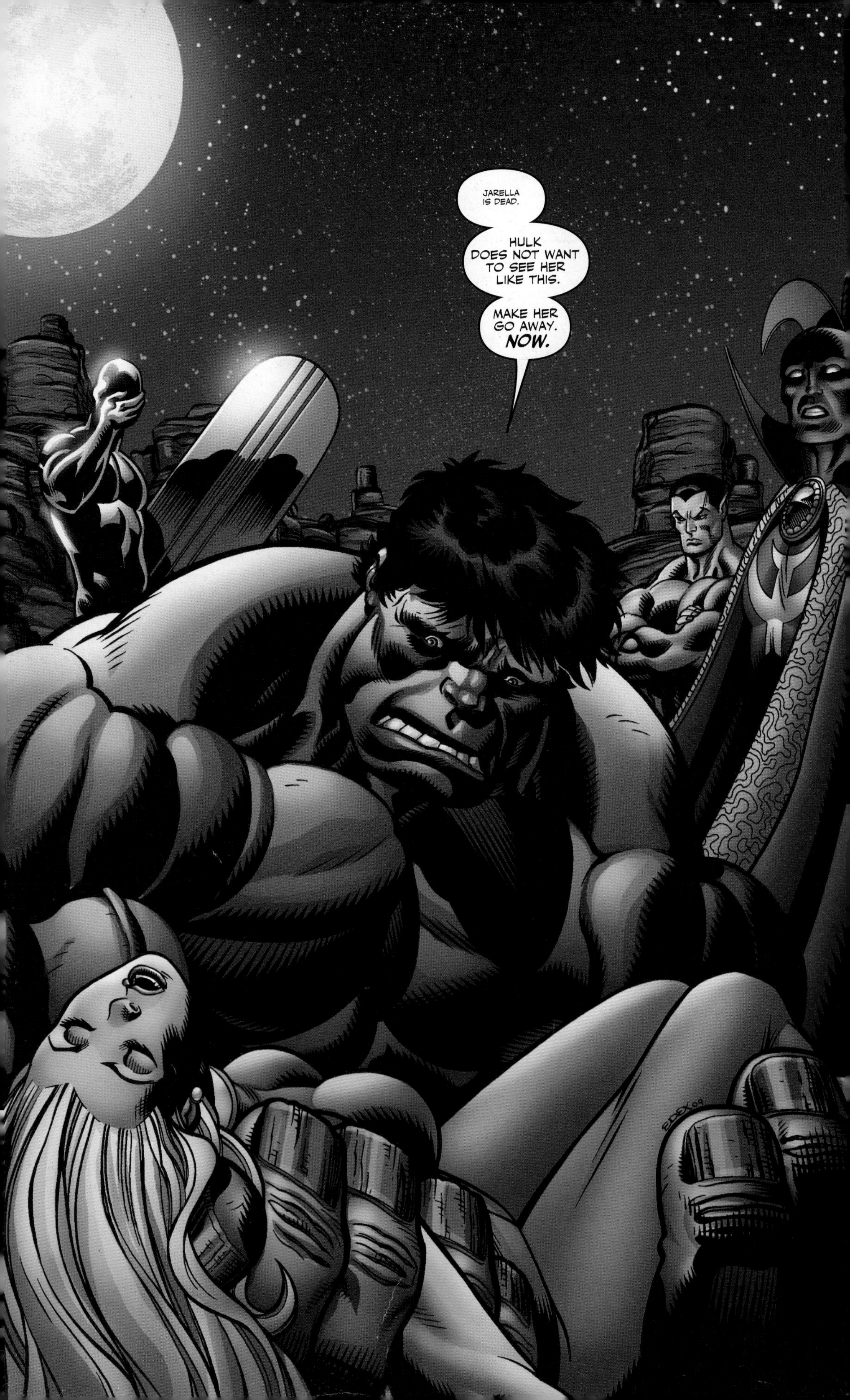
JARELLA IS DEAD.
HULK DOES NOT WANT TO SEE HER LIKE THIS.
MAKE HER GO AWAY. **NOW.**

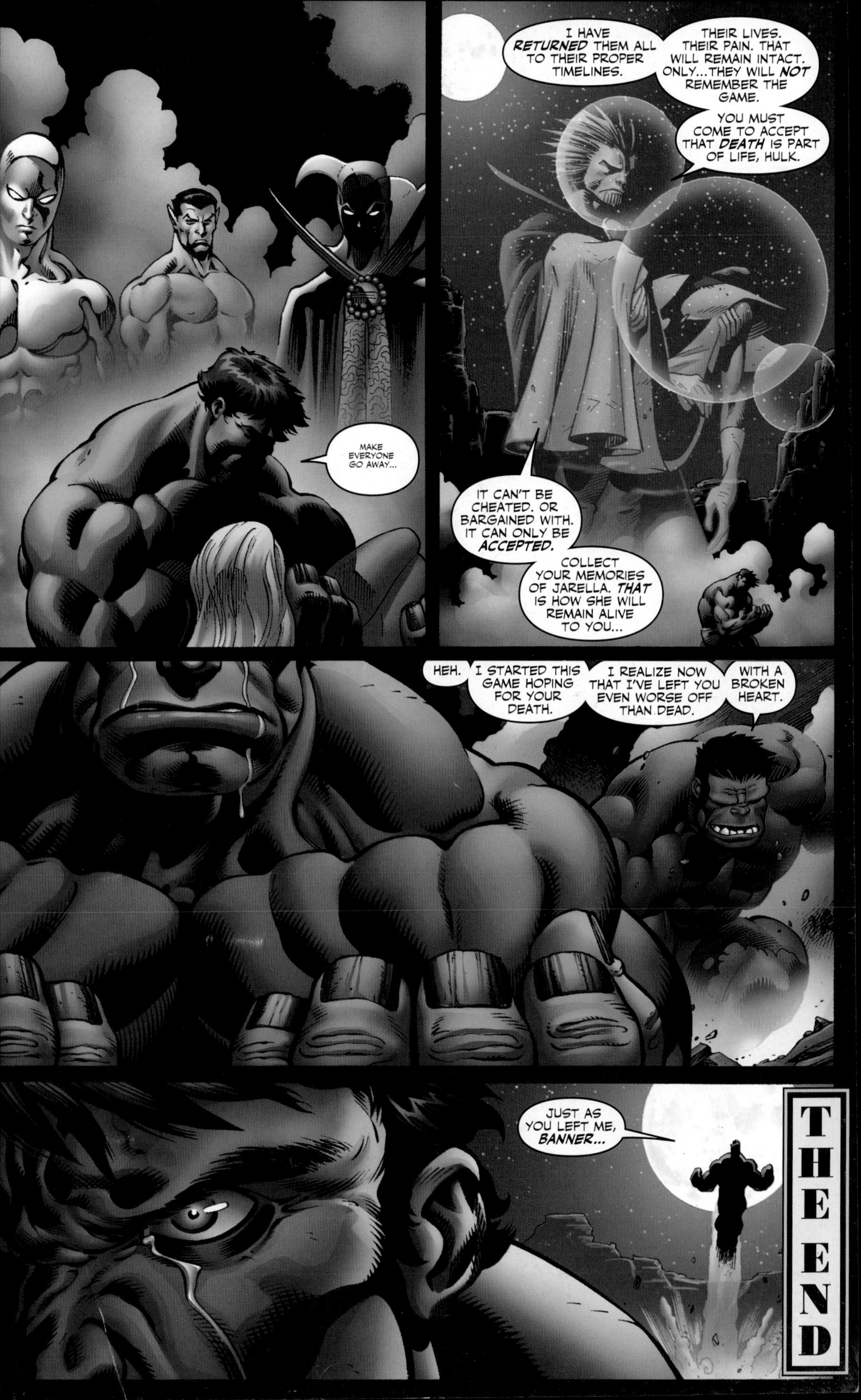
MAKE EVERYONE GO AWAY...
I HAVE *RETURNED* THEM ALL TO THEIR PROPER TIMELINES.
THEIR LIVES. THEIR PAIN. THAT WILL REMAIN INTACT. ONLY...THEY WILL *NOT* REMEMBER THE GAME.
YOU MUST COME TO ACCEPT THAT *DEATH* IS PART OF LIFE, HULK.
IT CAN'T BE CHEATED. OR BARGAINED WITH. IT CAN ONLY BE *ACCEPTED.*
COLLECT YOUR MEMORIES OF JARELLA. *THAT* IS HOW SHE WILL REMAIN ALIVE TO YOU...
HEH.
I STARTED THIS GAME HOPING FOR YOUR DEATH.
I REALIZE NOW THAT I'VE LEFT YOU EVEN WORSE OFF THAN DEAD.
WITH A BROKEN HEART.
JUST AS YOU LEFT ME, *BANNER...*
THE END

ROUND ★ FOUR

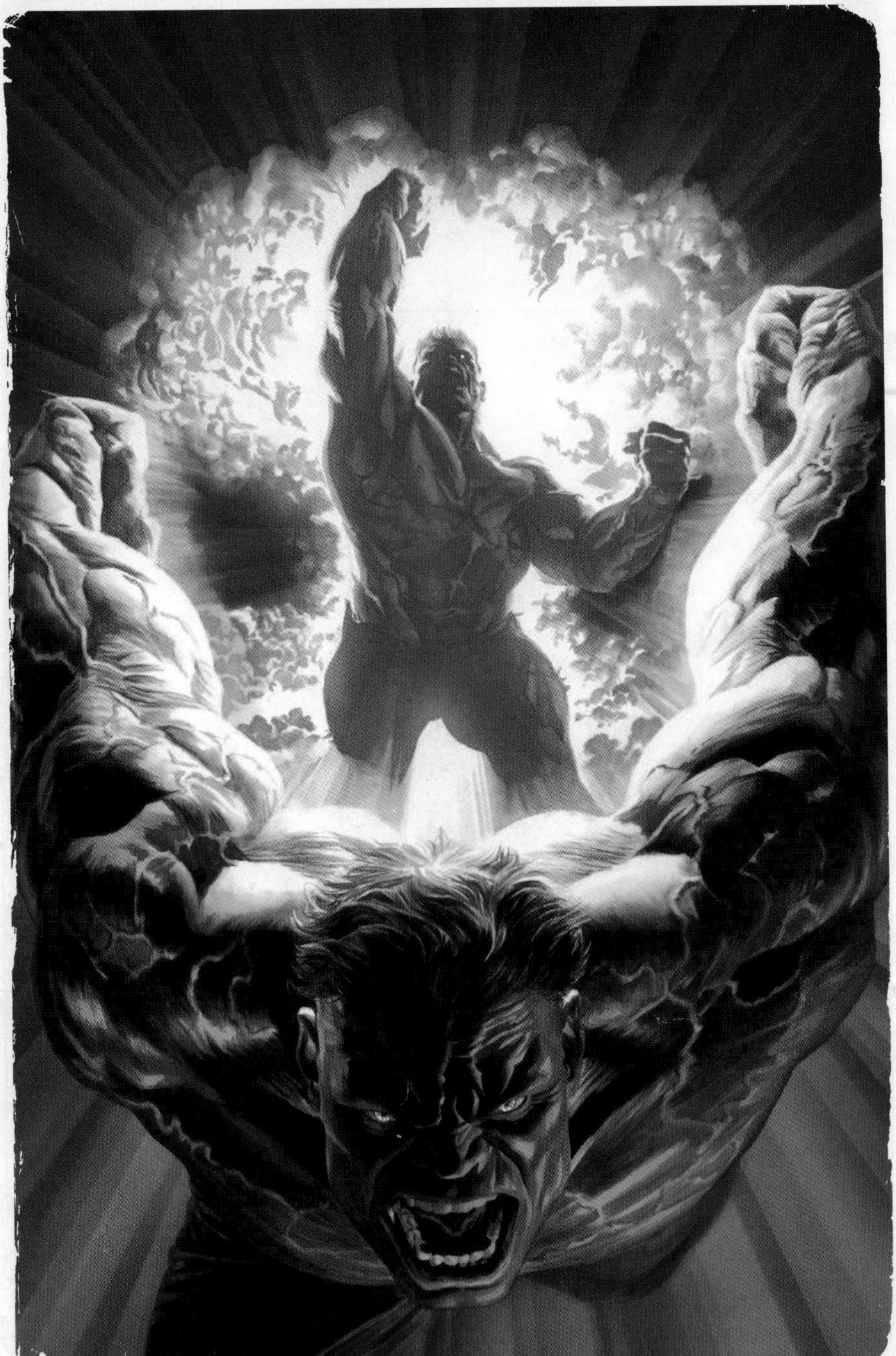

SEEING RED

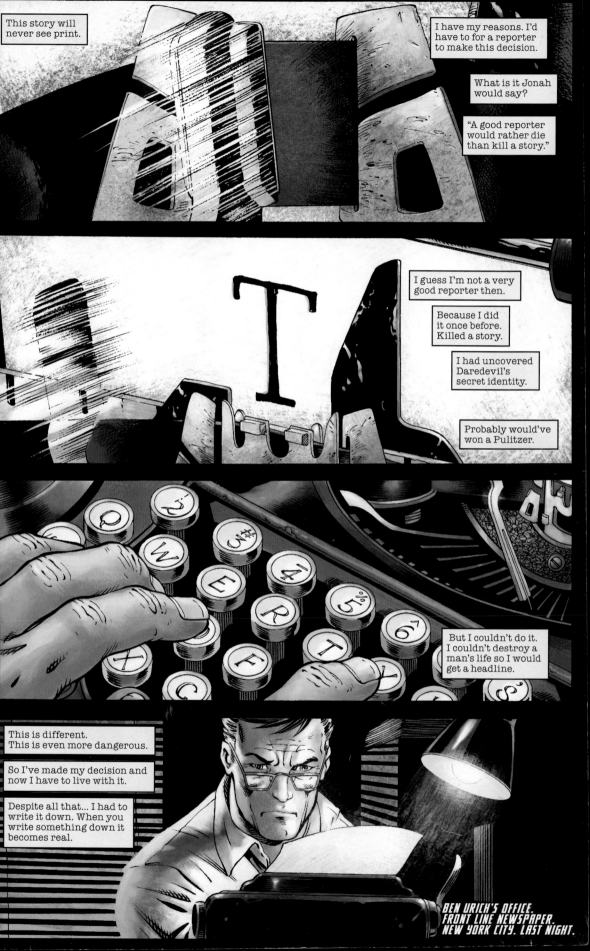

This story will never see print.

I have my reasons. I'd have to for a reporter to make this decision.

What is it Jonah would say?

"A good reporter would rather die than kill a story."

I guess I'm not a very good reporter then.

Because I did it once before. Killed a story.

I had uncovered Daredevil's secret identity.

Probably would've won a Pulitzer.

But I couldn't do it. I couldn't destroy a man's life so I would get a headline.

This is different. This is even more dangerous.

So I've made my decision and now I have to live with it.

Despite all that... I had to write it down. When you write something down it becomes real.

BEN URICH'S OFFICE. FRONT LINE NEWSPAPER. NEW YORK CITY. LAST NIGHT.

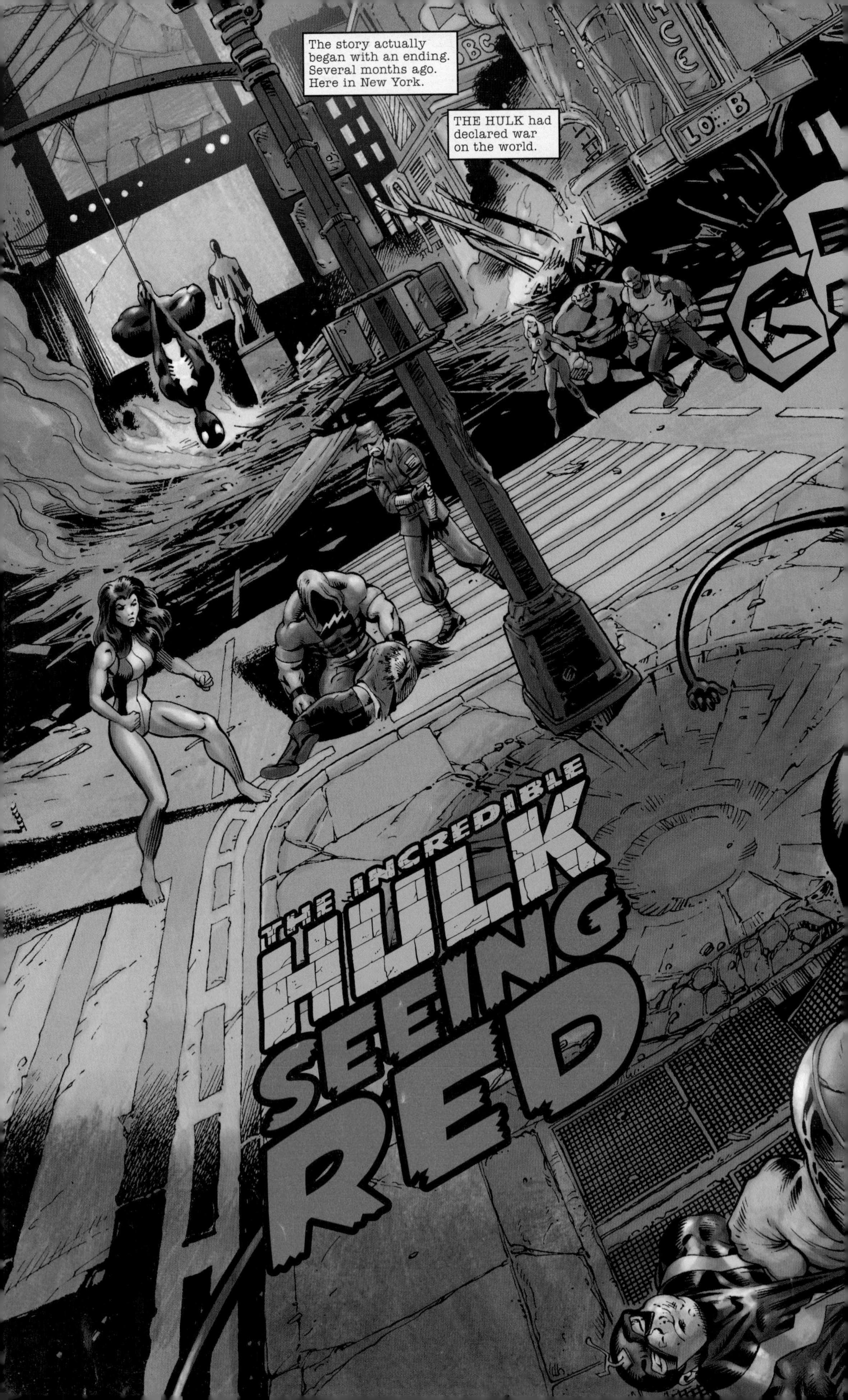
The story actually began with an ending. Several months ago. Here in New York.
THE HULK had declared war on the world.
THE INCREDIBLE HULK
SEEING RED

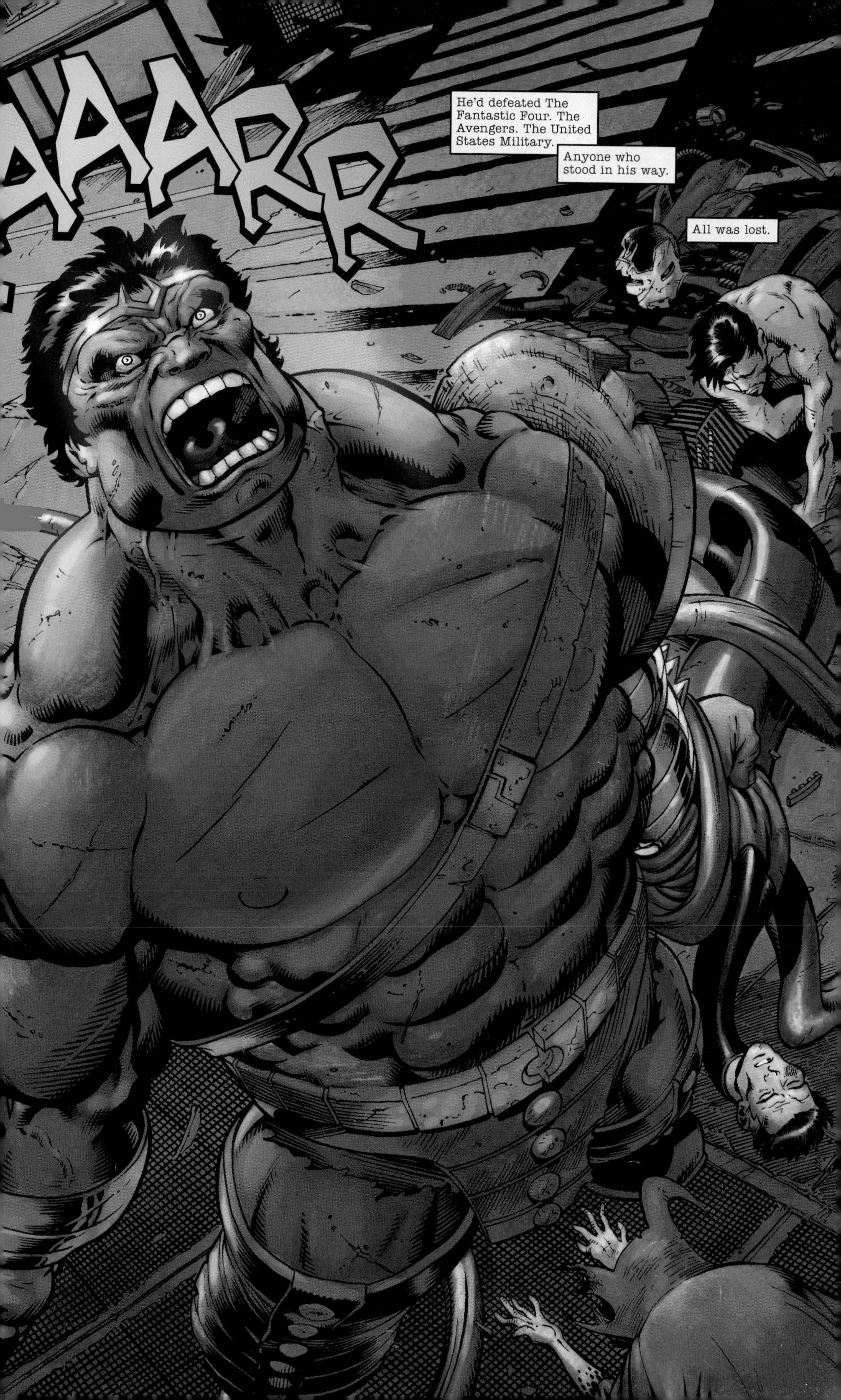
AAARR
He'd defeated The Fantastic Four. The Avengers. The United States Military.
Anyone who stood in his way.
All was lost.

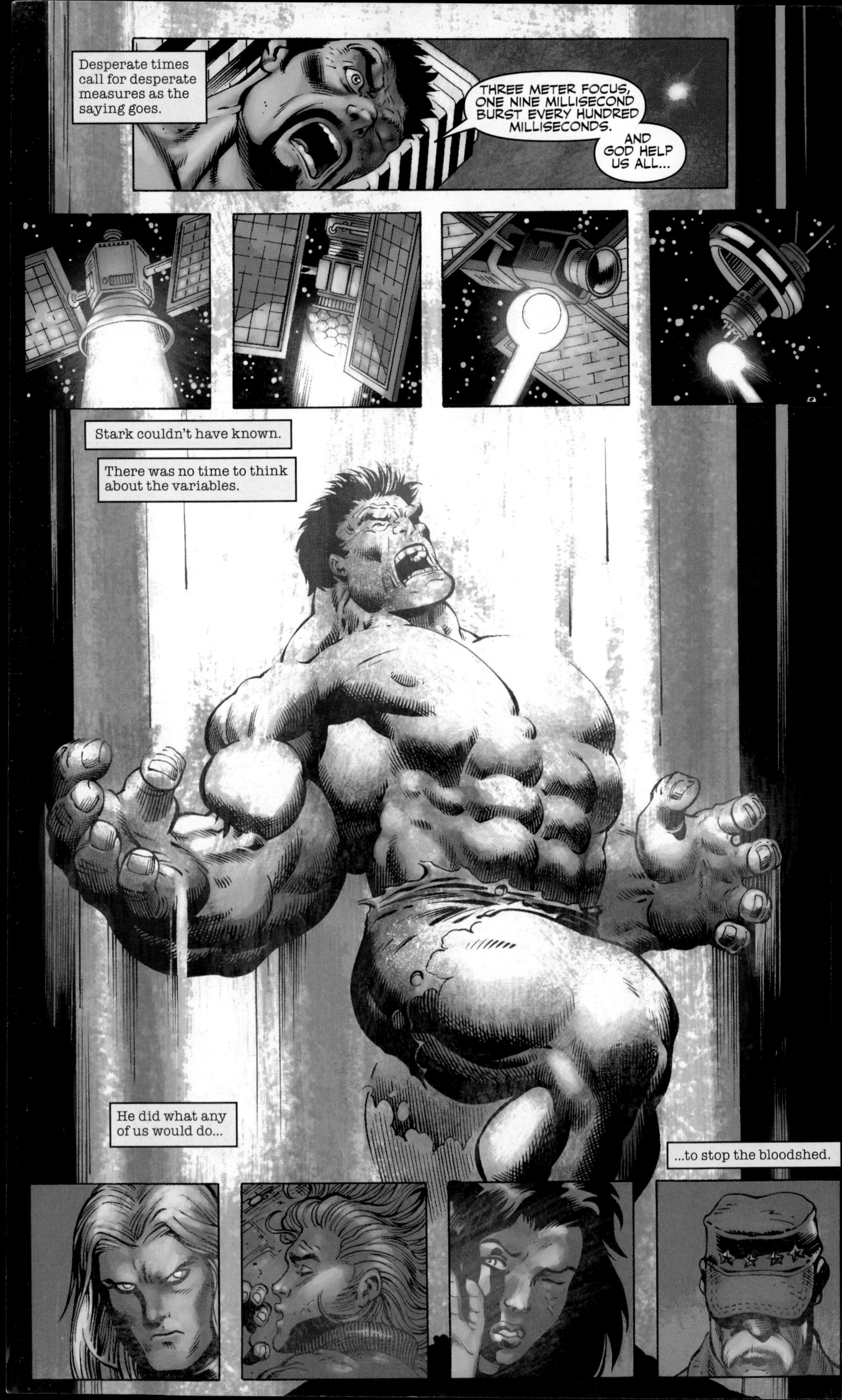

Desperate times call for desperate measures as the saying goes.
THREE METER FOCUS, ONE NINE MILLISECOND BURST EVERY HUNDRED MILLISECONDS.
AND GOD HELP US ALL...
Stark couldn't have known.
There was no time to think about the variables.
He did what any of us would do...
...to stop the bloodshed.

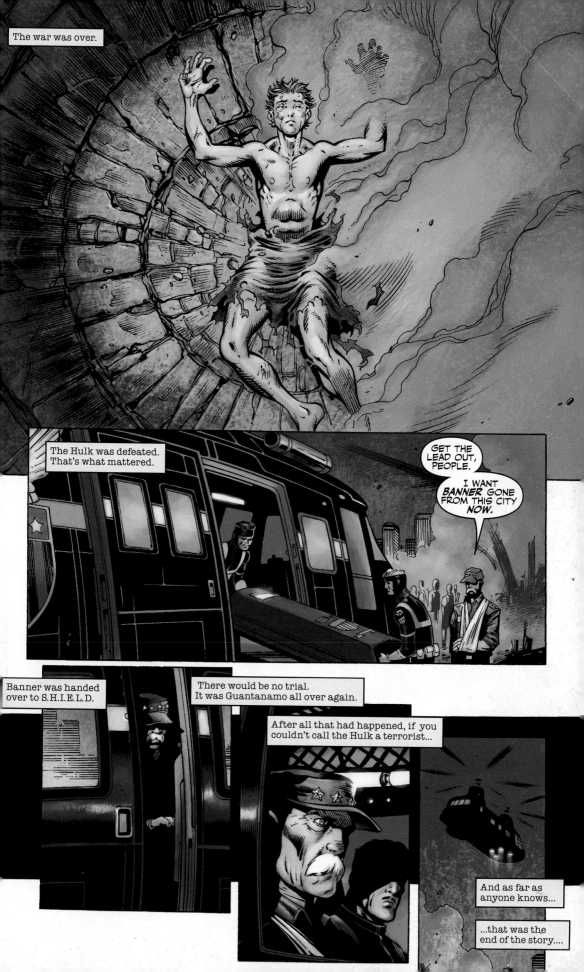

The war was over.

The Hulk was defeated. That's what mattered.

GET THE LEAD OUT, PEOPLE. I WANT *BANNER* GONE FROM THIS CITY *NOW.*

Banner was handed over to S.H.I.E.L.D.

There would be no trial. It was Guantanamo all over again.

After all that had happened, if you couldn't call the Hulk a terrorist...

And as far as anyone knows...

...that was the end of the story....

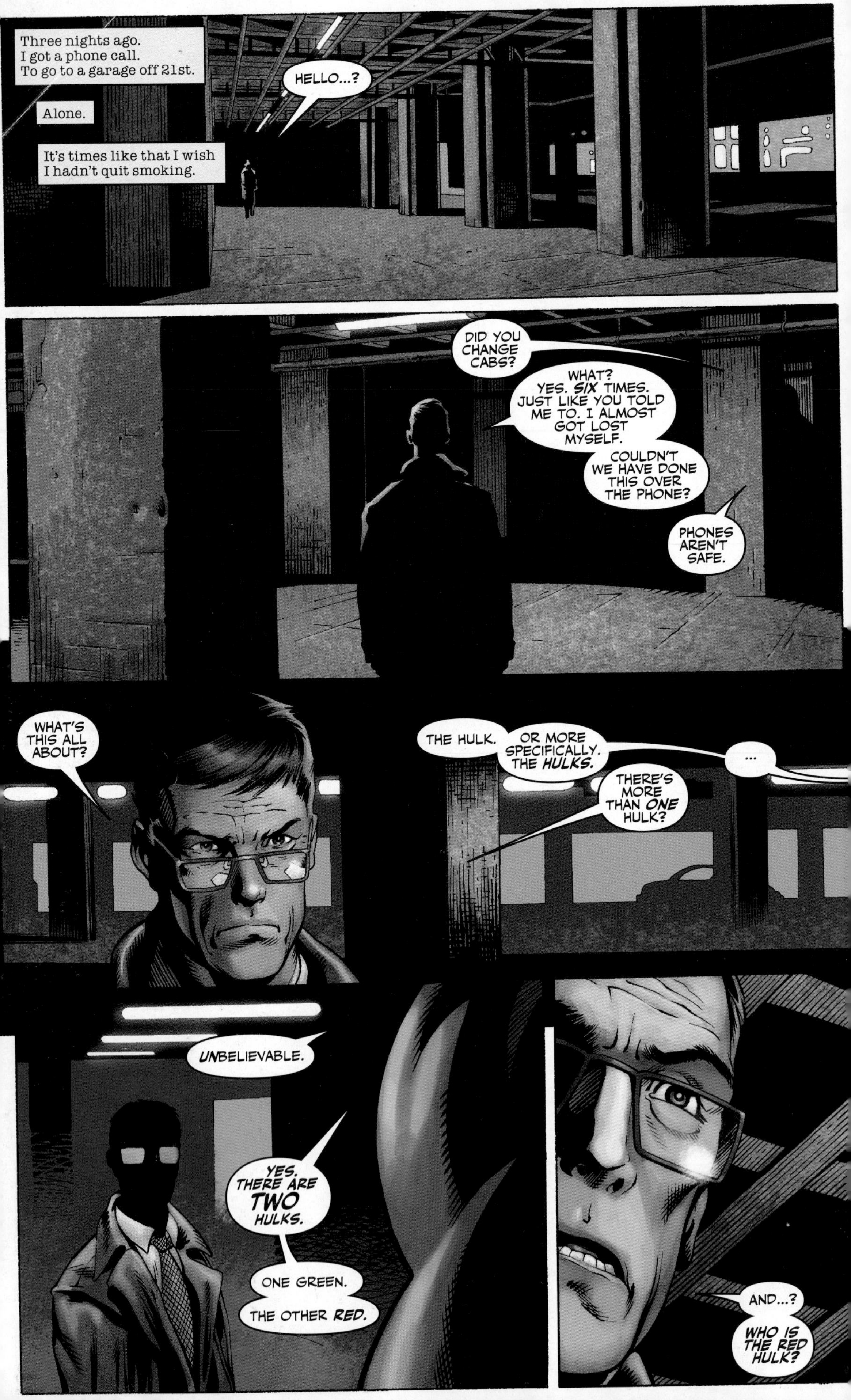

Three nights ago.
I got a phone call.
To go to a garage off 21st.
Alone.
It's times like that I wish I hadn't quit smoking.
HELLO...?
DID YOU CHANGE CABS?
WHAT? YES. SIX TIMES. JUST LIKE YOU TOLD ME TO. I ALMOST GOT LOST MYSELF.
COULDN'T WE HAVE DONE THIS OVER THE PHONE?
PHONES AREN'T SAFE.
WHAT'S THIS ALL ABOUT?
THE HULK.
OR MORE SPECIFICALLY. THE HULKS.
...
THERE'S MORE THAN ONE HULK?
UNBELIEVABLE.
YES. THERE ARE TWO HULKS.
ONE GREEN.
THE OTHER RED.
AND...?
WHO IS THE RED HULK?

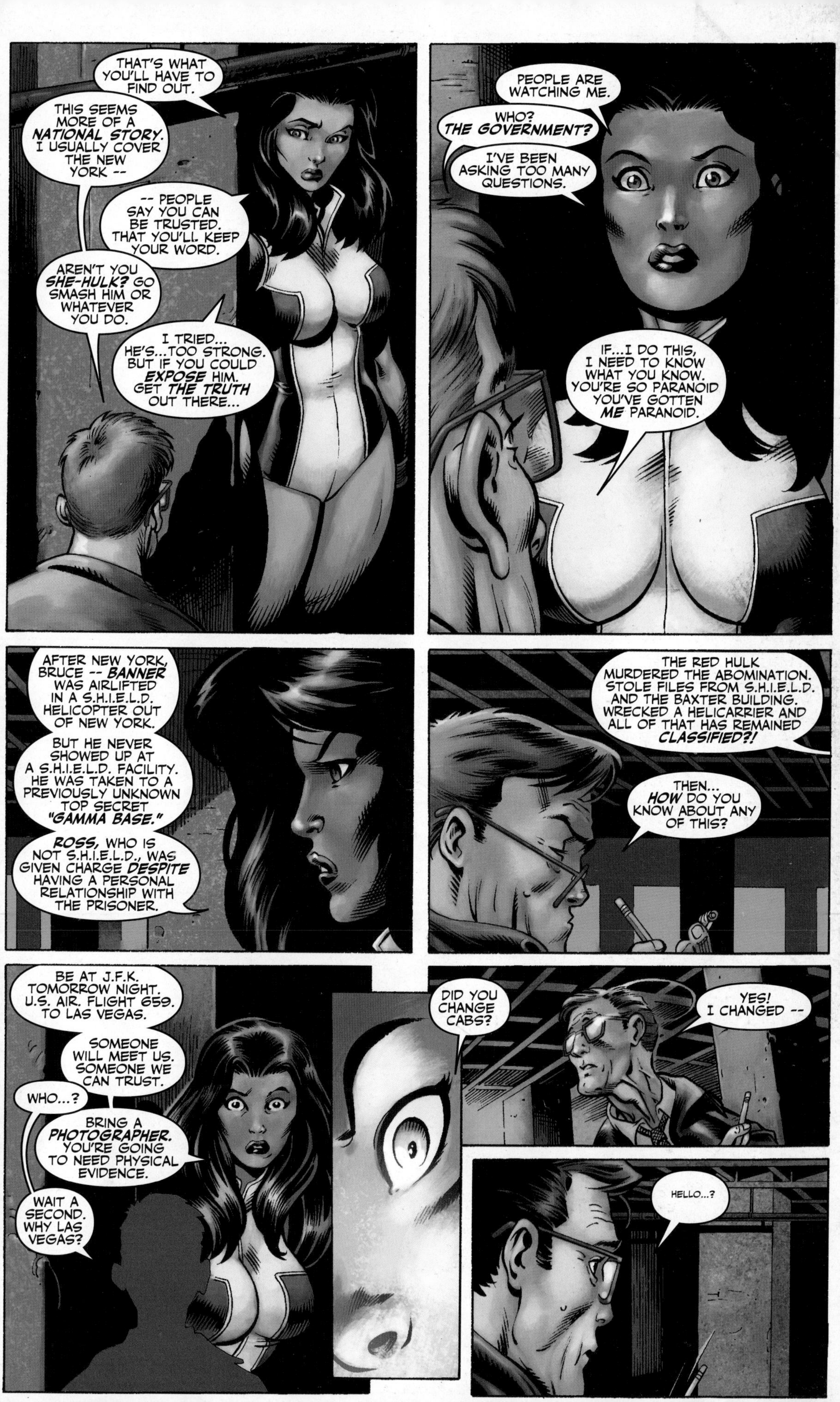

THAT'S WHAT YOU'LL HAVE TO FIND OUT.
THIS SEEMS MORE OF A NATIONAL STORY. I USUALLY COVER THE NEW YORK --
-- PEOPLE SAY YOU CAN BE TRUSTED. THAT YOU'LL KEEP YOUR WORD.
AREN'T YOU SHE-HULK? GO SMASH HIM OR WHATEVER YOU DO.
I TRIED... HE'S...TOO STRONG. BUT IF YOU COULD EXPOSE HIM. GET THE TRUTH OUT THERE...
PEOPLE ARE WATCHING ME.
WHO? THE GOVERNMENT?
I'VE BEEN ASKING TOO MANY QUESTIONS.
IF...I DO THIS, I NEED TO KNOW WHAT YOU KNOW. YOU'RE SO PARANOID YOU'VE GOTTEN ME PARANOID.
AFTER NEW YORK, BRUCE -- BANNER WAS AIRLIFTED IN A S.H.I.E.L.D. HELICOPTER OUT OF NEW YORK.
BUT HE NEVER SHOWED UP AT A S.H.I.E.L.D. FACILITY. HE WAS TAKEN TO A PREVIOUSLY UNKNOWN TOP SECRET "GAMMA BASE."
ROSS, WHO IS NOT S.H.I.E.L.D., WAS GIVEN CHARGE DESPITE HAVING A PERSONAL RELATIONSHIP WITH THE PRISONER.
THE RED HULK MURDERED THE ABOMINATION. STOLE FILES FROM S.H.I.E.L.D. AND THE BAXTER BUILDING. WRECKED A HELICARRIER AND ALL OF THAT HAS REMAINED CLASSIFIED?!
THEN... HOW DO YOU KNOW ABOUT ANY OF THIS?
BE AT J.F.K. TOMORROW NIGHT. U.S. AIR. FLIGHT 659. TO LAS VEGAS.
SOMEONE WILL MEET US. SOMEONE WE CAN TRUST.
WHO...?
BRING A PHOTOGRAPHER. YOU'RE GOING TO NEED PHYSICAL EVIDENCE.
WAIT A SECOND. WHY LAS VEGAS?
DID YOU CHANGE CABS?
YES! I CHANGED --
HELLO...?

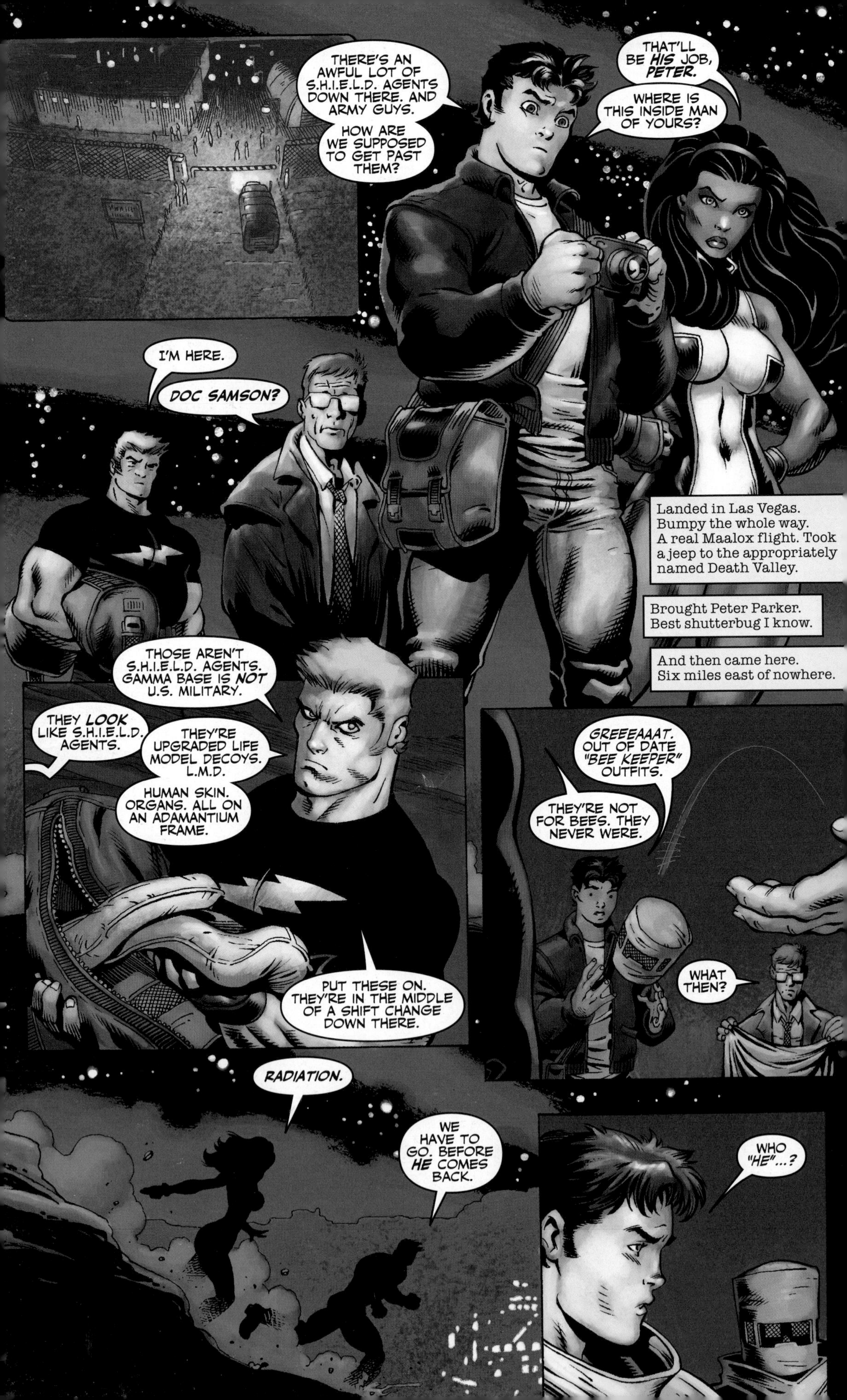
THERE'S AN AWFUL LOT OF S.H.I.E.L.D. AGENTS DOWN THERE. AND ARMY GUYS.
HOW ARE WE SUPPOSED TO GET PAST THEM?
THAT'LL BE HIS JOB, PETER.
WHERE IS THIS INSIDE MAN OF YOURS?
I'M HERE.
DOC SAMSON?
Landed in Las Vegas. Bumpy the whole way. A real Maalox flight. Took a jeep to the appropriately named Death Valley.
Brought Peter Parker. Best shutterbug I know.
And then came here. Six miles east of nowhere.
THOSE AREN'T S.H.I.E.L.D. AGENTS. GAMMA BASE IS NOT U.S. MILITARY.
THEY LOOK LIKE S.H.I.E.L.D. AGENTS.
THEY'RE UPGRADED LIFE MODEL DECOYS. L.M.D.
HUMAN SKIN. ORGANS. ALL ON AN ADAMANTIUM FRAME.
PUT THESE ON. THEY'RE IN THE MIDDLE OF A SHIFT CHANGE DOWN THERE.
GREEEAAAT. OUT OF DATE "BEE KEEPER" OUTFITS.
THEY'RE NOT FOR BEES. THEY NEVER WERE.
WHAT THEN?
RADIATION.
WE HAVE TO GO. BEFORE HE COMES BACK.
WHO "HE"...?

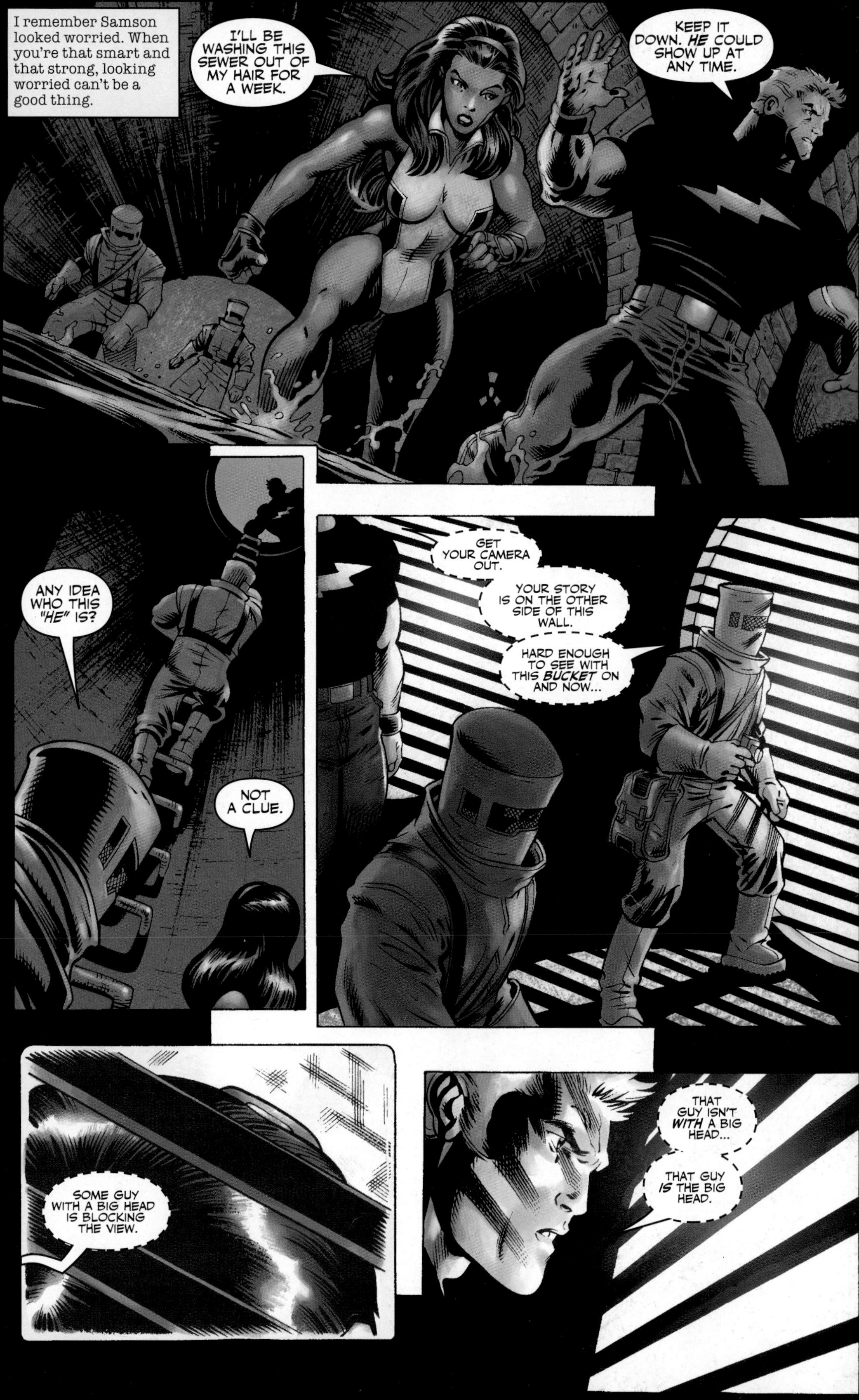

I remember Samson looked worried. When you're that smart and that strong, looking worried can't be a good thing.
I'LL BE WASHING THIS SEWER OUT OF MY HAIR FOR A WEEK.
KEEP IT DOWN. HE COULD SHOW UP AT ANY TIME.
ANY IDEA WHO THIS "HE" IS?
NOT A CLUE.
GET YOUR CAMERA OUT.
YOUR STORY IS ON THE OTHER SIDE OF THIS WALL.
HARD ENOUGH TO SEE WITH THIS BUCKET ON AND NOW...
SOME GUY WITH A BIG HEAD IS BLOCKING THE VIEW.
THAT GUY ISN'T WITH A BIG HEAD...
THAT GUY IS THE BIG HEAD.

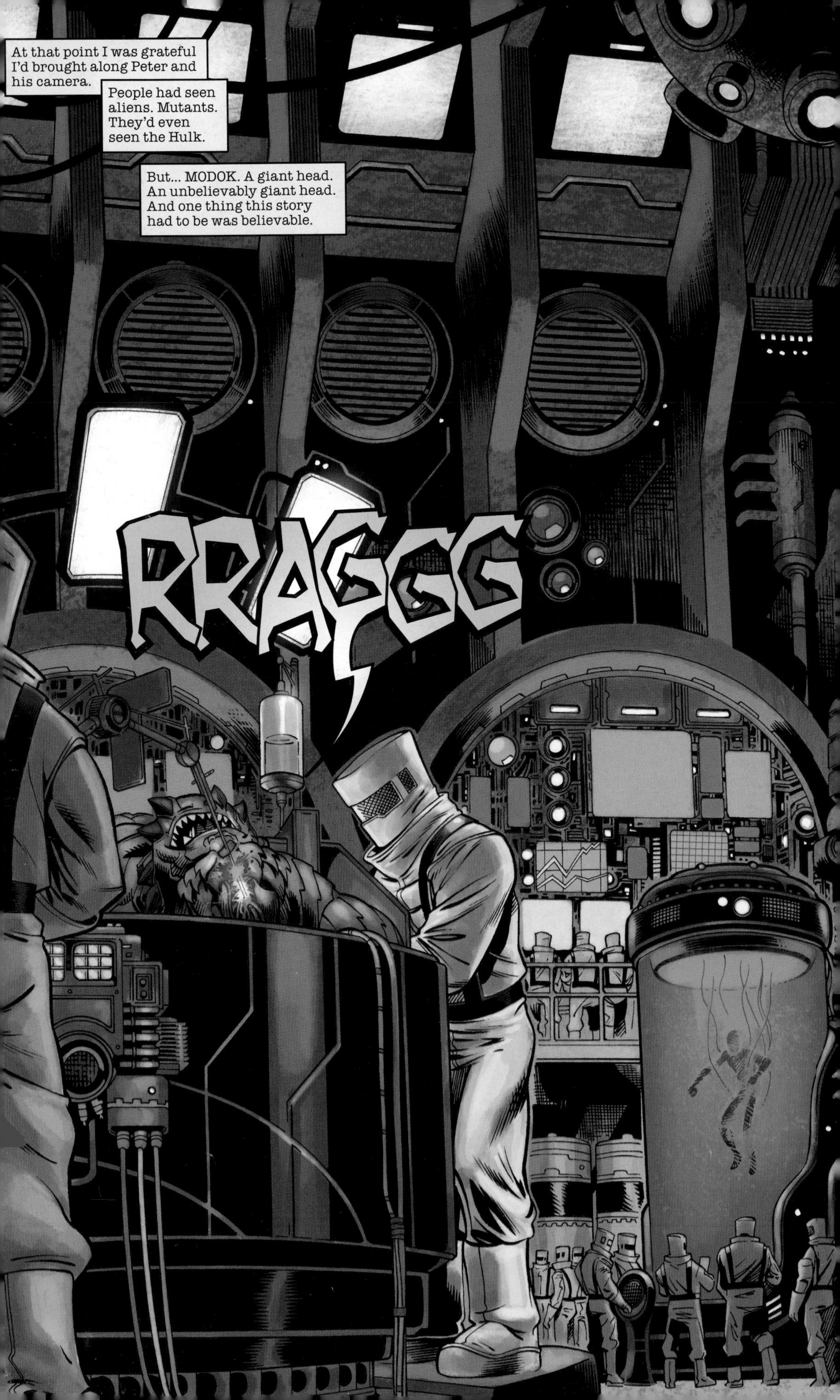
At that point I was grateful I'd brought along Peter and his camera.
People had seen aliens. Mutants. They'd even seen the Hulk.
But... MODOK. A giant head. An unbelievably giant head. And one thing this story had to be was believable.
RRAGGG

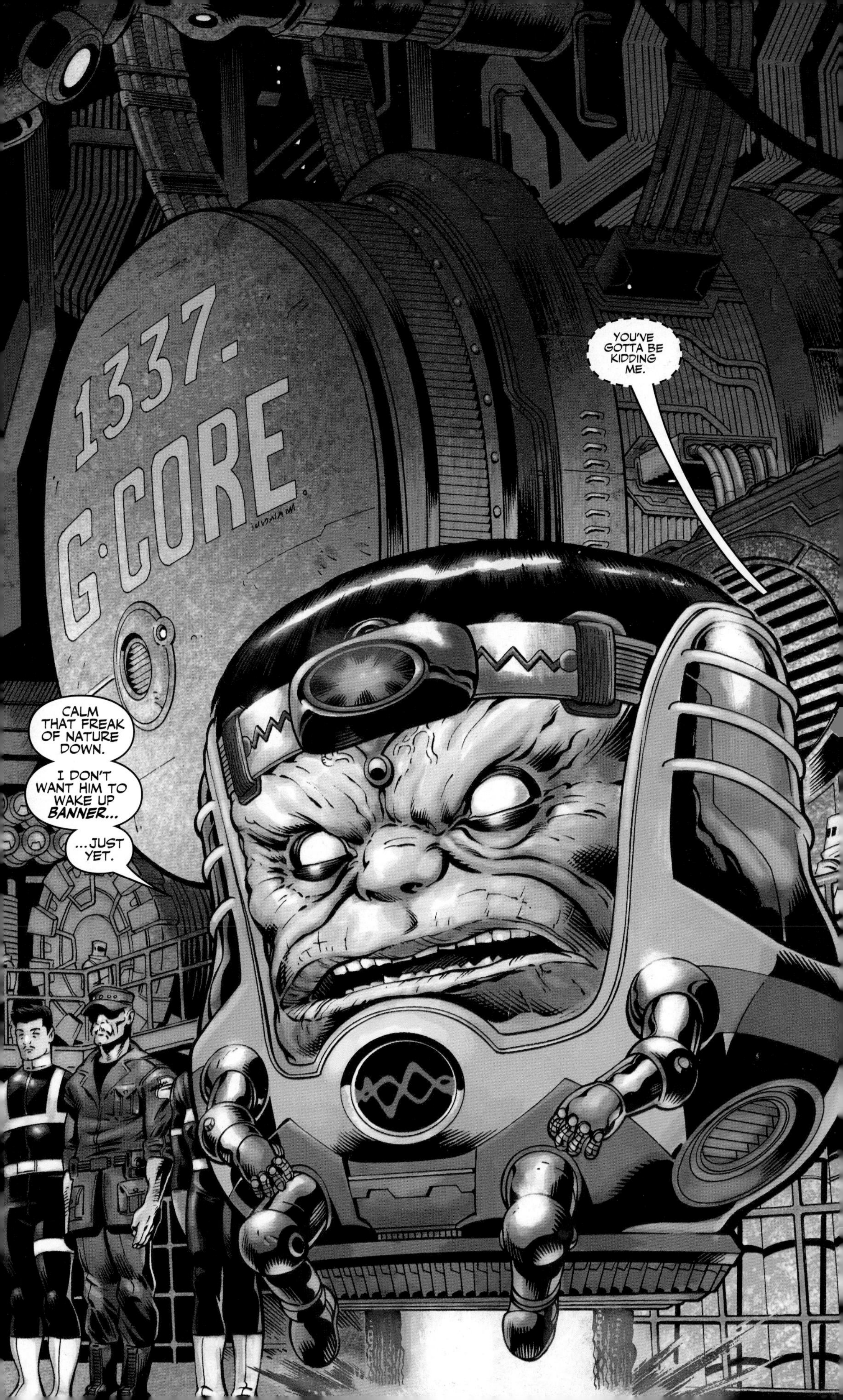
1337-
G-CORE
YOU'VE GOTTA BE KIDDING ME.
CALM THAT FREAK OF NATURE DOWN.
I DON'T WANT HIM TO WAKE UP BANNER...
...JUST YET.

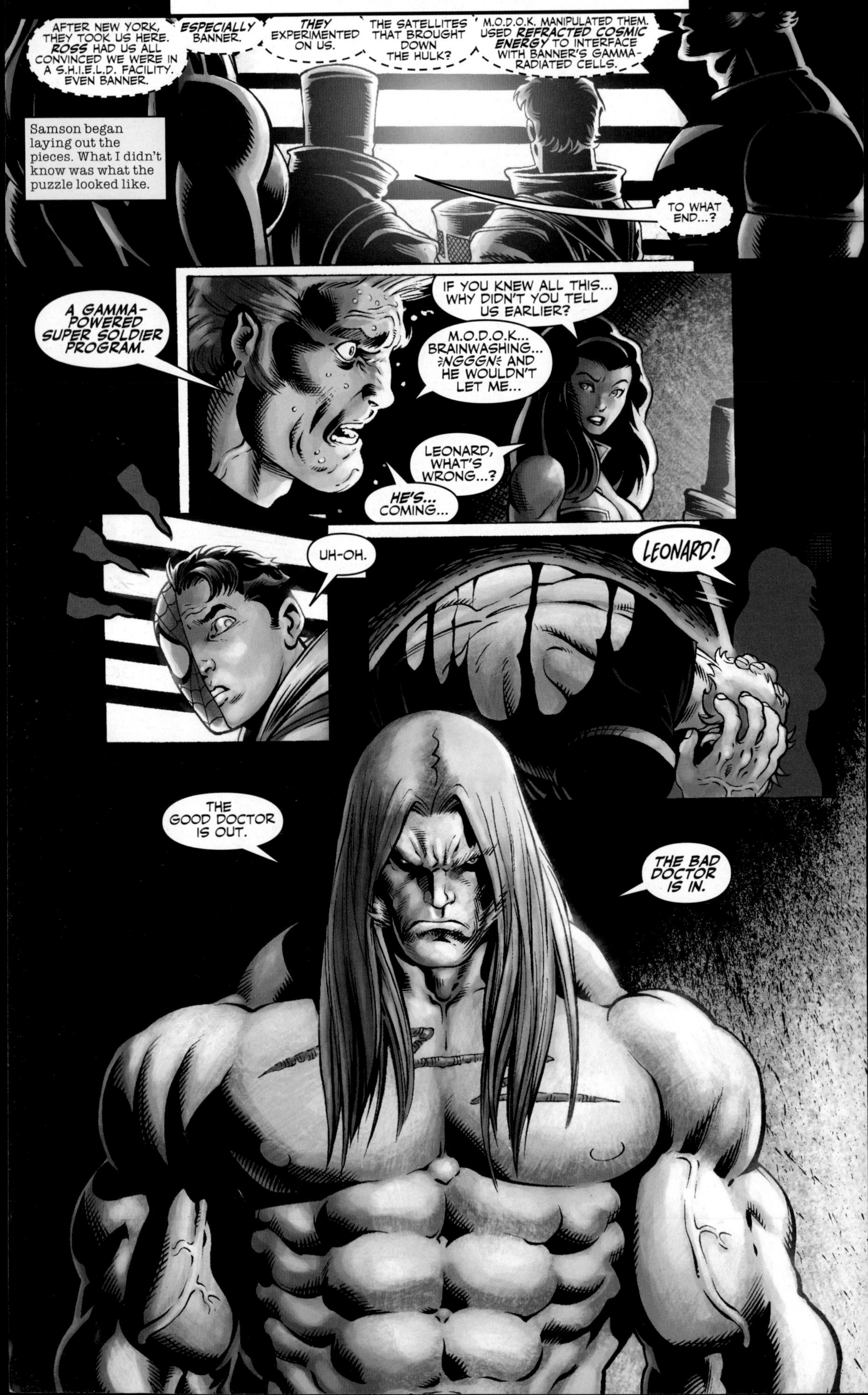
AFTER NEW YORK, THEY TOOK US HERE. ROSS HAD US ALL CONVINCED WE WERE IN A S.H.I.E.L.D. FACILITY. EVEN BANNER.
ESPECIALLY BANNER.
THEY EXPERIMENTED ON US.
THE SATELLITES THAT BROUGHT DOWN THE HULK?
M.O.D.O.K. MANIPULATED THEM. USED REFRACTED COSMIC ENERGY TO INTERFACE WITH BANNER'S GAMMA-RADIATED CELLS.
Samson began laying out the pieces. What I didn't know was what the puzzle looked like.
TO WHAT END...?
A GAMMA-POWERED SUPER SOLDIER PROGRAM.
IF YOU KNEW ALL THIS... WHY DIDN'T YOU TELL US EARLIER?
M.O.D.O.K... BRAINWASHING... NGGGN AND HE WOULDN'T LET ME...
LEONARD, WHAT'S WRONG...?
HE'S... COMING...
UH-OH.
LEONARD!
THE GOOD DOCTOR IS OUT.
THE BAD DOCTOR IS IN.

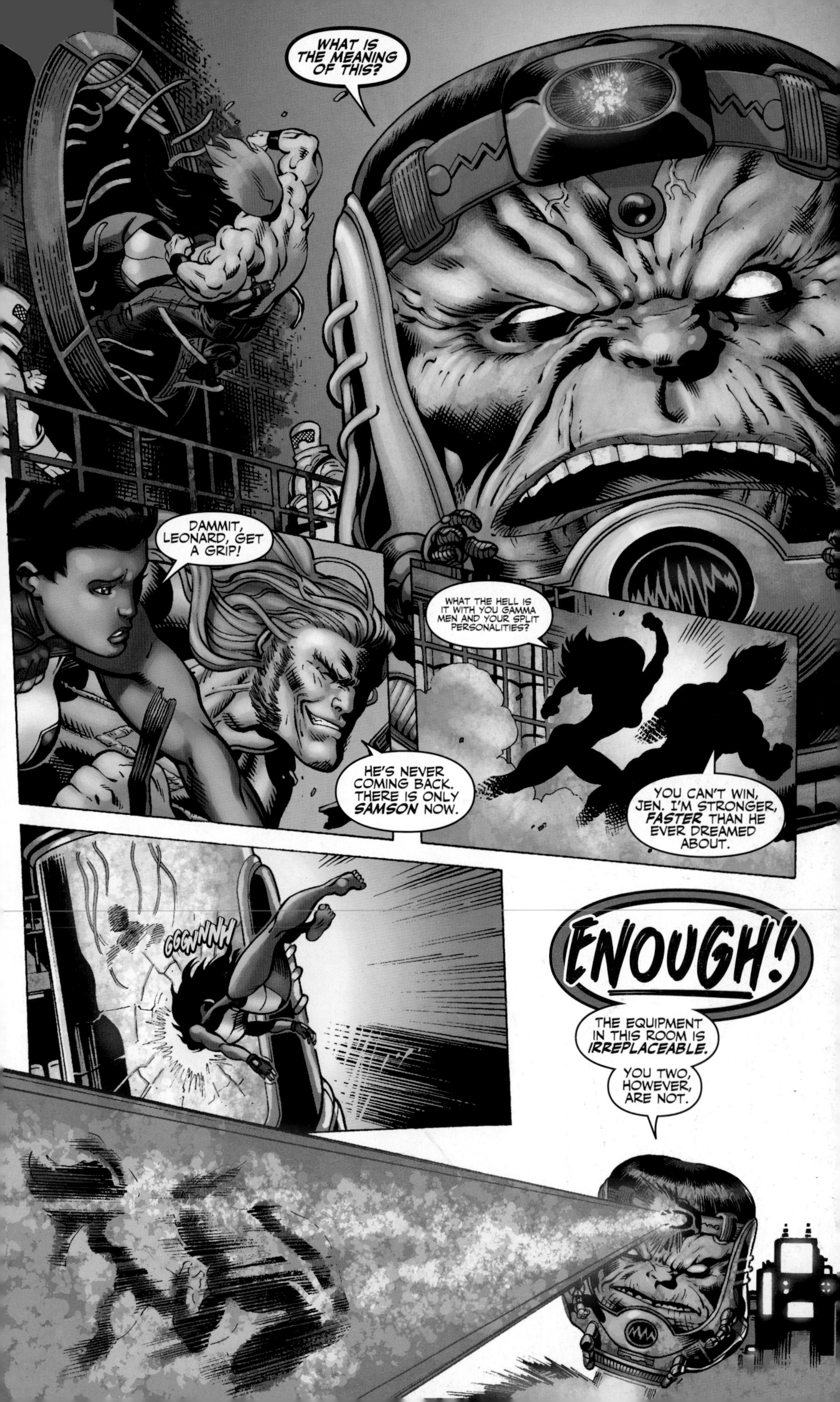

WHAT IS THE MEANING OF THIS?
DAMMIT, LEONARD, GET A GRIP!
HE'S NEVER COMING BACK. THERE IS ONLY SAMSON NOW.
WHAT THE HELL IS IT WITH YOU GAMMA MEN AND YOUR SPLIT PERSONALITIES?
YOU CAN'T WIN, JEN. I'M STRONGER, FASTER THAN HE EVER DREAMED ABOUT.
GGGNNNH
ENOUGH!
THE EQUIPMENT IN THIS ROOM IS IRREPLACEABLE.
YOU TWO, HOWEVER, ARE NOT.

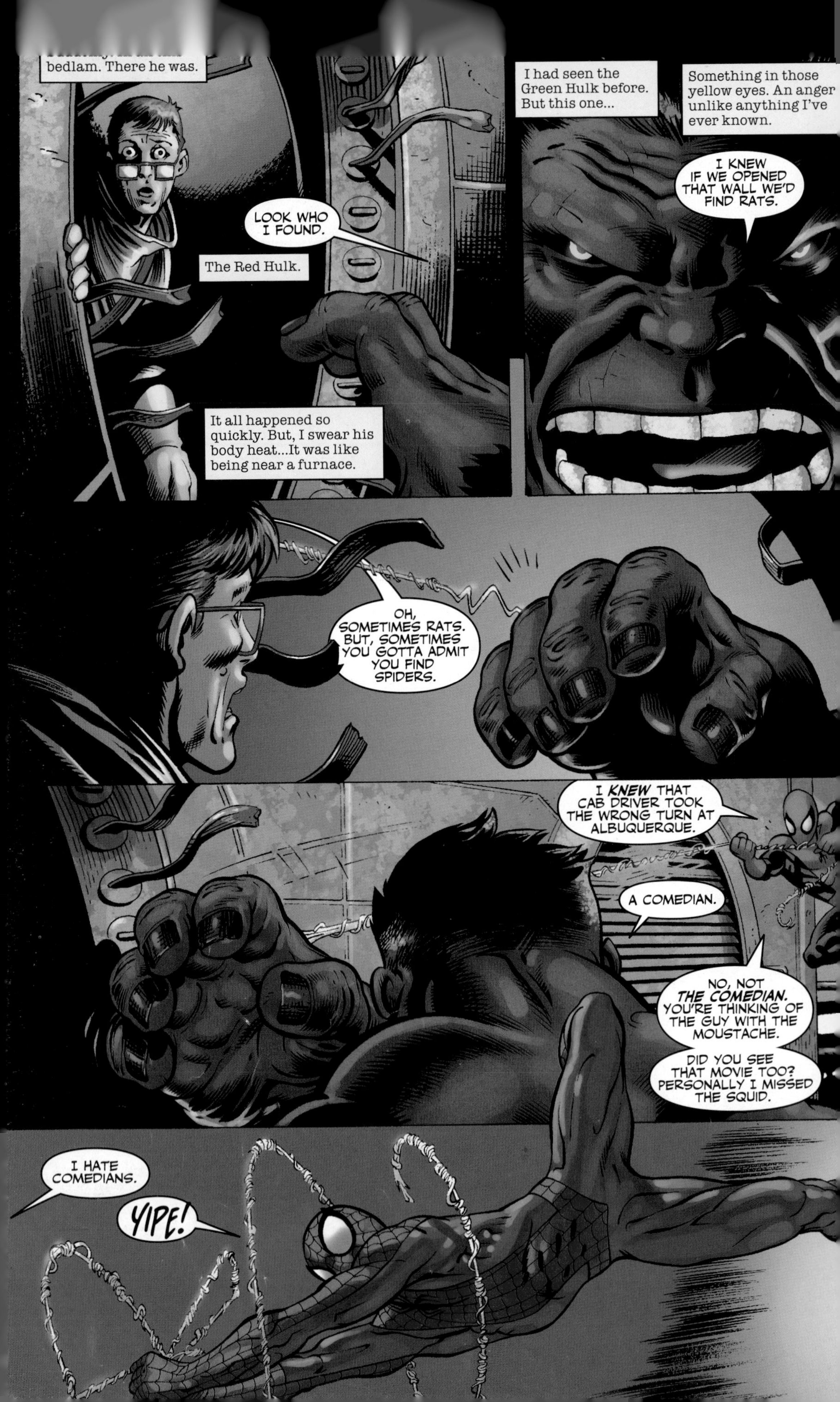
bedlam. There he was.
LOOK WHO I FOUND.
The Red Hulk.
It all happened so quickly. But, I swear his body heat...It was like being near a furnace.
I had seen the Green Hulk before. But this one...
Something in those yellow eyes. An anger unlike anything I've ever known.
I KNEW IF WE OPENED THAT WALL WE'D FIND RATS.
OH, SOMETIMES RATS. BUT, SOMETIMES YOU GOTTA ADMIT YOU FIND SPIDERS.
I KNEW THAT CAB DRIVER TOOK THE WRONG TURN AT ALBUQUERQUE.
A COMEDIAN.
NO, NOT THE COMEDIAN. YOU'RE THINKING OF THE GUY WITH THE MOUSTACHE.
DID YOU SEE THAT MOVIE TOO? PERSONALLY I MISSED THE SQUID.
I HATE COMEDIANS.
YIPE!

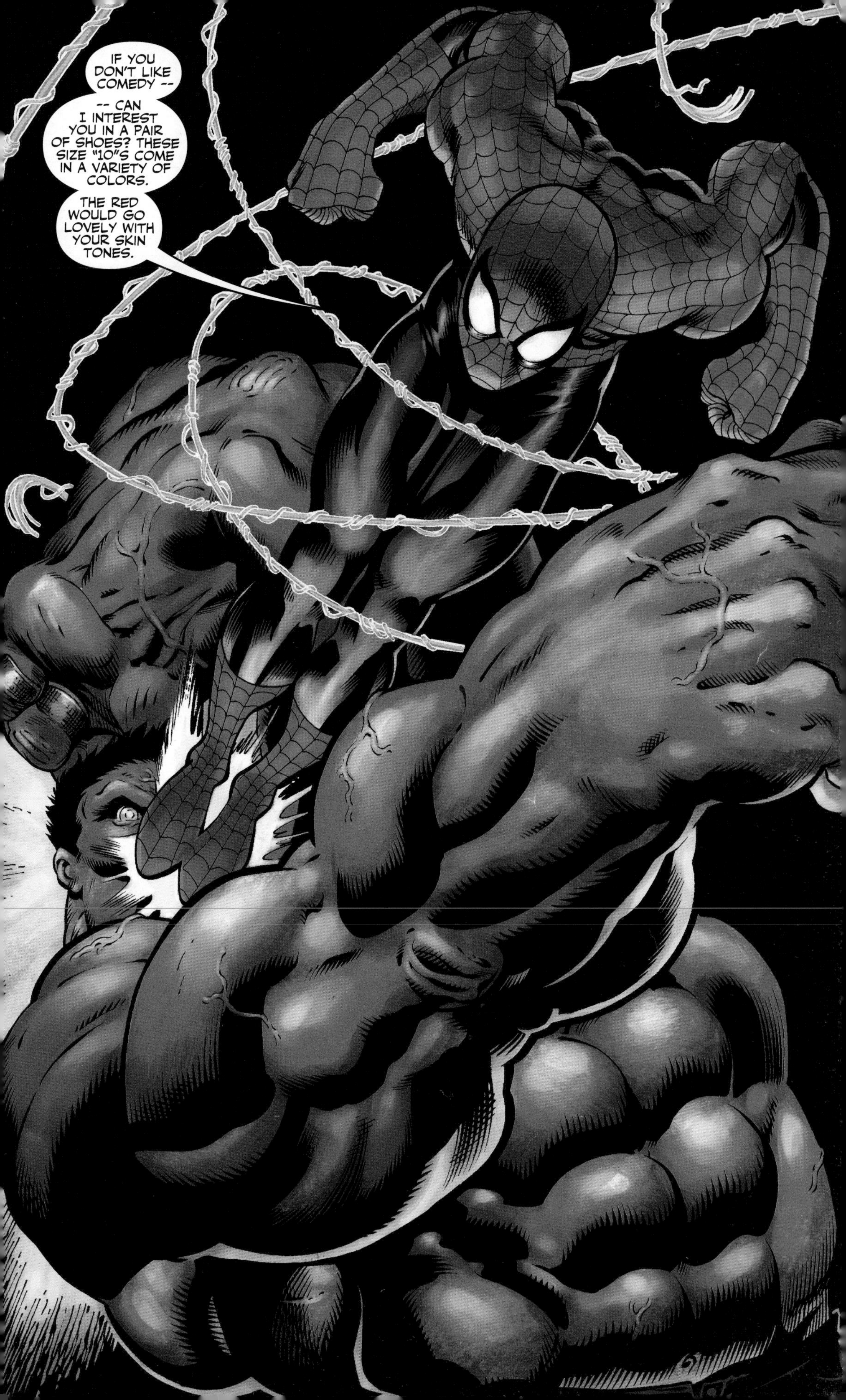
IF YOU DON'T LIKE COMEDY --
-- CAN I INTEREST YOU IN A PAIR OF SHOES? THESE SIZE "10"S COME IN A VARIETY OF COLORS.
THE RED WOULD GO LOVELY WITH YOUR SKIN TONES.

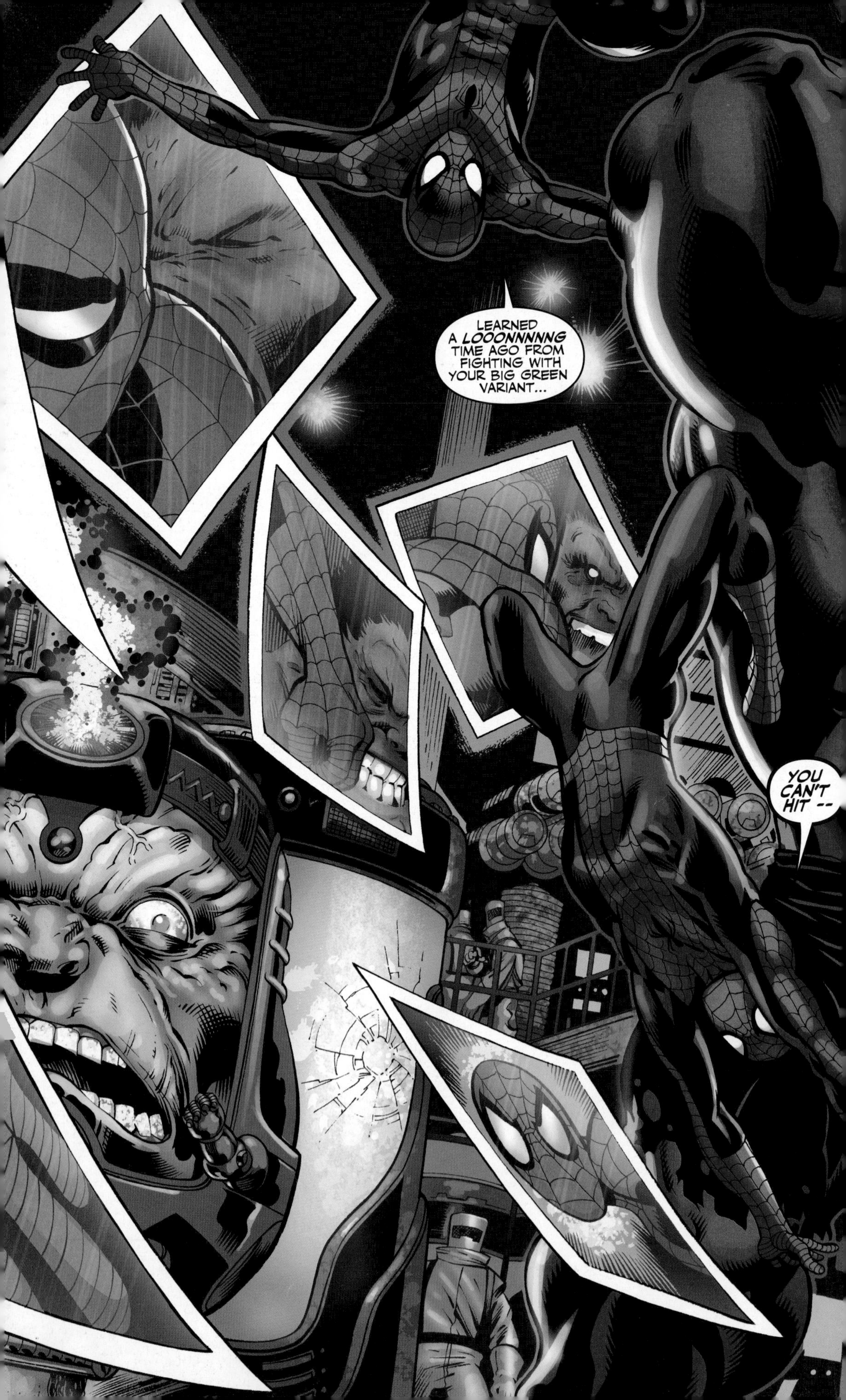
LEARNED A *LOOONNNNNG* TIME AGO FROM FIGHTING WITH YOUR BIG GREEN VARIANT...
YOU CAN'T HIT --

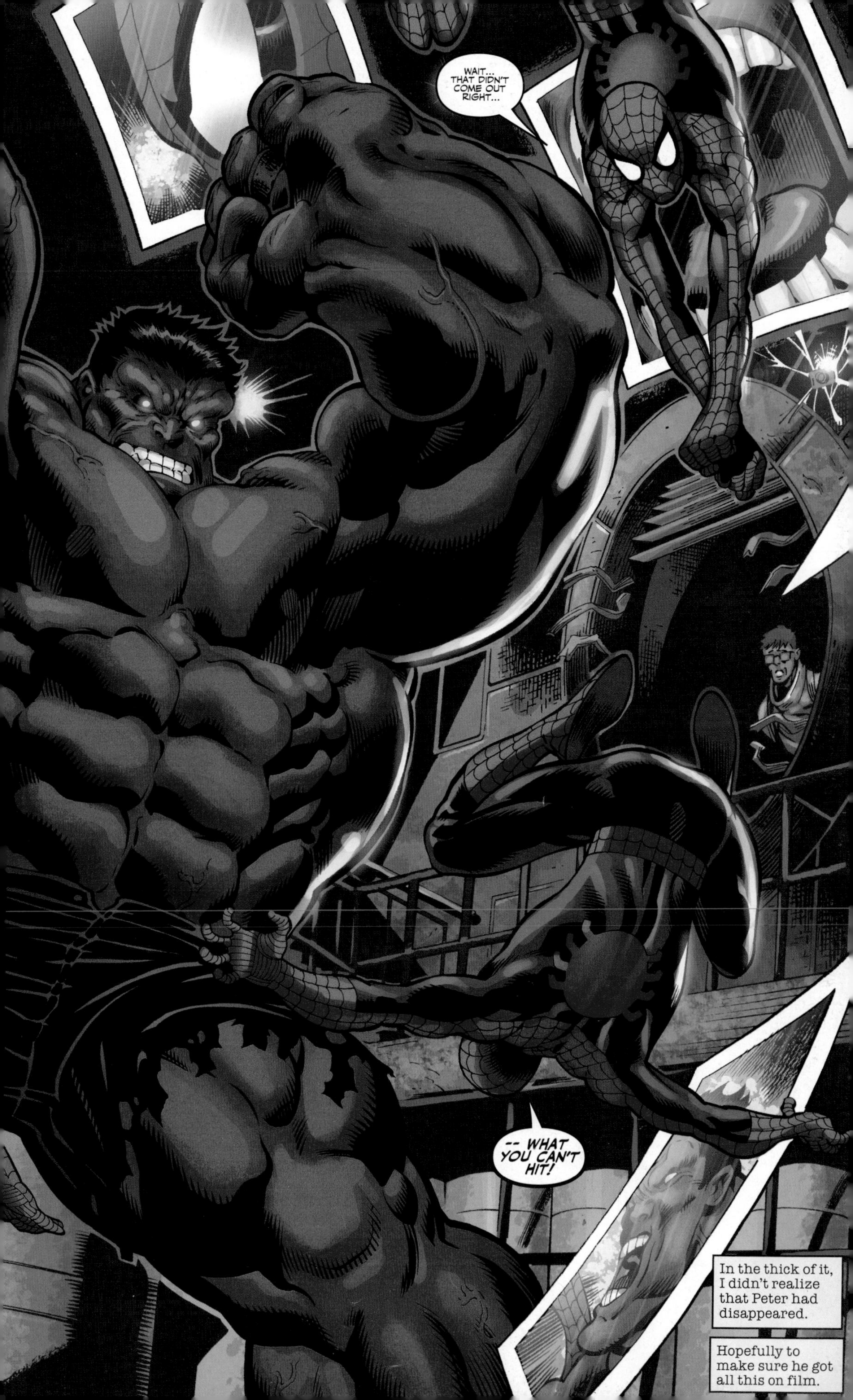
WAIT... THAT DIDN'T COME OUT RIGHT...
-- WHAT YOU CAN'T HIT!
In the thick of it, I didn't realize that Peter had disappeared.
Hopefully to make sure he got all this on film.

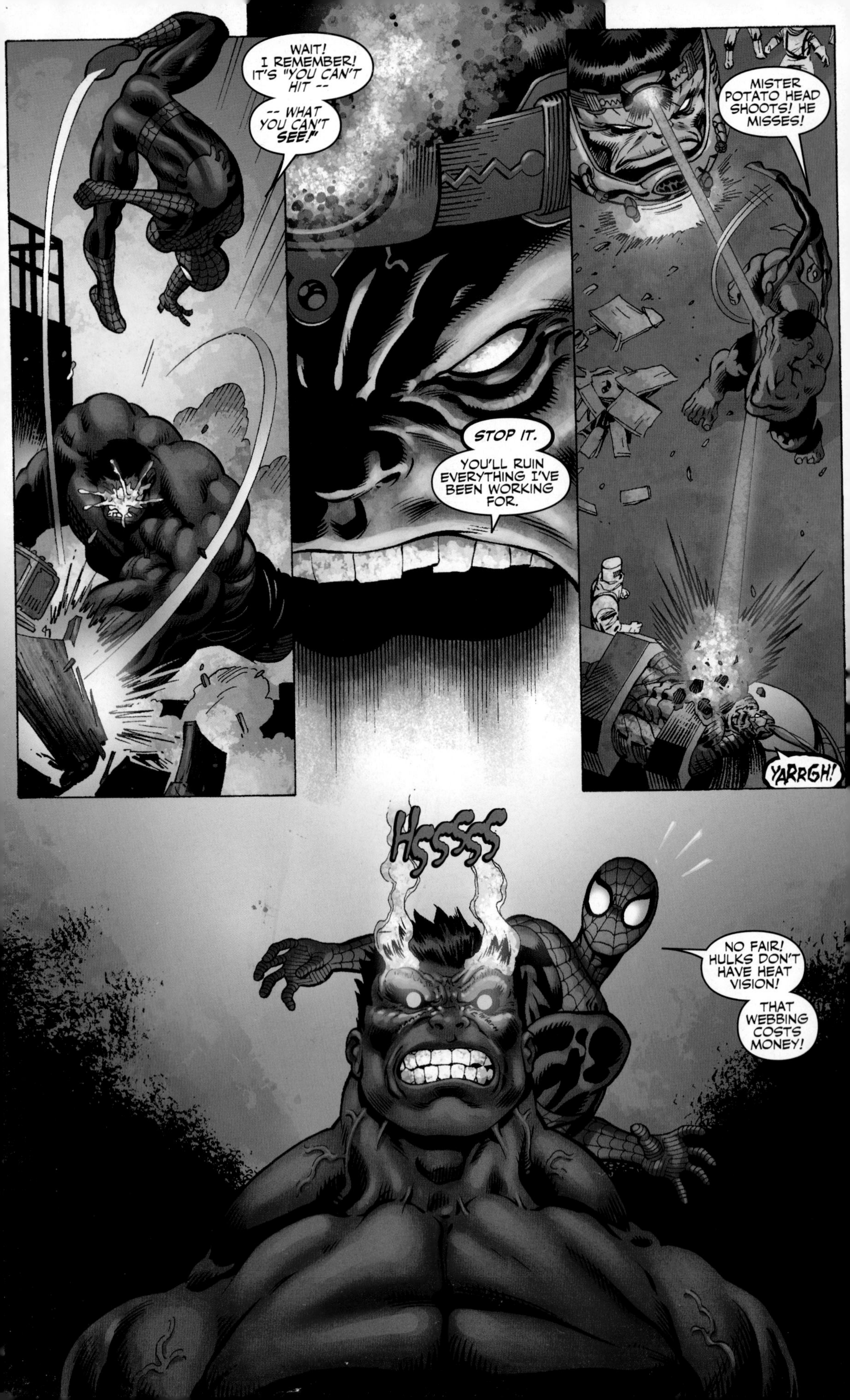
WAIT! I REMEMBER! IT'S "YOU CAN'T HIT --
-- WHAT YOU CAN'T SEE!"
STOP IT.
YOU'LL RUIN EVERYTHING I'VE BEEN WORKING FOR.
MISTER POTATO HEAD SHOOTS! HE MISSES!
YARRGH!
HSSSS
NO FAIR! HULKS DON'T HAVE HEAT VISION!
THAT WEBBING COSTS MONEY!

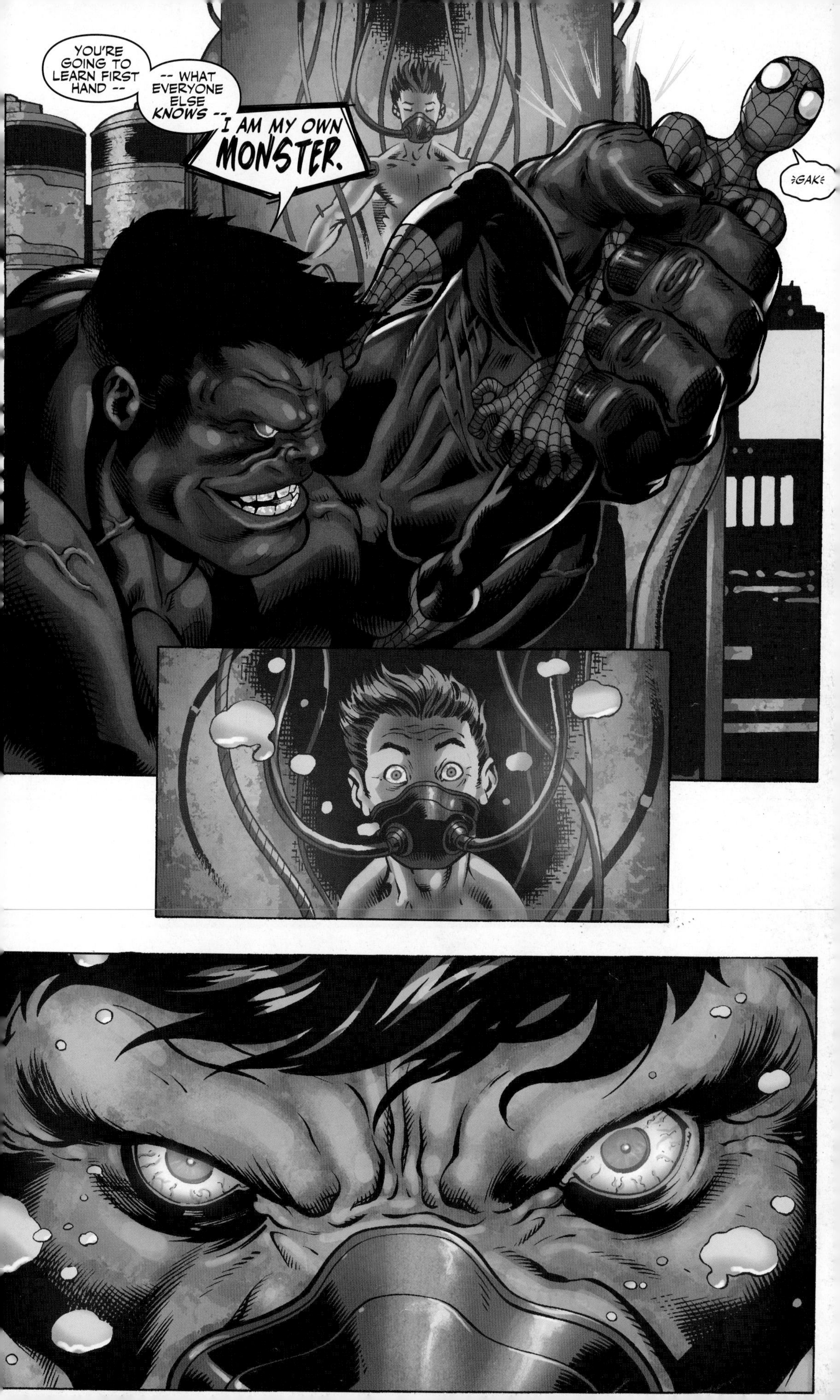
YOU'RE GOING TO LEARN FIRST HAND --
-- WHAT EVERYONE ELSE KNOWS --
I AM MY OWN MONSTER.
GAK

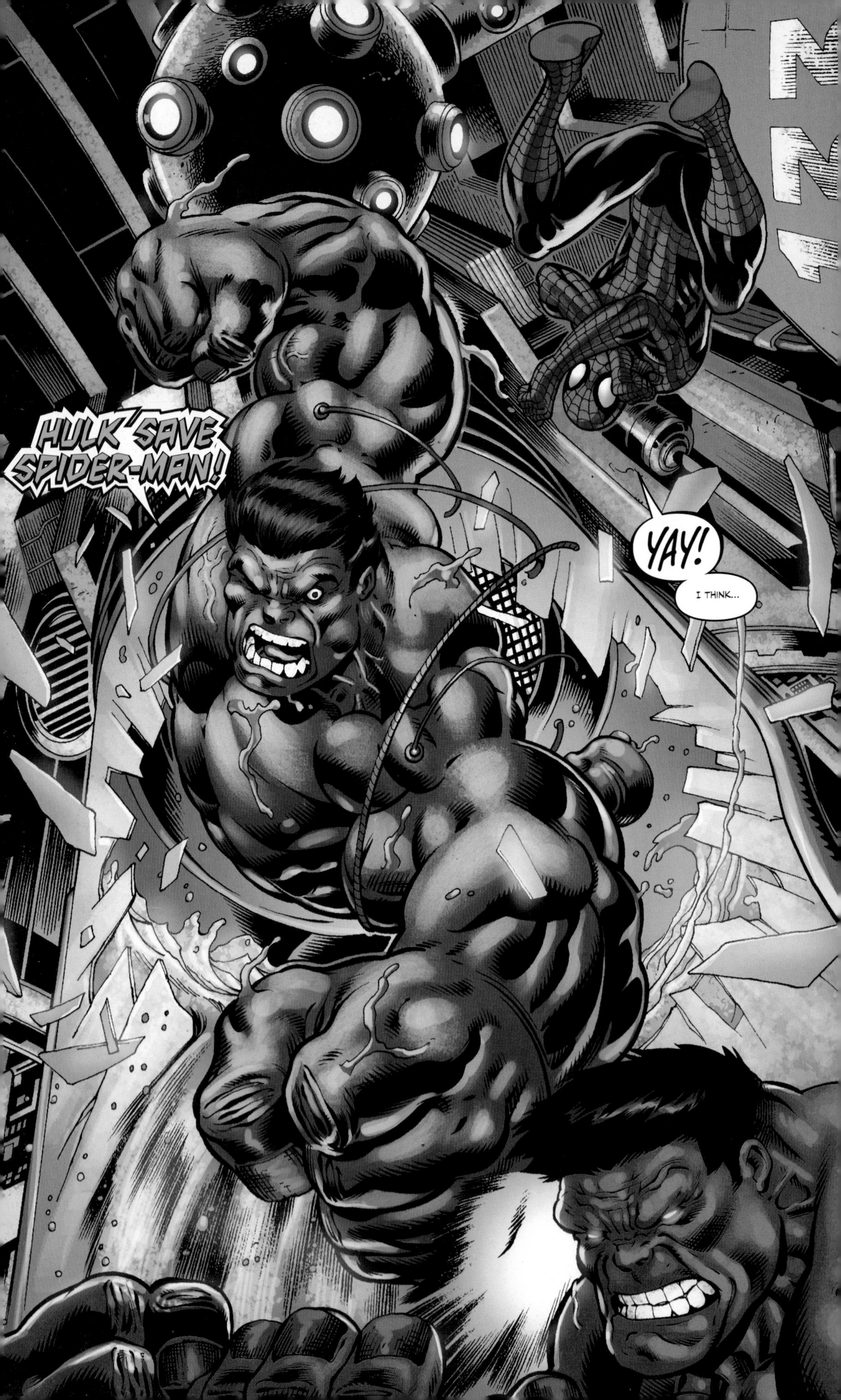

HULK SAVE SPIDER-MAN!
YAY!
I THINK...

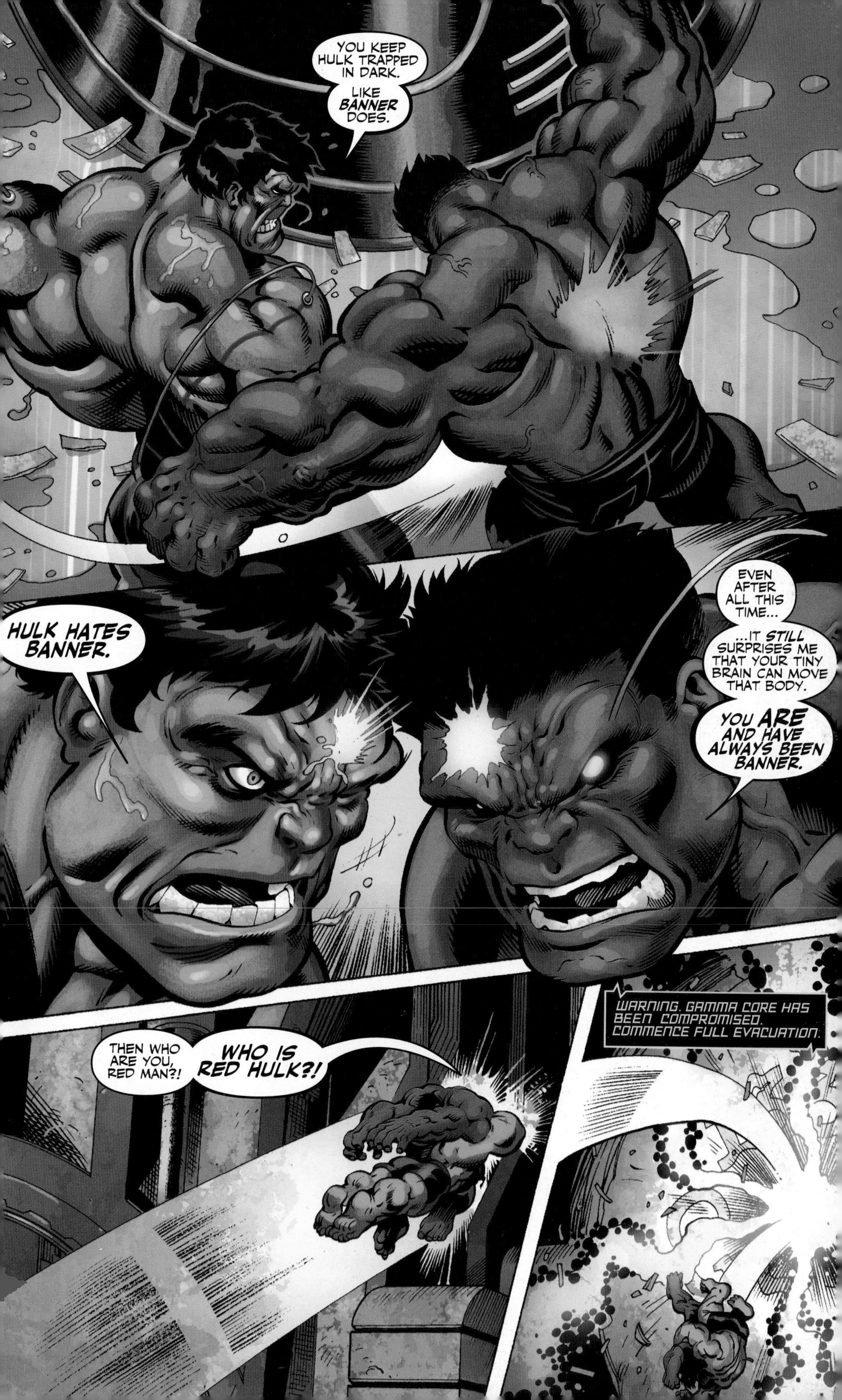
YOU KEEP HULK TRAPPED IN DARK.
LIKE BANNER DOES.
HULK HATES BANNER.
EVEN AFTER ALL THIS TIME...
...IT STILL SURPRISES ME THAT YOUR TINY BRAIN CAN MOVE THAT BODY.
YOU ARE AND HAVE ALWAYS BEEN BANNER.
THEN WHO ARE YOU, RED MAN?!
WHO IS RED HULK?!
WARNING. GAMMA CORE HAS BEEN COMPROMISED. COMMENCE FULL EVACUATION.

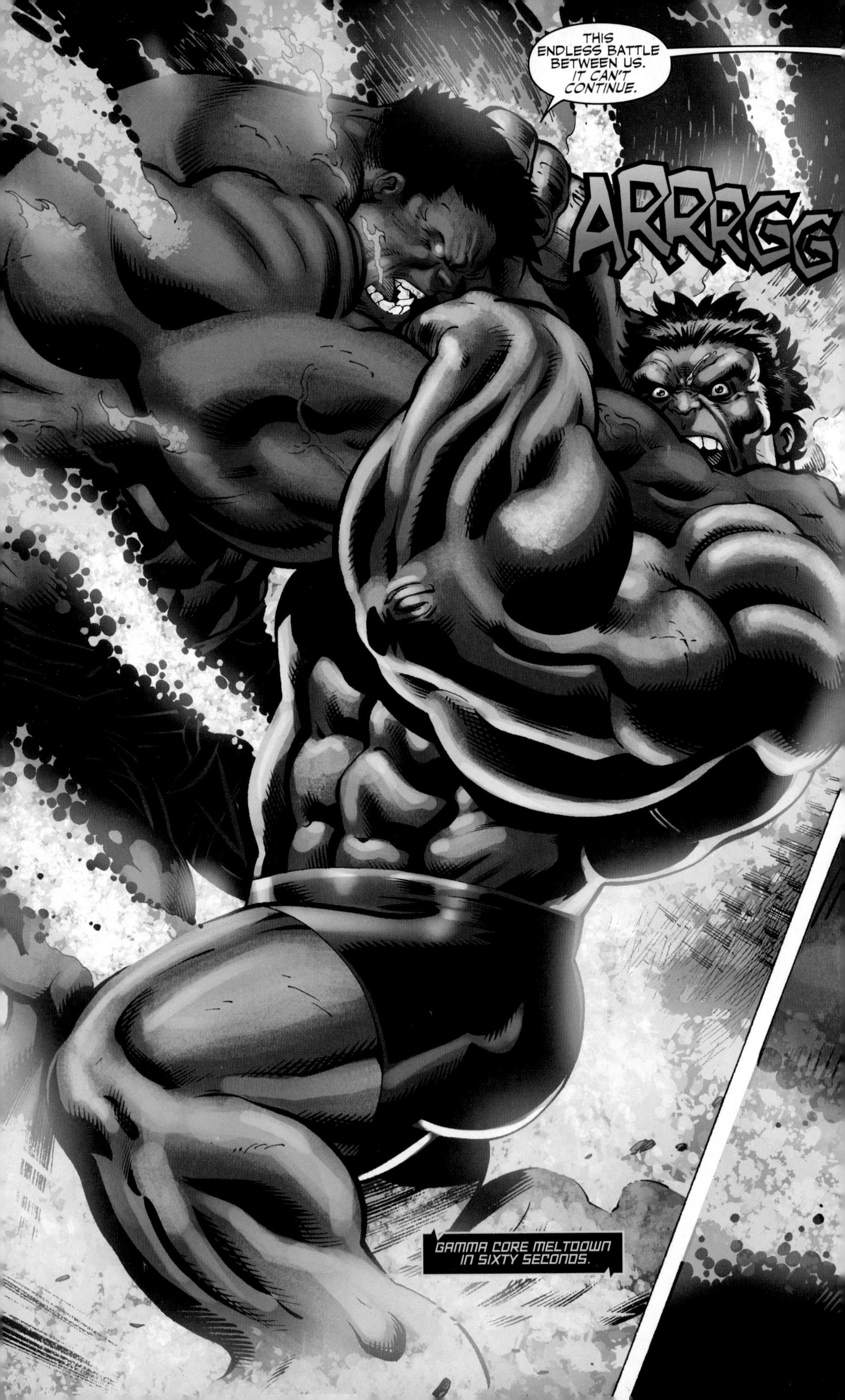
THIS ENDLESS BATTLE BETWEEN US. IT CAN'T CONTINUE.
ARRRGG
GAMMA CORE MELTDOWN IN SIXTY SECONDS.

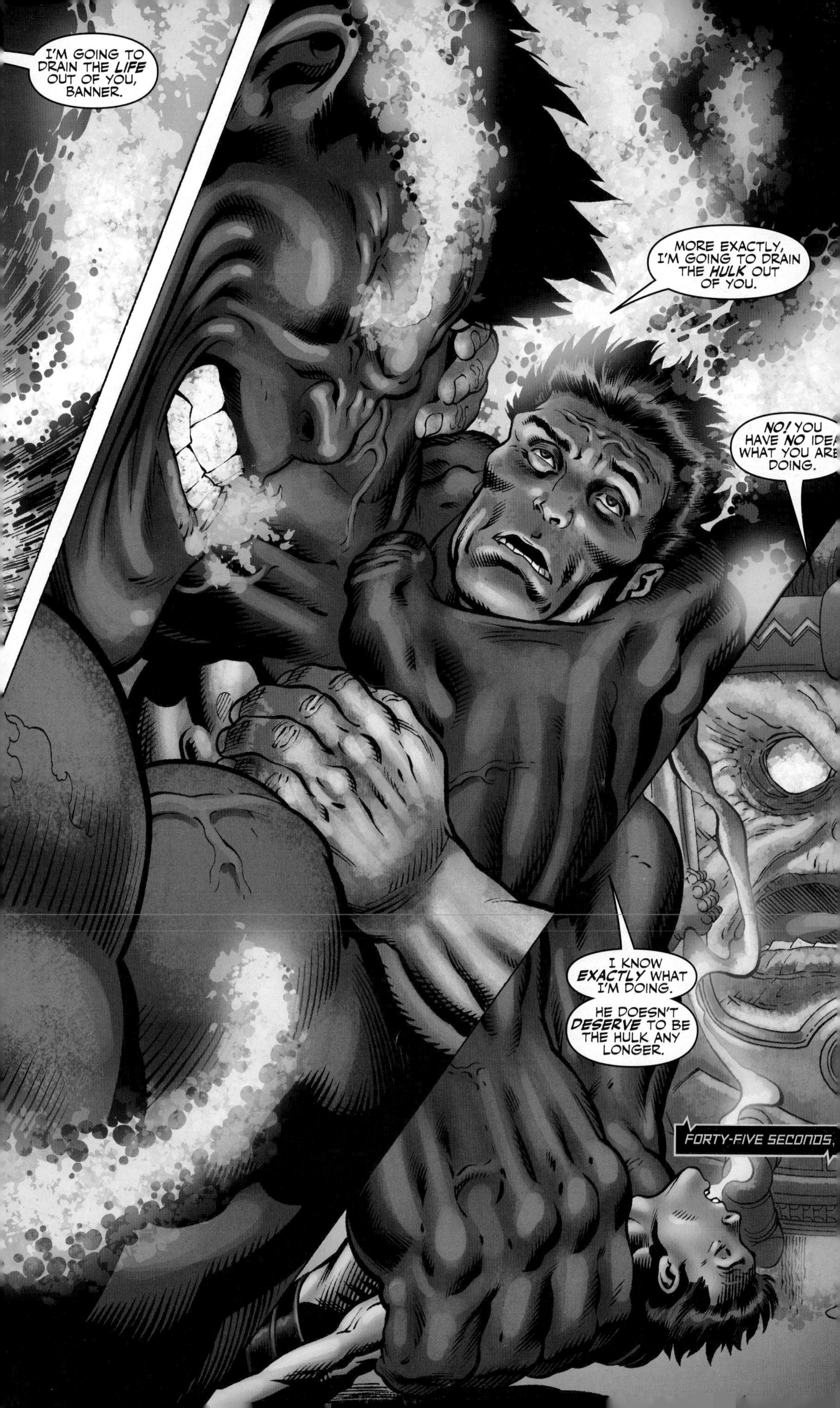
I'M GOING TO DRAIN THE LIFE OUT OF YOU, BANNER.
MORE EXACTLY, I'M GOING TO DRAIN THE HULK OUT OF YOU.
NO! YOU HAVE NO IDEA WHAT YOU ARE DOING.
I KNOW EXACTLY WHAT I'M DOING.
HE DOESN'T DESERVE TO BE THE HULK ANY LONGER.
FORTY-FIVE SECONDS.

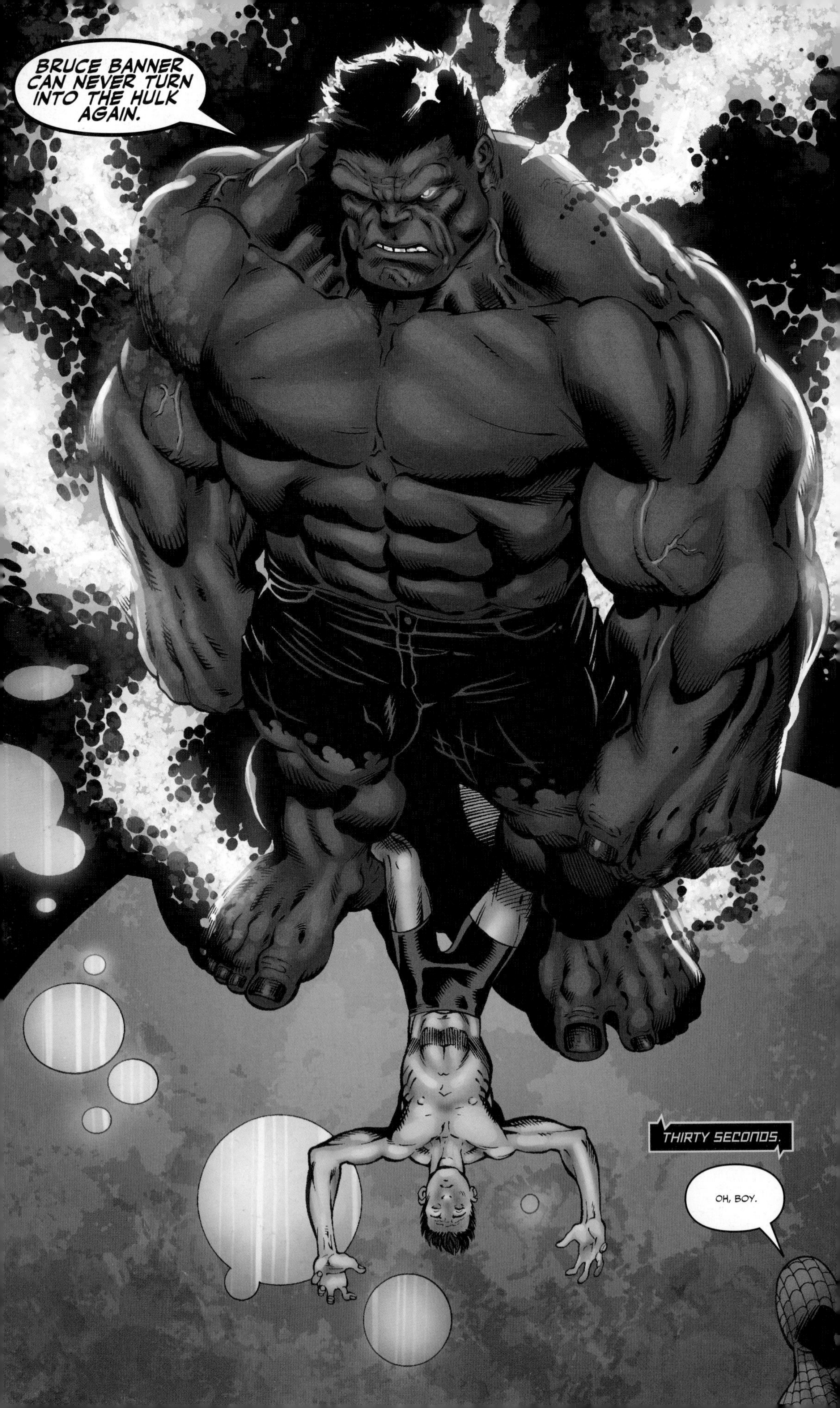
BRUCE BANNER CAN NEVER TURN INTO THE HULK AGAIN.
THIRTY SECONDS.
OH, BOY.

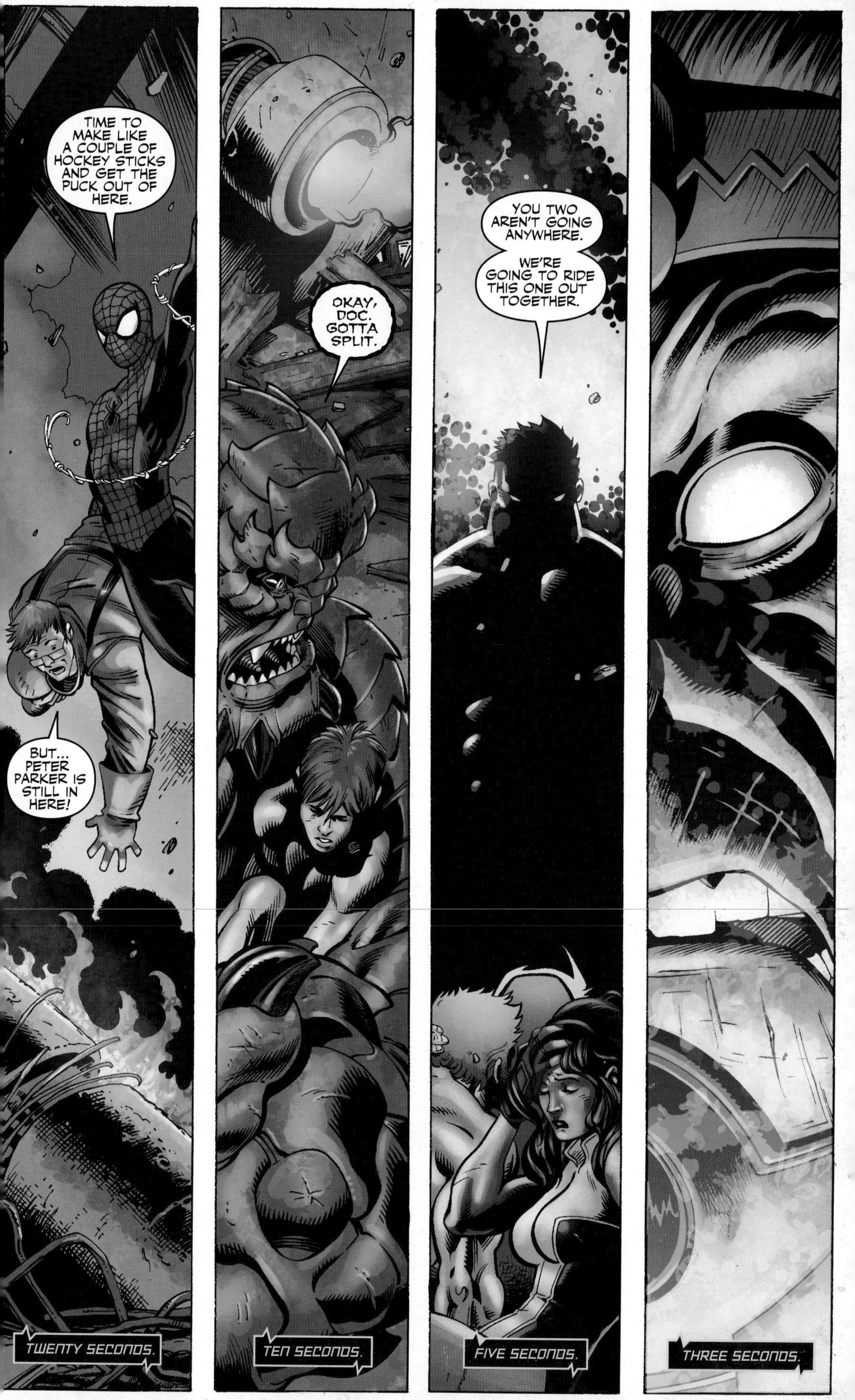
TIME TO MAKE LIKE A COUPLE OF HOCKEY STICKS AND GET THE PUCK OUT OF HERE.
BUT... PETER PARKER IS STILL IN HERE!
TWENTY SECONDS.
OKAY, DOC. GOTTA SPLIT.
TEN SECONDS.
YOU TWO AREN'T GOING ANYWHERE.
WE'RE GOING TO RIDE THIS ONE OUT TOGETHER.
FIVE SECONDS.
THREE SECONDS.

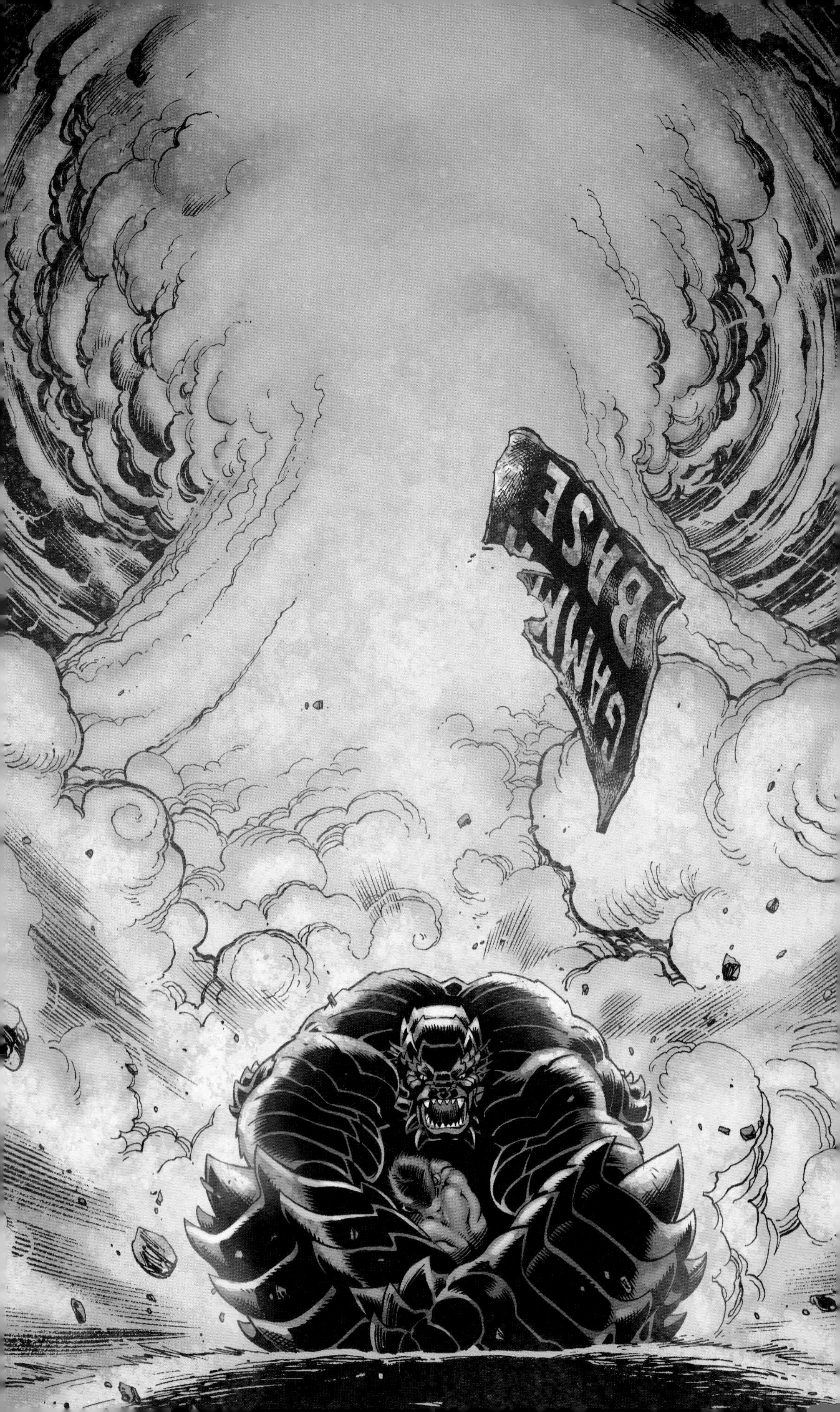

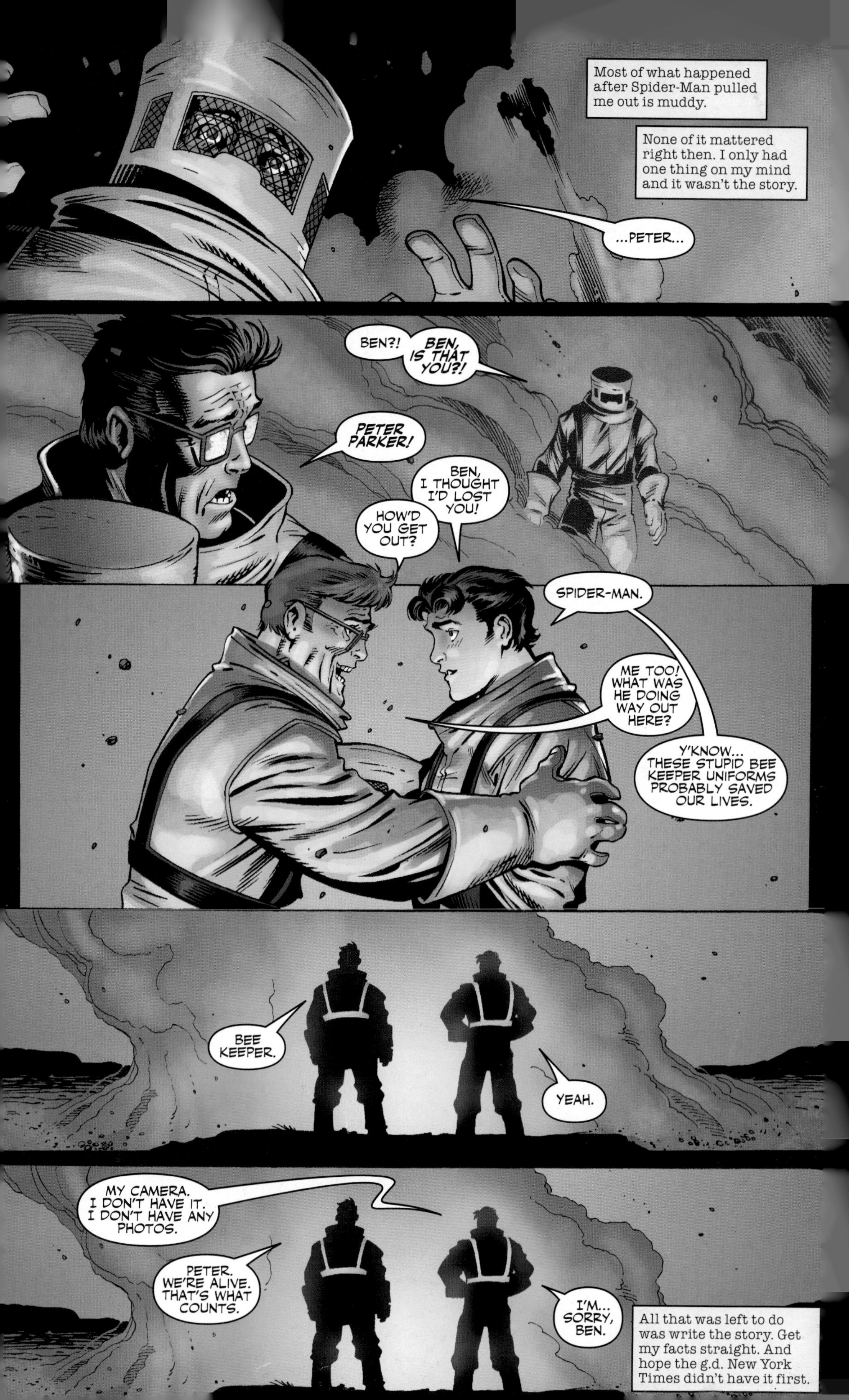
Most of what happened after Spider-Man pulled me out is muddy.
None of it mattered right then. I only had one thing on my mind and it wasn't the story.
...PETER...
BEN?!
BEN, IS THAT YOU?!
PETER PARKER!
BEN, I THOUGHT I'D LOST YOU!
HOW'D YOU GET OUT?
SPIDER-MAN.
ME TOO! WHAT WAS HE DOING WAY OUT HERE?
Y'KNOW... THESE STUPID BEE KEEPER UNIFORMS PROBABLY SAVED OUR LIVES.
BEE KEEPER.
YEAH.
MY CAMERA. I DON'T HAVE IT. I DON'T HAVE ANY PHOTOS.
PETER. WE'RE ALIVE. THAT'S WHAT COUNTS.
I'M... SORRY, BEN.
All that was left to do was write the story. Get my facts straight. And hope the g.d. New York Times didn't have it first.

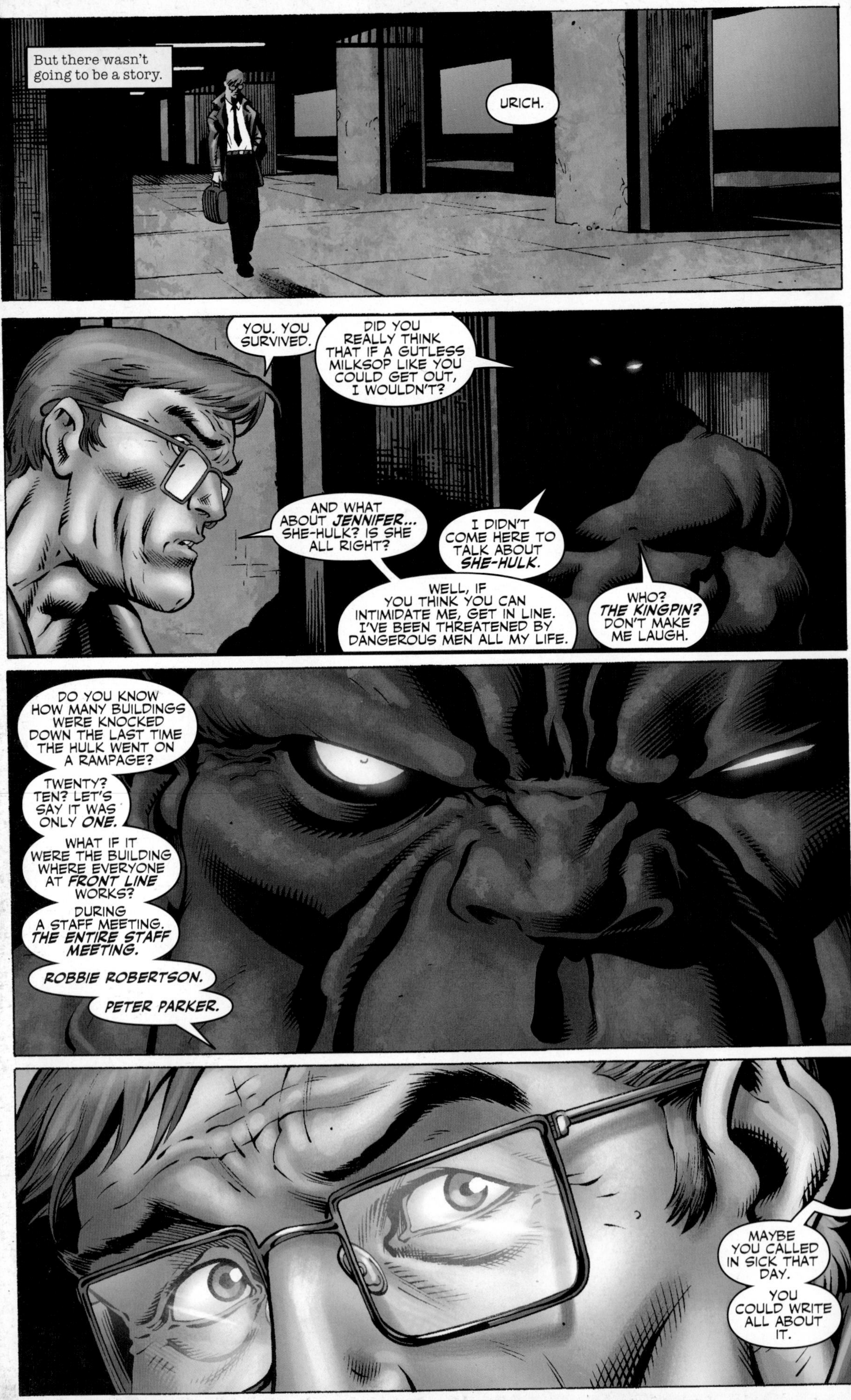

But there wasn't going to be a story.
URICH.
YOU. YOU SURVIVED.
DID YOU REALLY THINK THAT IF A GUTLESS MILKSOP LIKE YOU COULD GET OUT, I WOULDN'T?
AND WHAT ABOUT *JENNIFER...* SHE-HULK? IS SHE ALL RIGHT?
I DIDN'T COME HERE TO TALK ABOUT *SHE-HULK.*
WELL, IF YOU THINK YOU CAN INTIMIDATE ME, GET IN LINE. I'VE BEEN THREATENED BY DANGEROUS MEN ALL MY LIFE.
WHO? *THE KINGPIN?* DON'T MAKE ME LAUGH.
DO YOU KNOW HOW MANY BUILDINGS WERE KNOCKED DOWN THE LAST TIME THE HULK WENT ON A RAMPAGE?
TWENTY? TEN? LET'S SAY IT WAS ONLY *ONE.*
WHAT IF IT WERE THE BUILDING WHERE EVERYONE AT *FRONT LINE* WORKS?
DURING A STAFF MEETING. *THE ENTIRE STAFF MEETING.*
ROBBIE ROBERTSON.
PETER PARKER.
MAYBE YOU CALLED IN SICK THAT DAY.
YOU COULD WRITE ALL ABOUT IT.

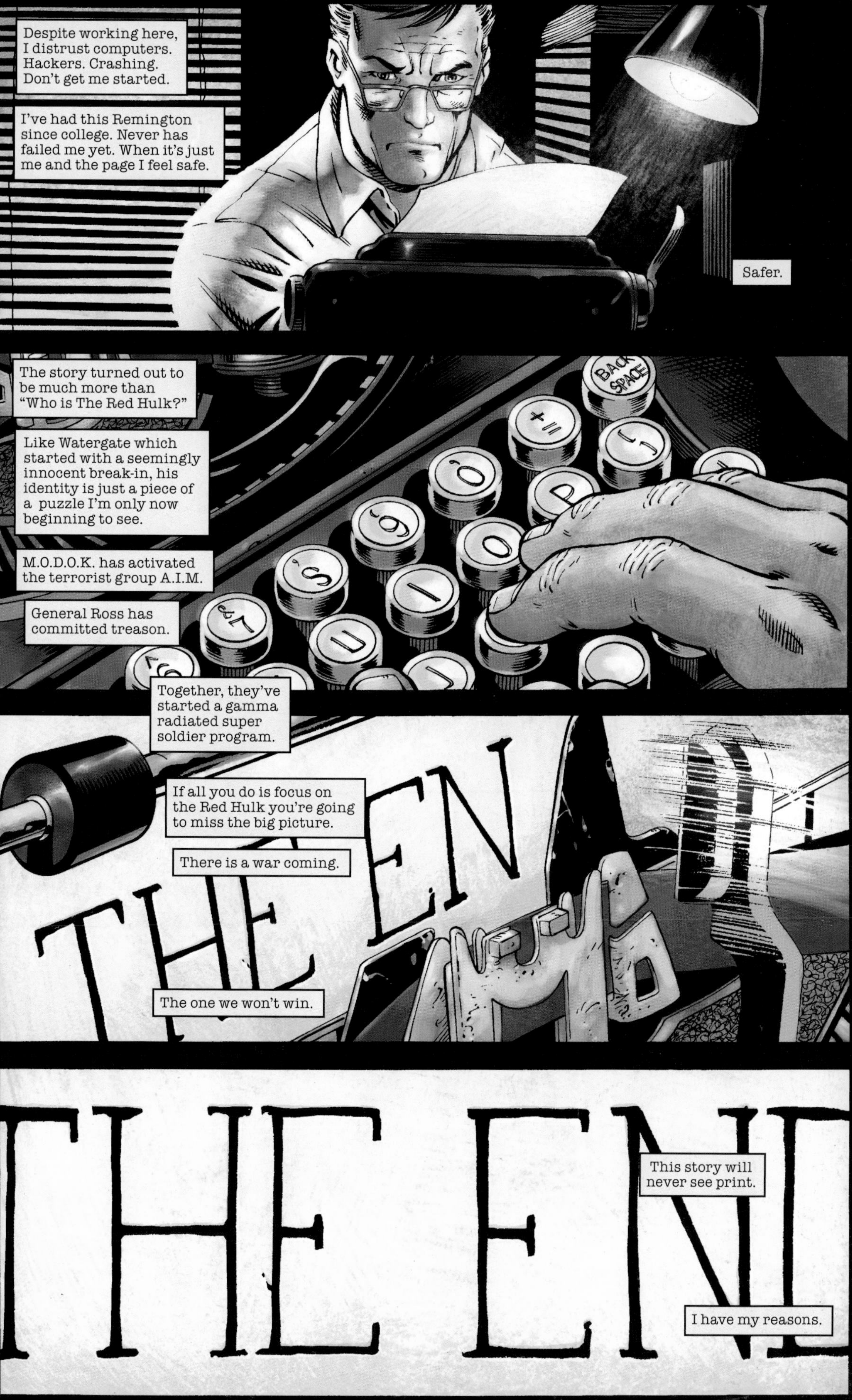

Despite working here, I distrust computers. Hackers. Crashing. Don't get me started.
I've had this Remington since college. Never has failed me yet. When it's just me and the page I feel safe.
Safer.
The story turned out to be much more than "Who is The Red Hulk?"
Like Watergate which started with a seemingly innocent break-in, his identity is just a piece of a puzzle I'm only now beginning to see.
M.O.D.O.K. has activated the terrorist group A.I.M.
General Ross has committed treason.
Together, they've started a gamma radiated super soldier program.
If all you do is focus on the Red Hulk you're going to miss the big picture.
There is a war coming.
The one we won't win.
This story will never see print.
I have my reasons.

ROUND ★ FIVE

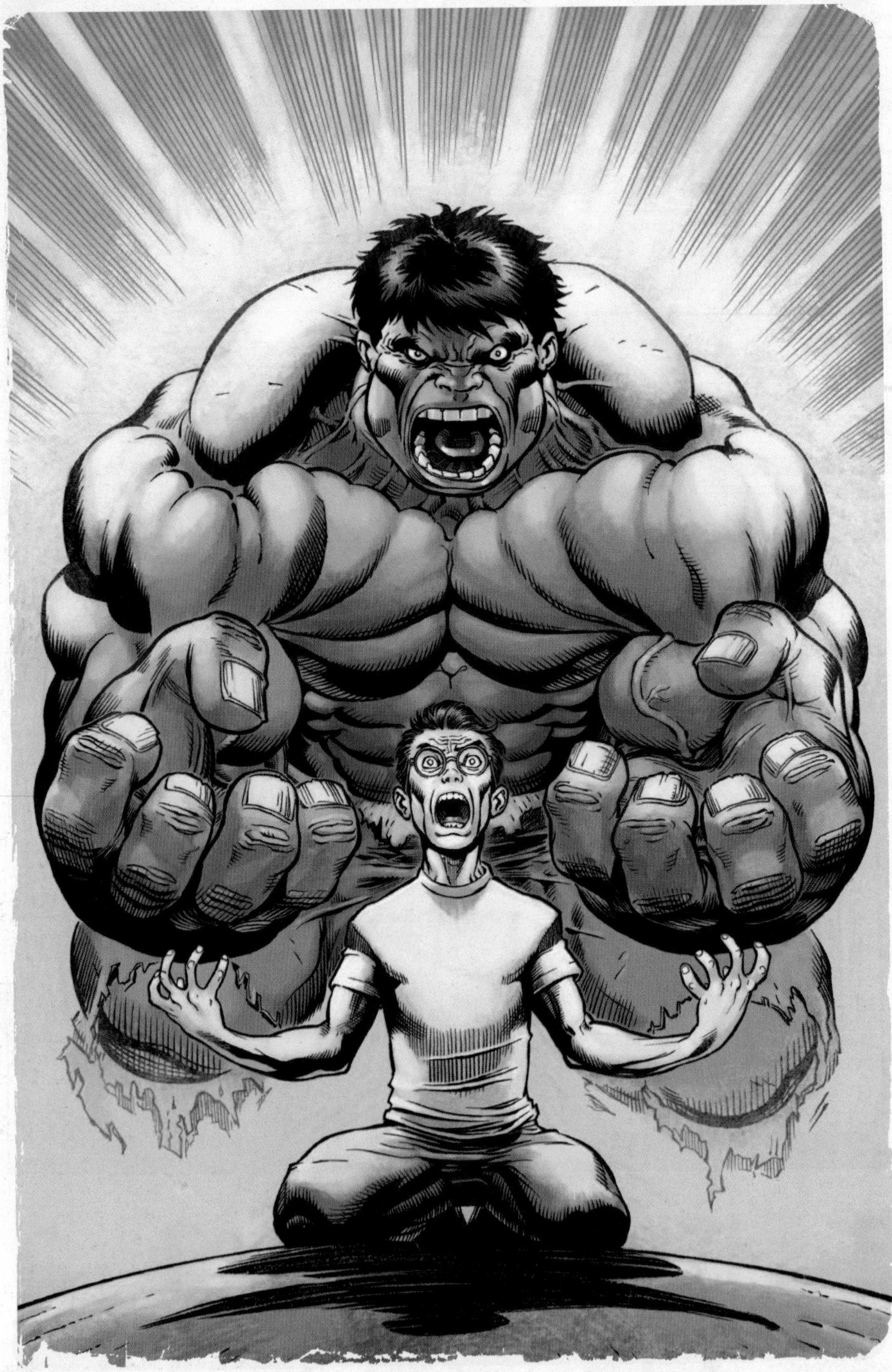

HULK NO MORE

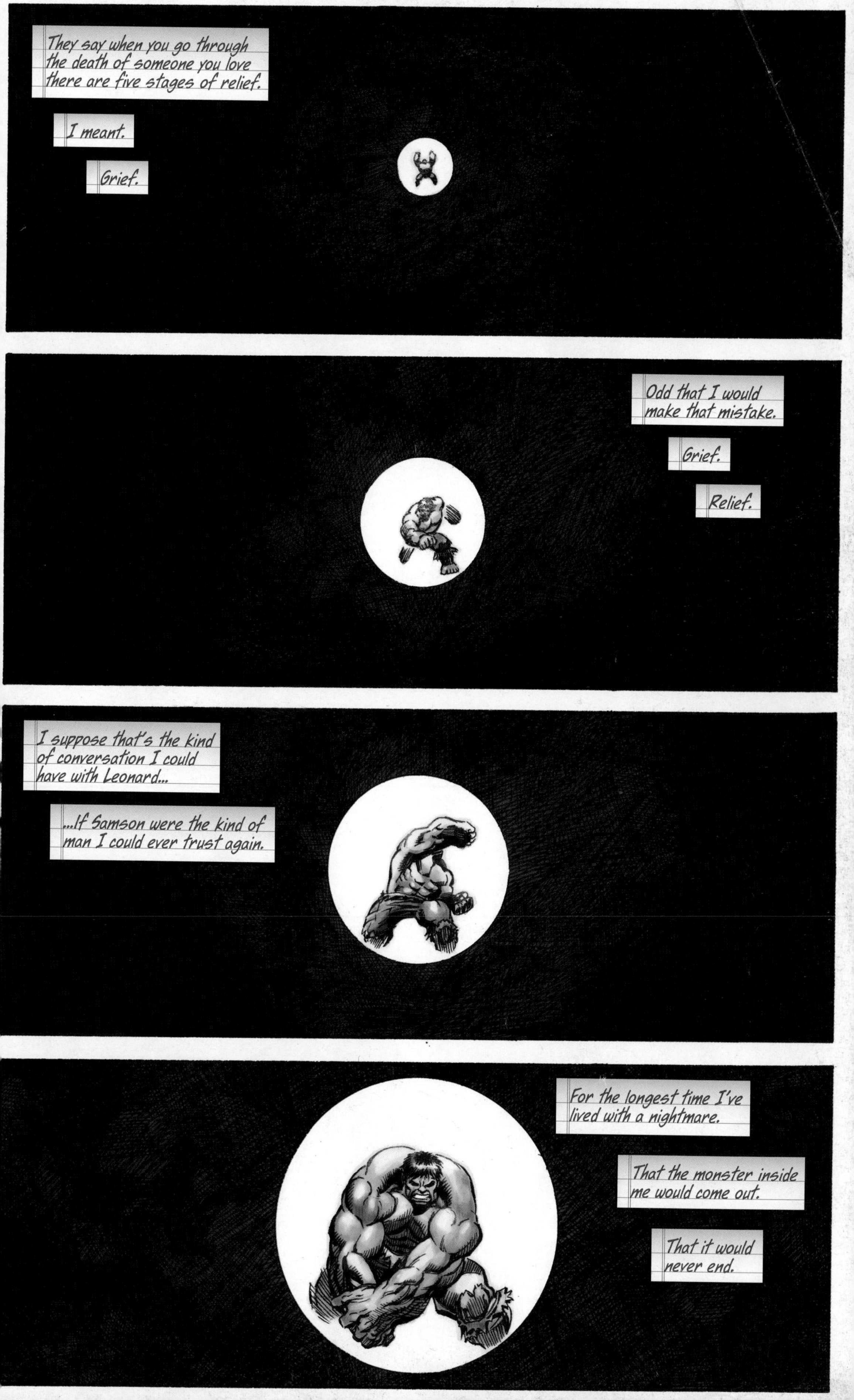
They say when you go through the death of someone you love there are five stages of relief.
I meant.
Grief.
Odd that I would make that mistake.
Grief.
Relief.
I suppose that's the kind of conversation I could have with Leonard...
...If Samson were the kind of man I could ever trust again.
For the longest time I've lived with a nightmare.
That the monster inside me would come out.
That it would never end.

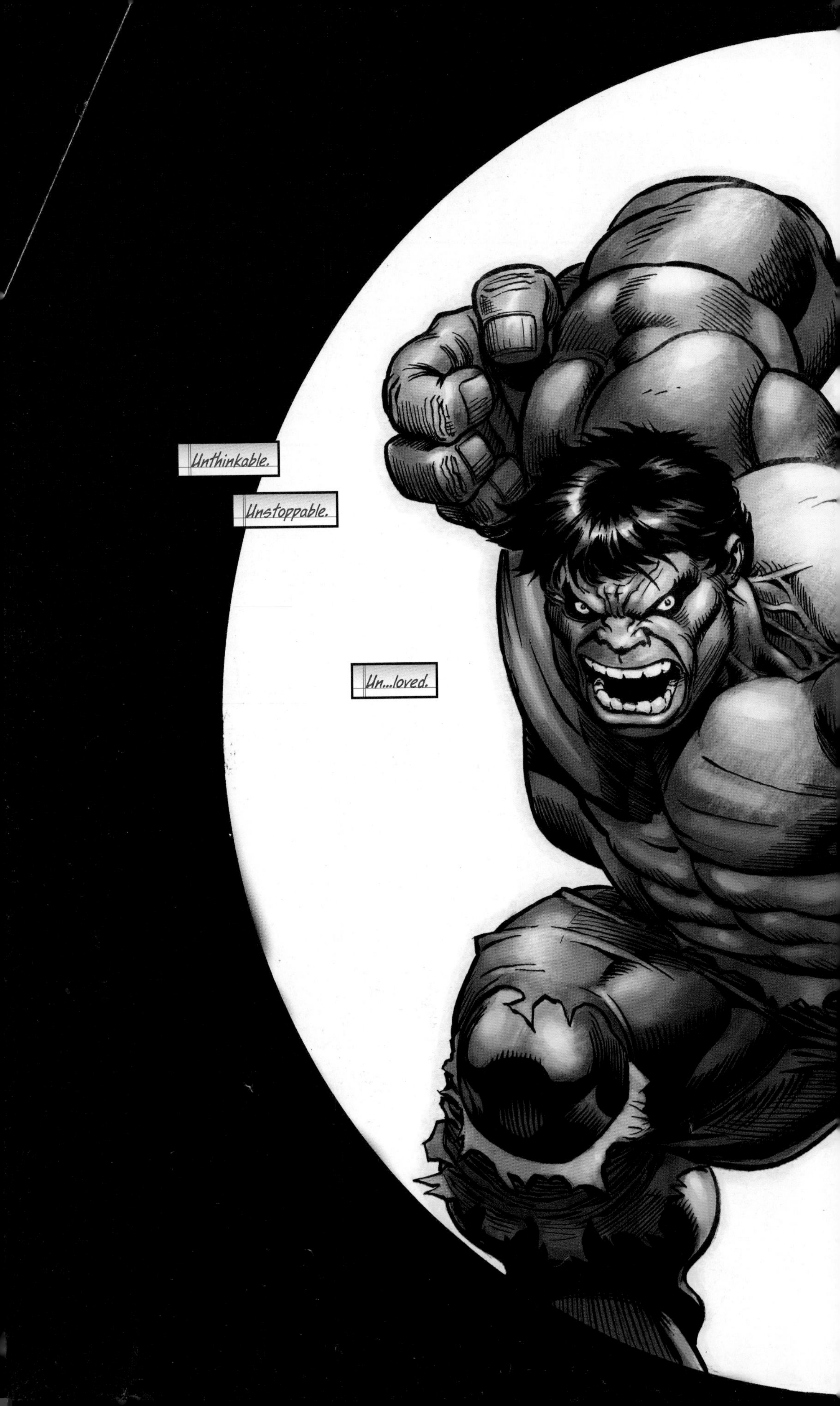
Unthinkable.
Unstoppable.
Un...loved.

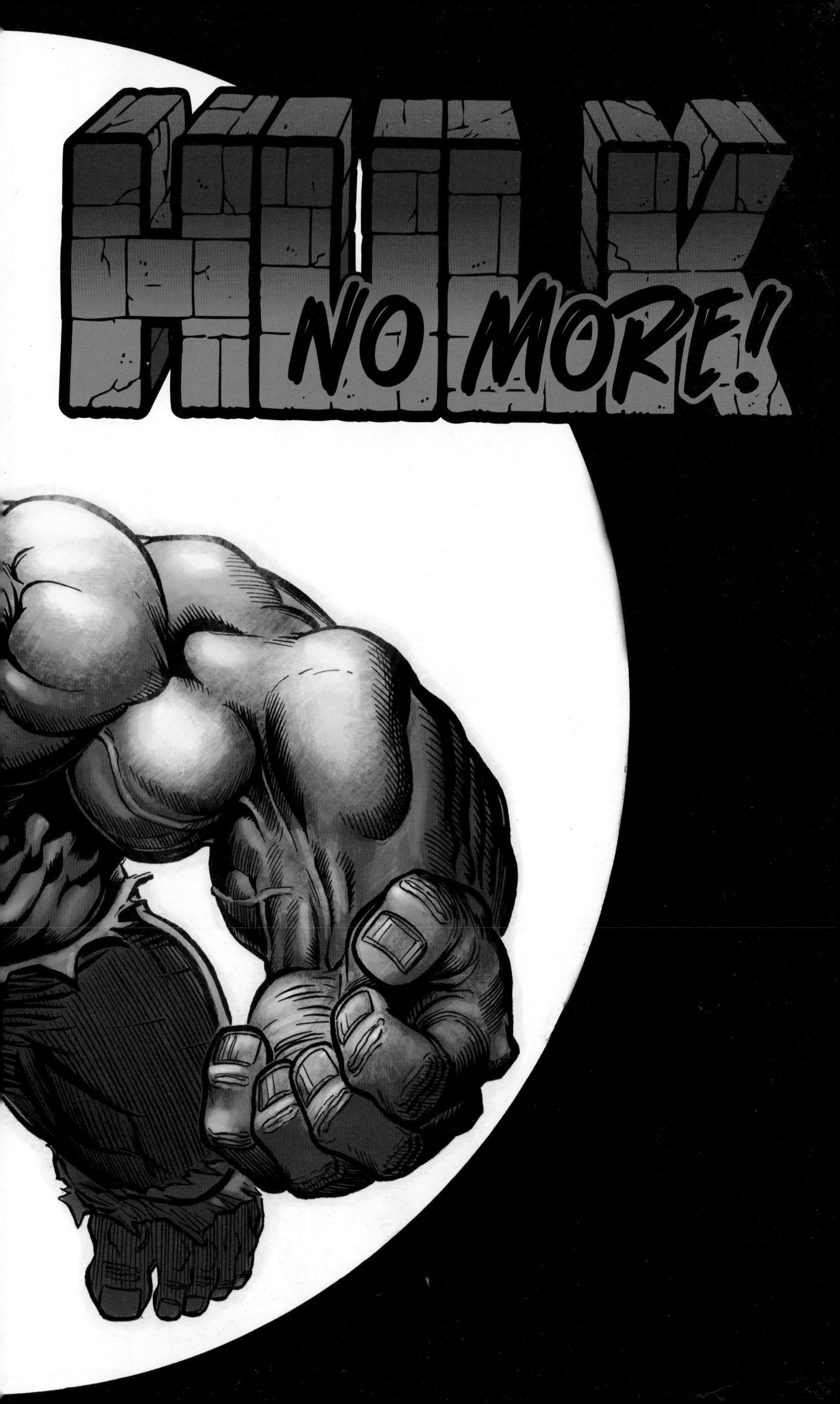
HULK
NO MORE!

A monster that I, alone, created.

Causing destruction in every aspect of my life. Love. Family.

Everything.

And now that I've woken up from the nightmare...

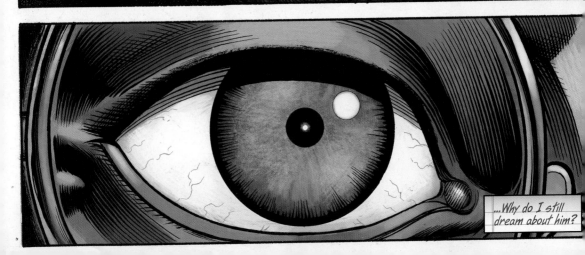

...Why do I still dream about him?

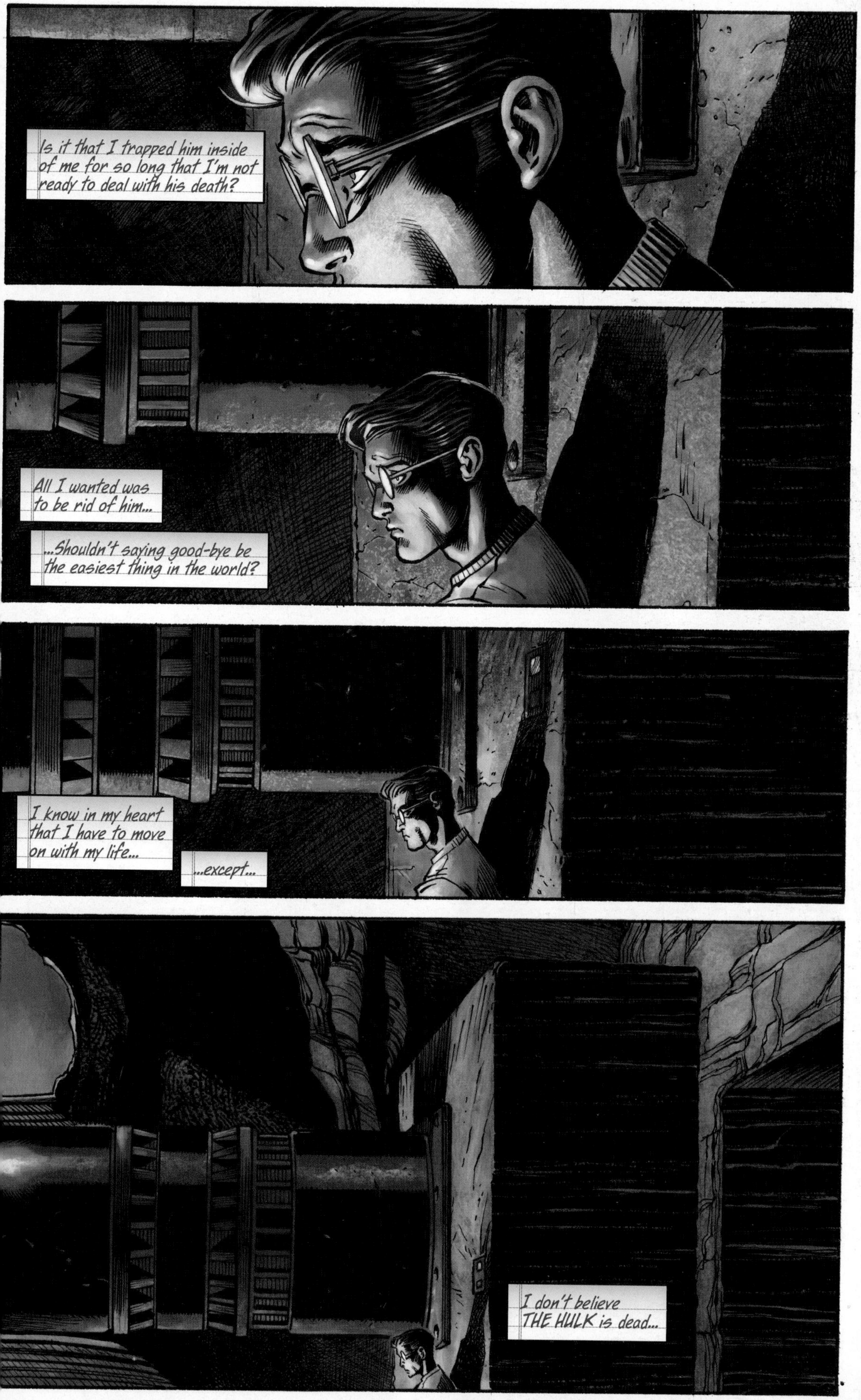
Is it that I trapped him inside of me for so long that I'm not ready to deal with his death?
All I wanted was to be rid of him...
...Shouldn't saying good-bye be the easiest thing in the world?
I know in my heart that I have to move on with my life...
...except...
I don't believe THE HULK is dead...

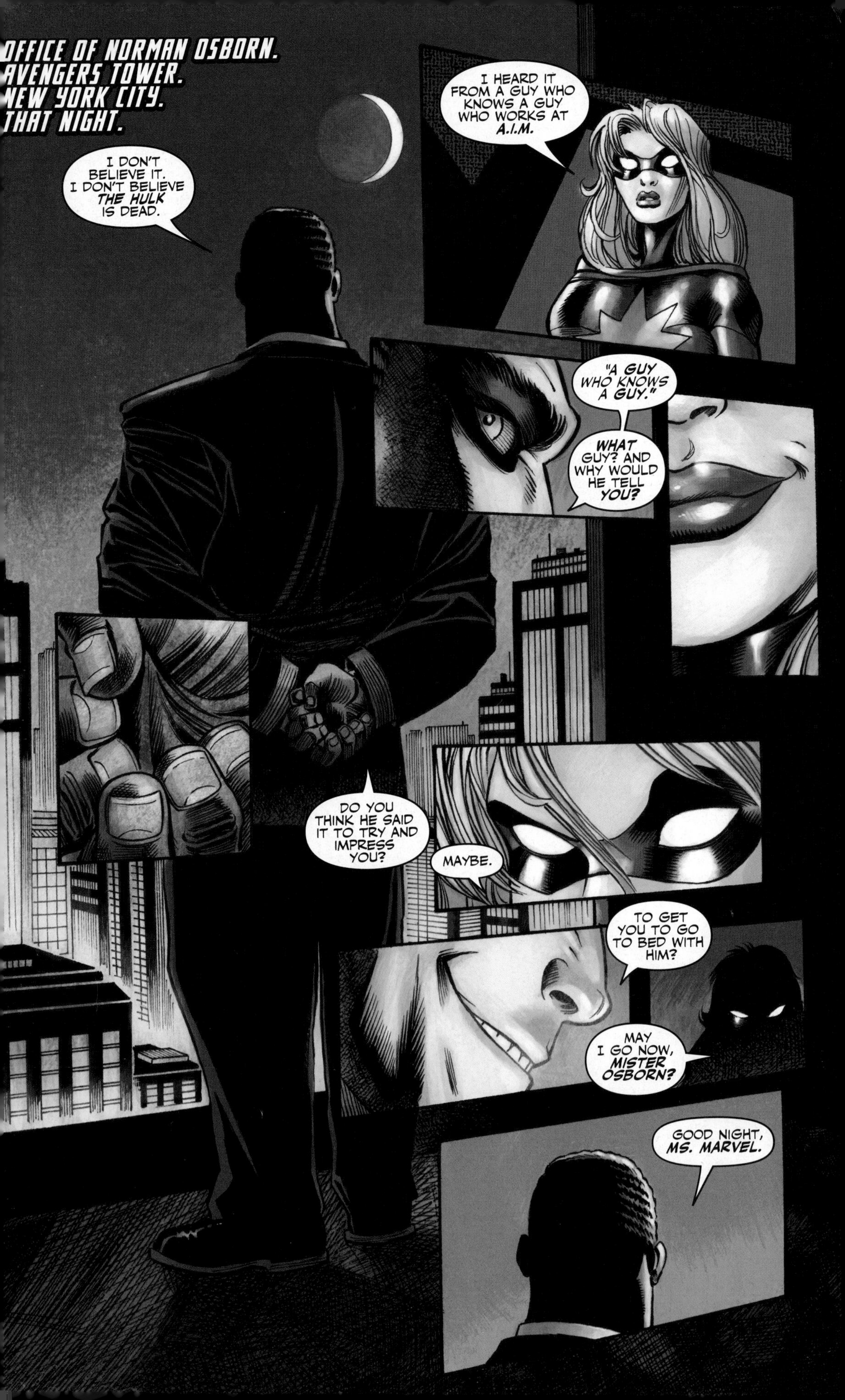
OFFICE OF NORMAN OSBORN.
AVENGERS TOWER.
NEW YORK CITY.
THAT NIGHT.
I DON'T BELIEVE IT. I DON'T BELIEVE THE HULK IS DEAD.
I HEARD IT FROM A GUY WHO KNOWS A GUY WHO WORKS AT A.I.M.
"A GUY WHO KNOWS A GUY."
WHAT GUY? AND WHY WOULD HE TELL YOU?
DO YOU THINK HE SAID IT TO TRY AND IMPRESS YOU?
MAYBE.
TO GET YOU TO GO TO BED WITH HIM?
MAY I GO NOW, MISTER OSBORN?
GOOD NIGHT, MS. MARVEL.

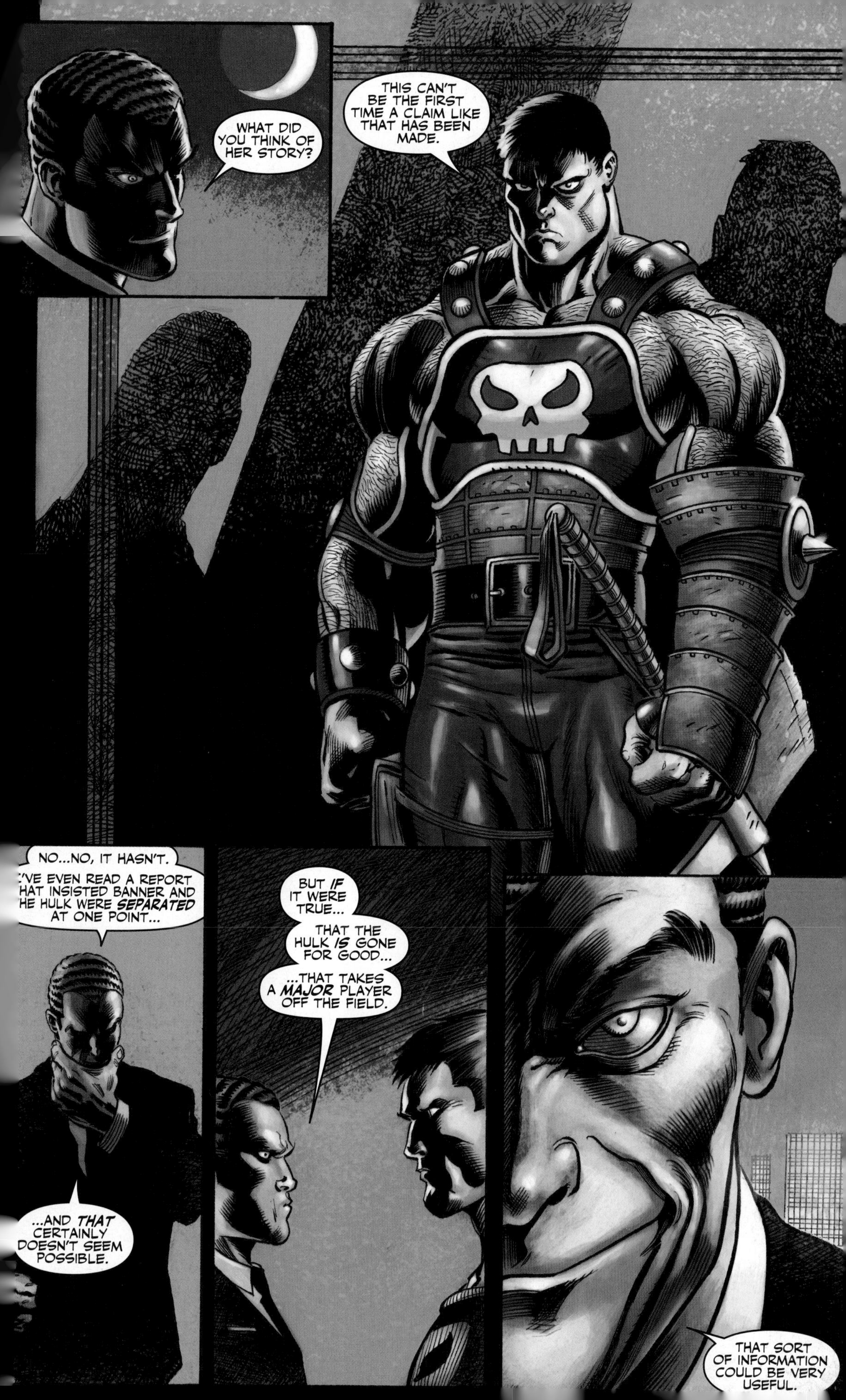
WHAT DID YOU THINK OF HER STORY?
THIS CAN'T BE THE FIRST TIME A CLAIM LIKE THAT HAS BEEN MADE.
NO...NO, IT HASN'T.
I'VE EVEN READ A REPORT THAT INSISTED BANNER AND THE HULK WERE SEPARATED AT ONE POINT...
...AND THAT CERTAINLY DOESN'T SEEM POSSIBLE.
BUT IF IT WERE TRUE...
THAT THE HULK IS GONE FOR GOOD...
...THAT TAKES A MAJOR PLAYER OFF THE FIELD.
THAT SORT OF INFORMATION COULD BE VERY USEFUL.

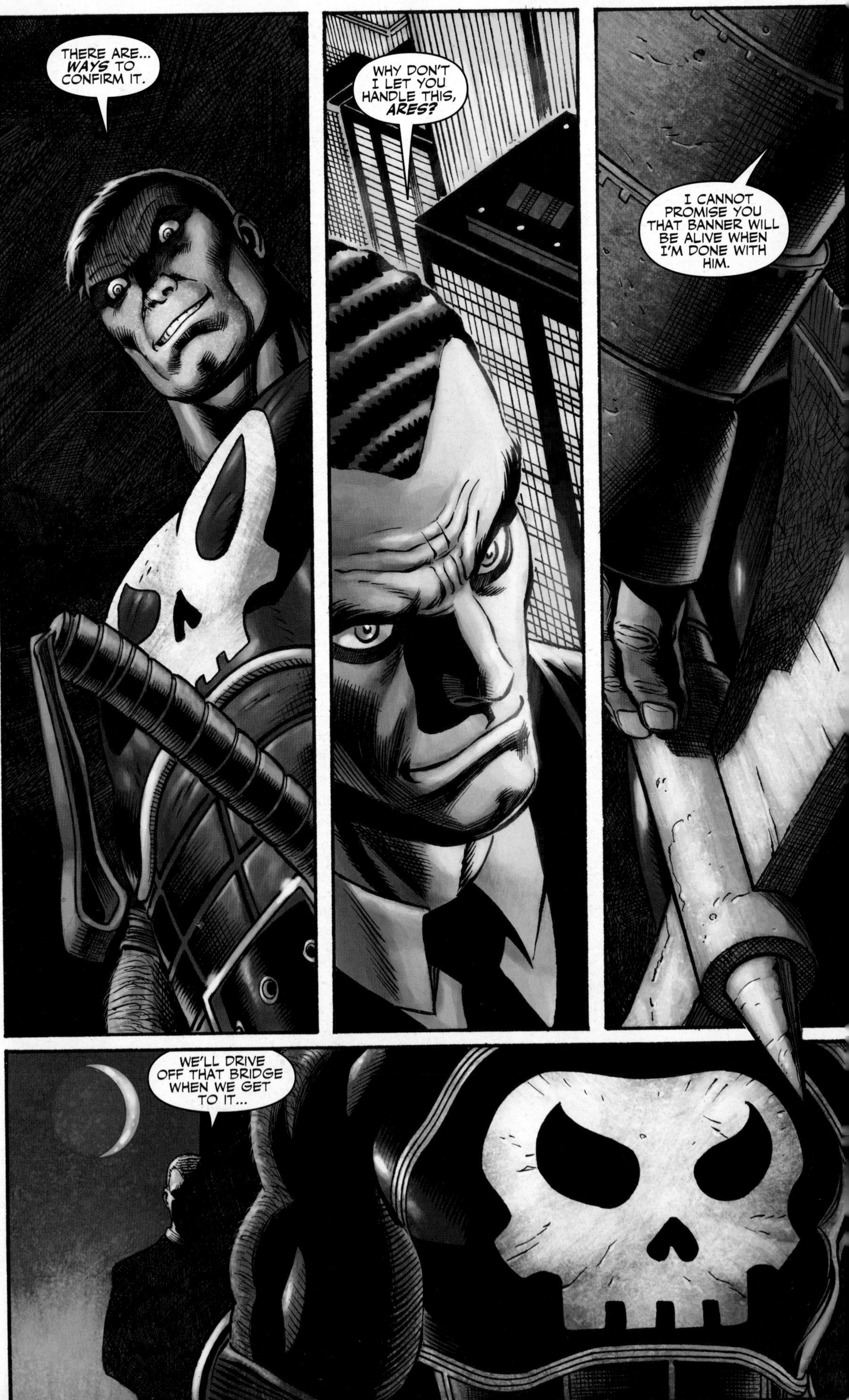

THERE ARE... WAYS TO CONFIRM IT.
WHY DON'T I LET YOU HANDLE THIS, ARES?
I CANNOT PROMISE YOU THAT BANNER WILL BE ALIVE WHEN I'M DONE WITH HIM.
WE'LL DRIVE OFF THAT BRIDGE WHEN WE GET TO IT...

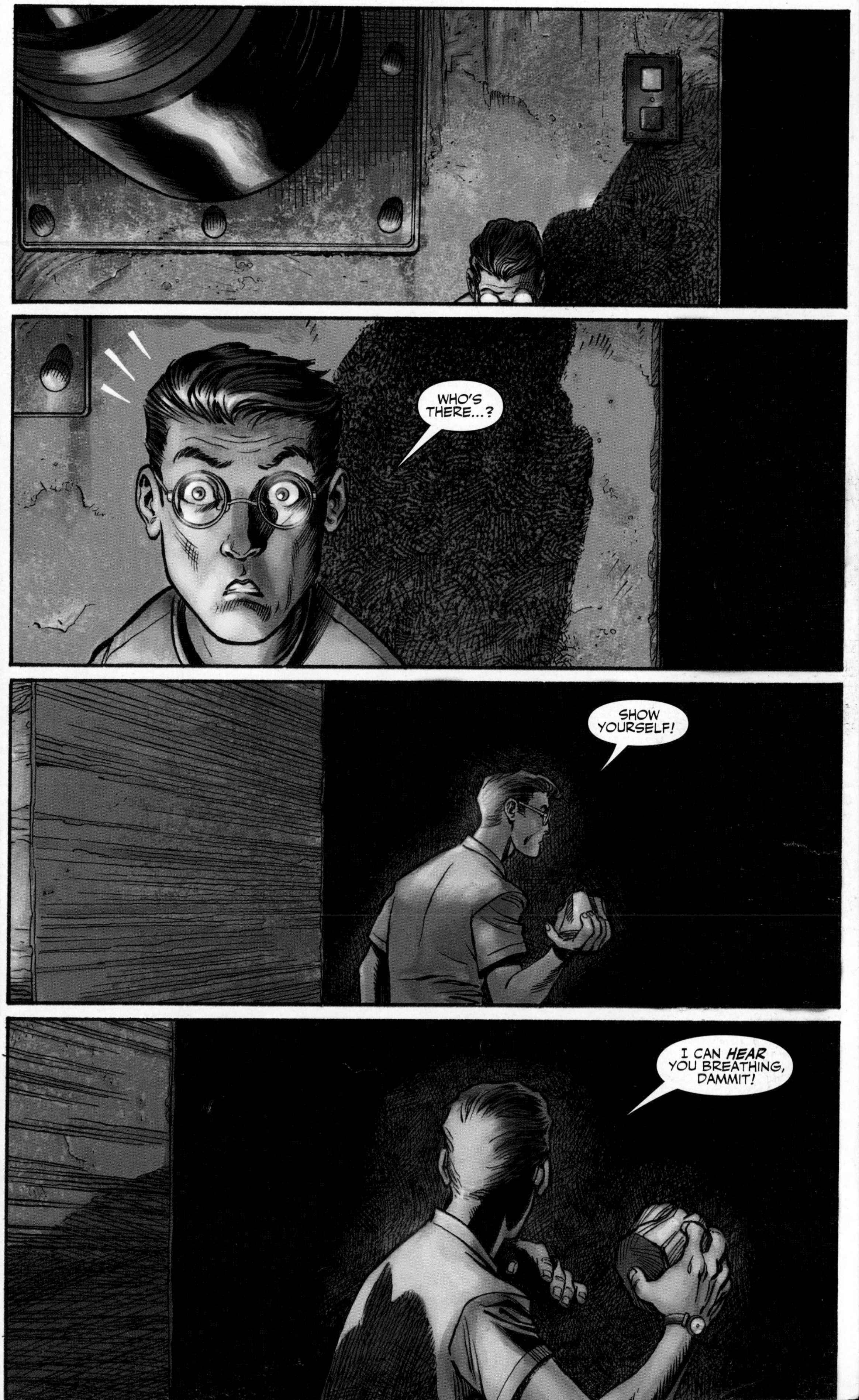
WHO'S THERE...?
SHOW YOURSELF!
I CAN *HEAR* YOU BREATHING, DAMMIT!

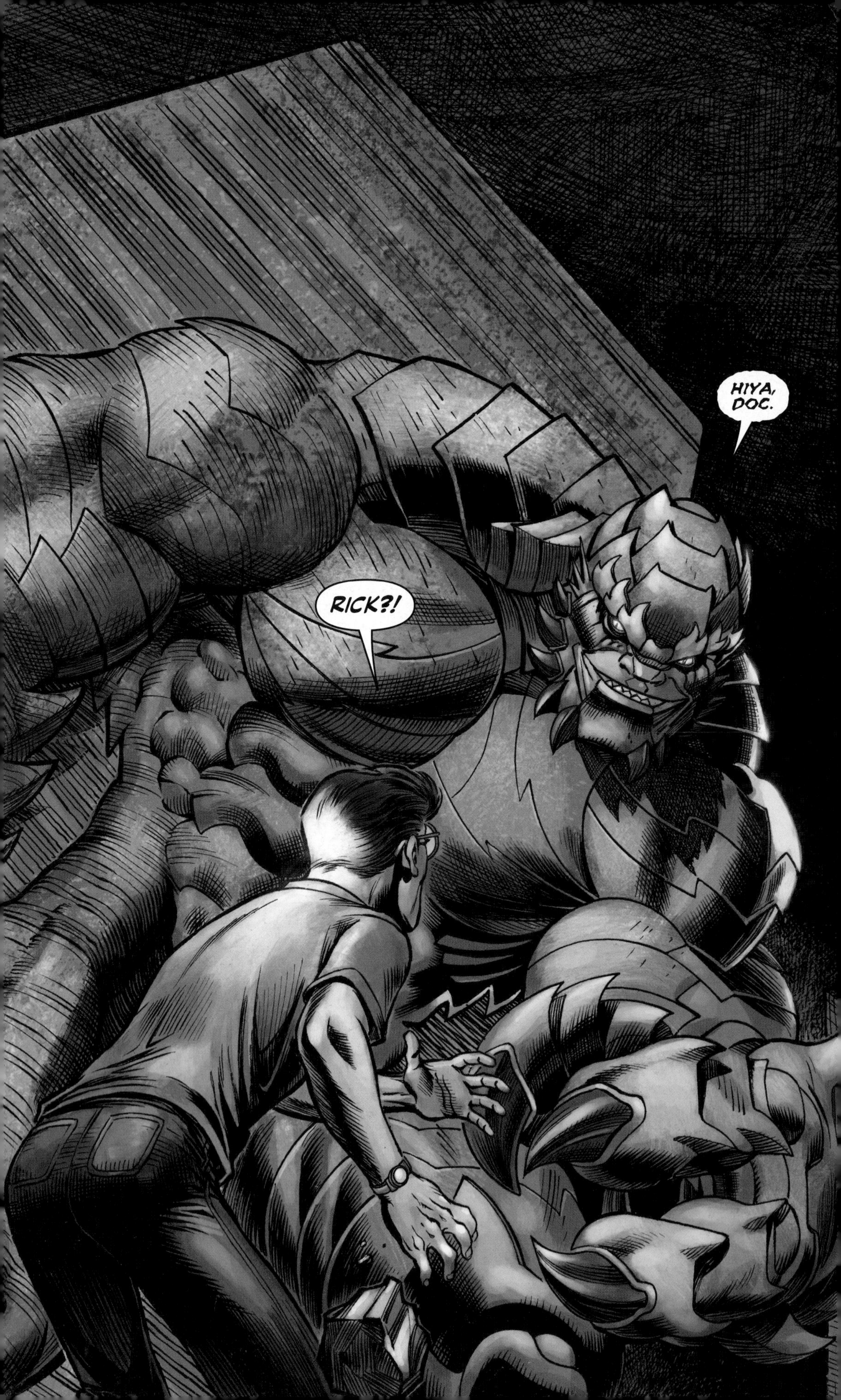
HIYA, DOC.
RICK?!

HOW--HOW DID YOU DO THAT? ADAPT TO THE ENVIRONMENT LIKE THAT?

ALWAYS THE SCIENTIST, HUH, BRUCE?

I'M NOT SURE, REALLY.

SOMETHING ELSE M.O.D.O.K. DID TO ME. OR I COULD ALWAYS DO ONCE I BECAME...A-BOMB.

AND I JUST DIDN'T KNOW HOW.

PRETTY FRICKIN' COOL.

I GUESS NOW WE KNOW WHAT'D HAPPEN IF AN ARMADILLO AND A CHAMELEON HAD A BABY.

A REALLY FUGLY BABY --

-- WHO'S STRONG AS ALL GET OUT!

I'M STILL AMAZED THAT YOU'VE TAKEN CONTROL OF A-BOMB'S PERSONALITY.

YOU NO LONGER REFER TO YOURSELF IN THE THIRD PERSON.

LIKE I USED TO...

"HULK AM STRONGEST THERE IS..."

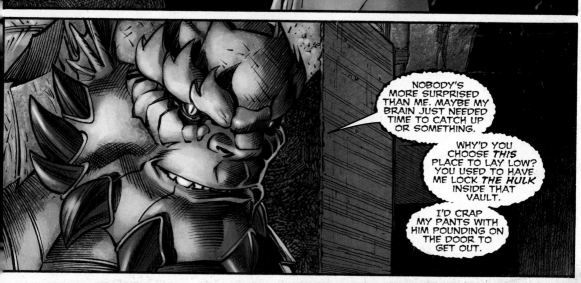

NOBODY'S MORE SURPRISED THAN ME. MAYBE MY BRAIN JUST NEEDED TIME TO CATCH UP OR SOMETHING.

WHY'D YOU CHOOSE THIS PLACE TO LAY LOW? YOU USED TO HAVE ME LOCK THE HULK INSIDE THAT VAULT.

I'D CRAP MY PANTS WITH HIM POUNDING ON THE DOOR TO GET OUT.

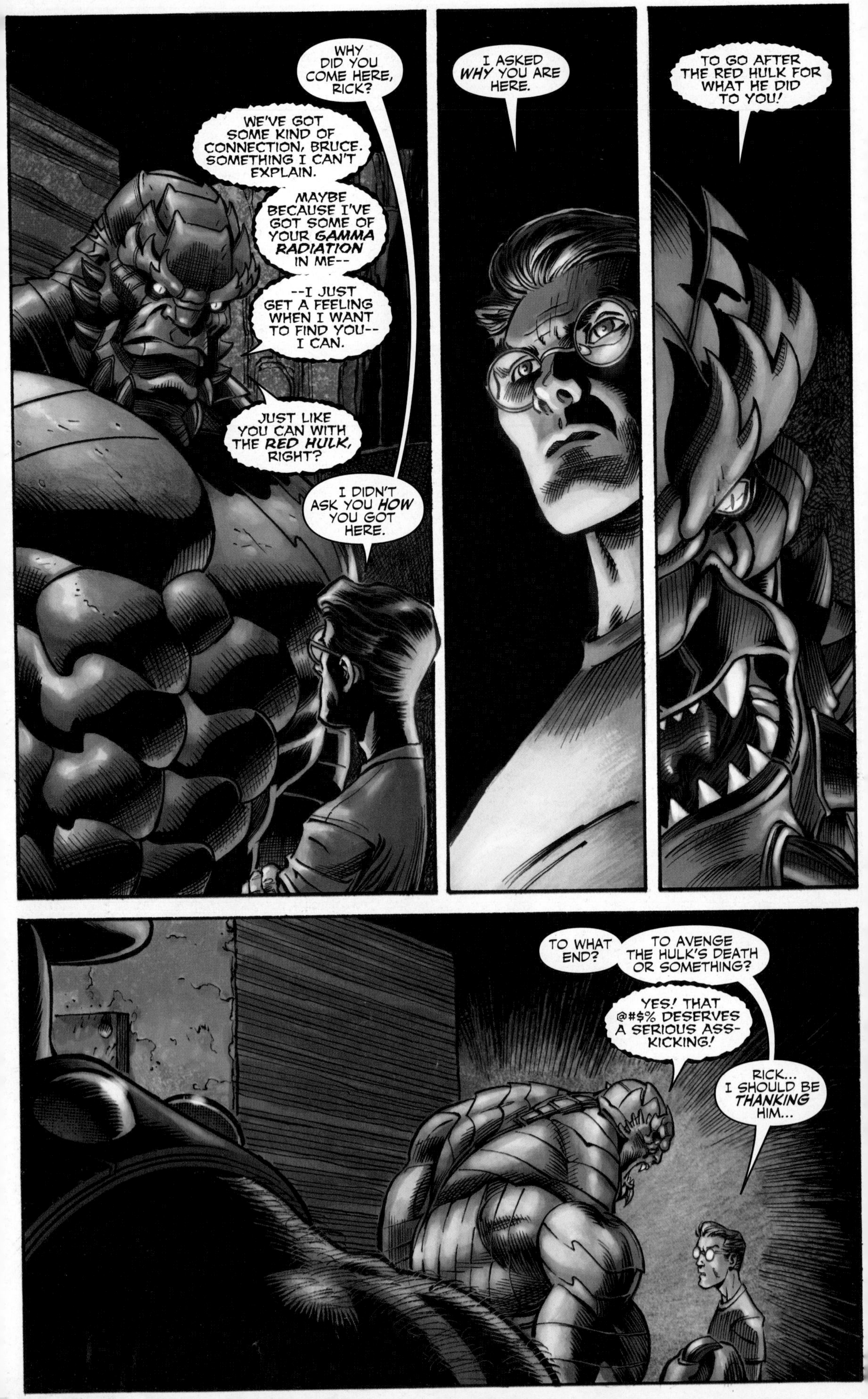
WHY DID YOU COME HERE, RICK?
WE'VE GOT SOME KIND OF CONNECTION, BRUCE. SOMETHING I CAN'T EXPLAIN.
MAYBE BECAUSE I'VE GOT SOME OF YOUR GAMMA RADIATION IN ME--
--I JUST GET A FEELING WHEN I WANT TO FIND YOU-- I CAN.
JUST LIKE YOU CAN WITH THE RED HULK, RIGHT?
I DIDN'T ASK YOU HOW YOU GOT HERE.
I ASKED WHY YOU ARE HERE.
TO GO AFTER THE RED HULK FOR WHAT HE DID TO YOU!
TO WHAT END?
TO AVENGE THE HULK'S DEATH OR SOMETHING?
YES! THAT @#$% DESERVES A SERIOUS ASS-KICKING!
RICK... I SHOULD BE THANKING HIM...

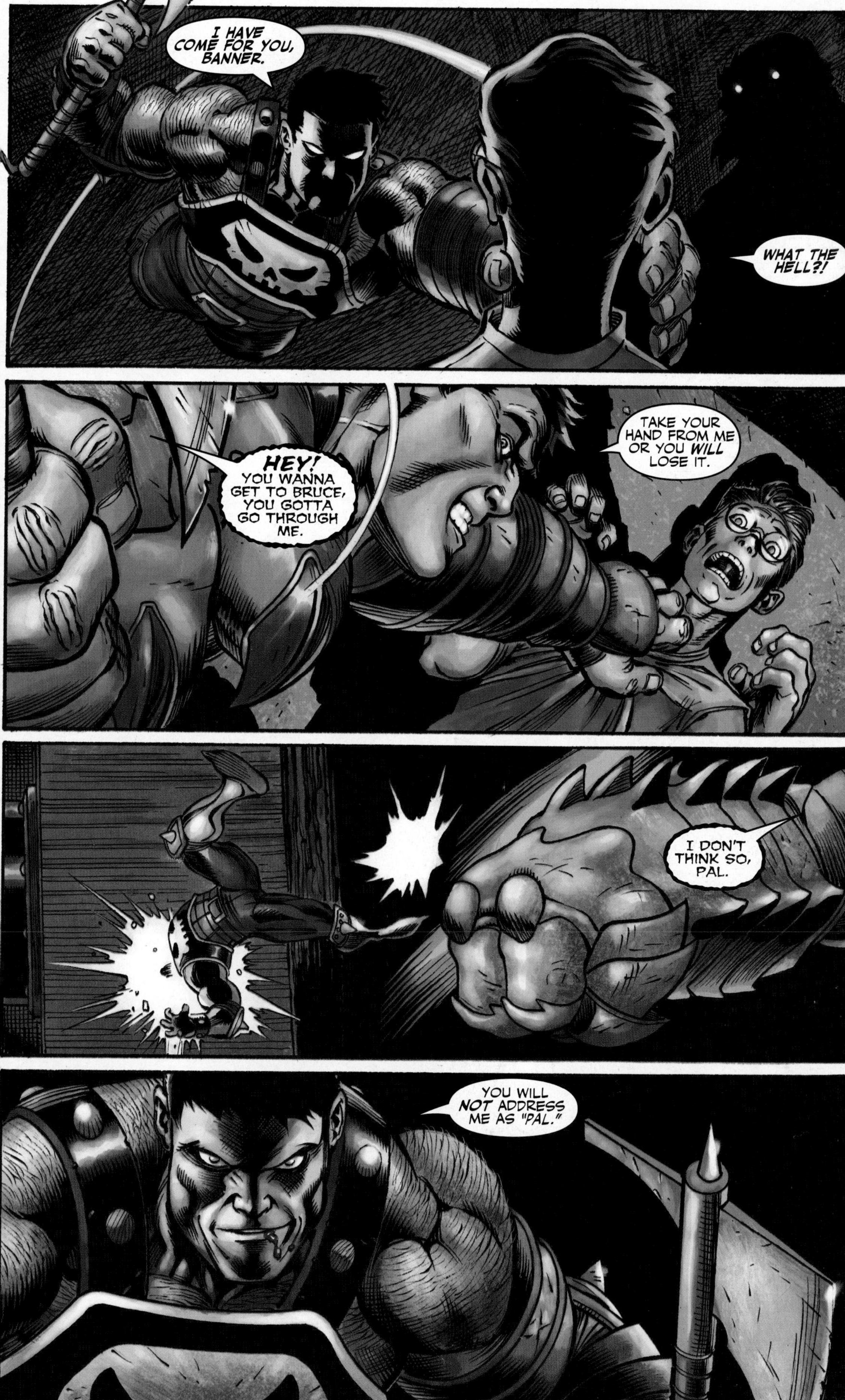
I HAVE COME FOR YOU, BANNER.
WHAT THE HELL?!
HEY! YOU WANNA GET TO BRUCE, YOU GOTTA GO THROUGH ME.
TAKE YOUR HAND FROM ME OR YOU WILL LOSE IT.
I DON'T THINK SO, PAL.
YOU WILL NOT ADDRESS ME AS "PAL."

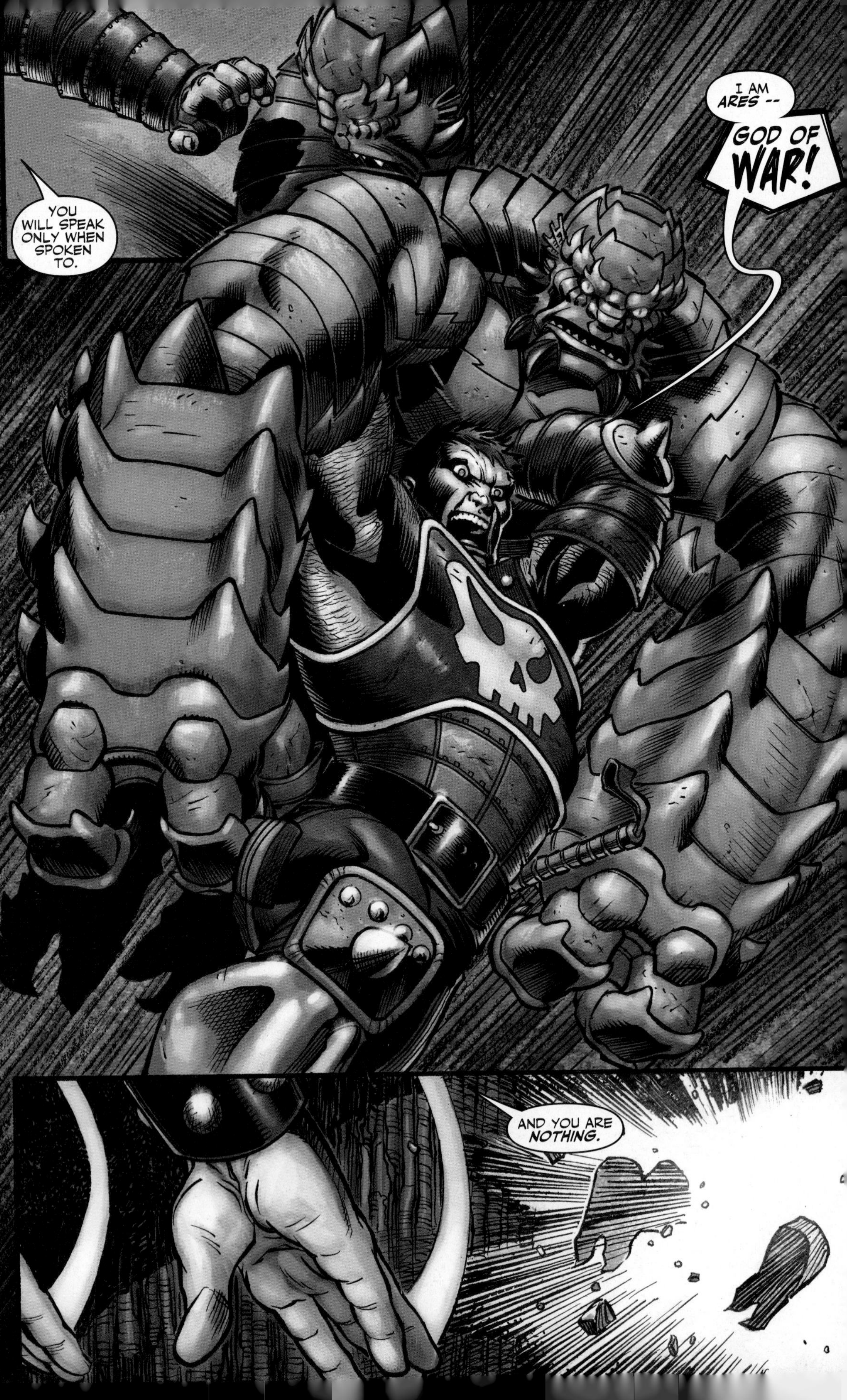
YOU WILL SPEAK ONLY WHEN SPOKEN TO.
I AM ARES --
GOD OF WAR!
AND YOU ARE NOTHING.

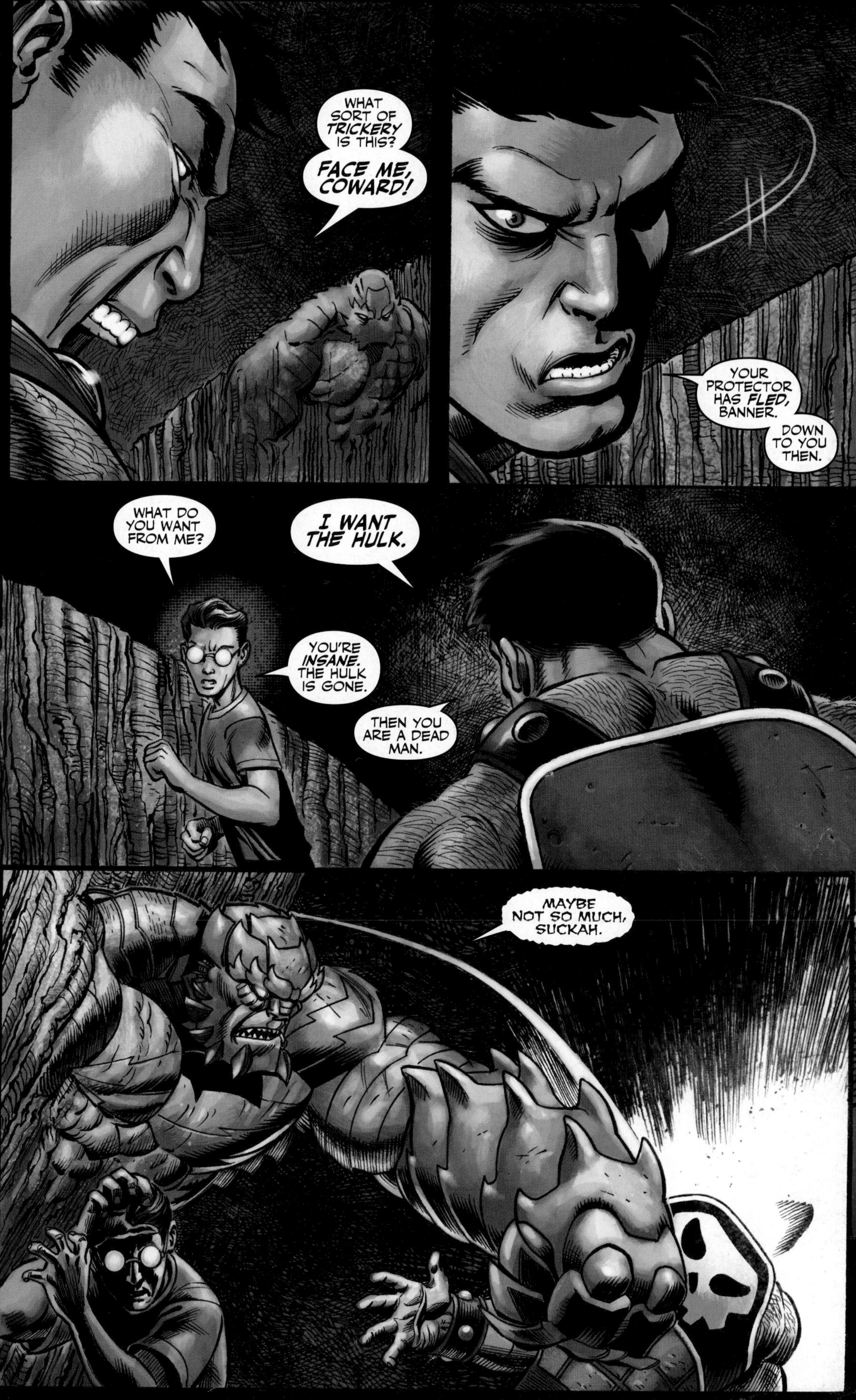
WHAT SORT OF TRICKERY IS THIS?
FACE ME, COWARD!
YOUR PROTECTOR HAS FLED, BANNER.
DOWN TO YOU THEN.
WHAT DO YOU WANT FROM ME?
I WANT THE HULK.
YOU'RE INSANE. THE HULK IS GONE.
THEN YOU ARE A DEAD MAN.
MAYBE NOT SO MUCH, SUCKAH.

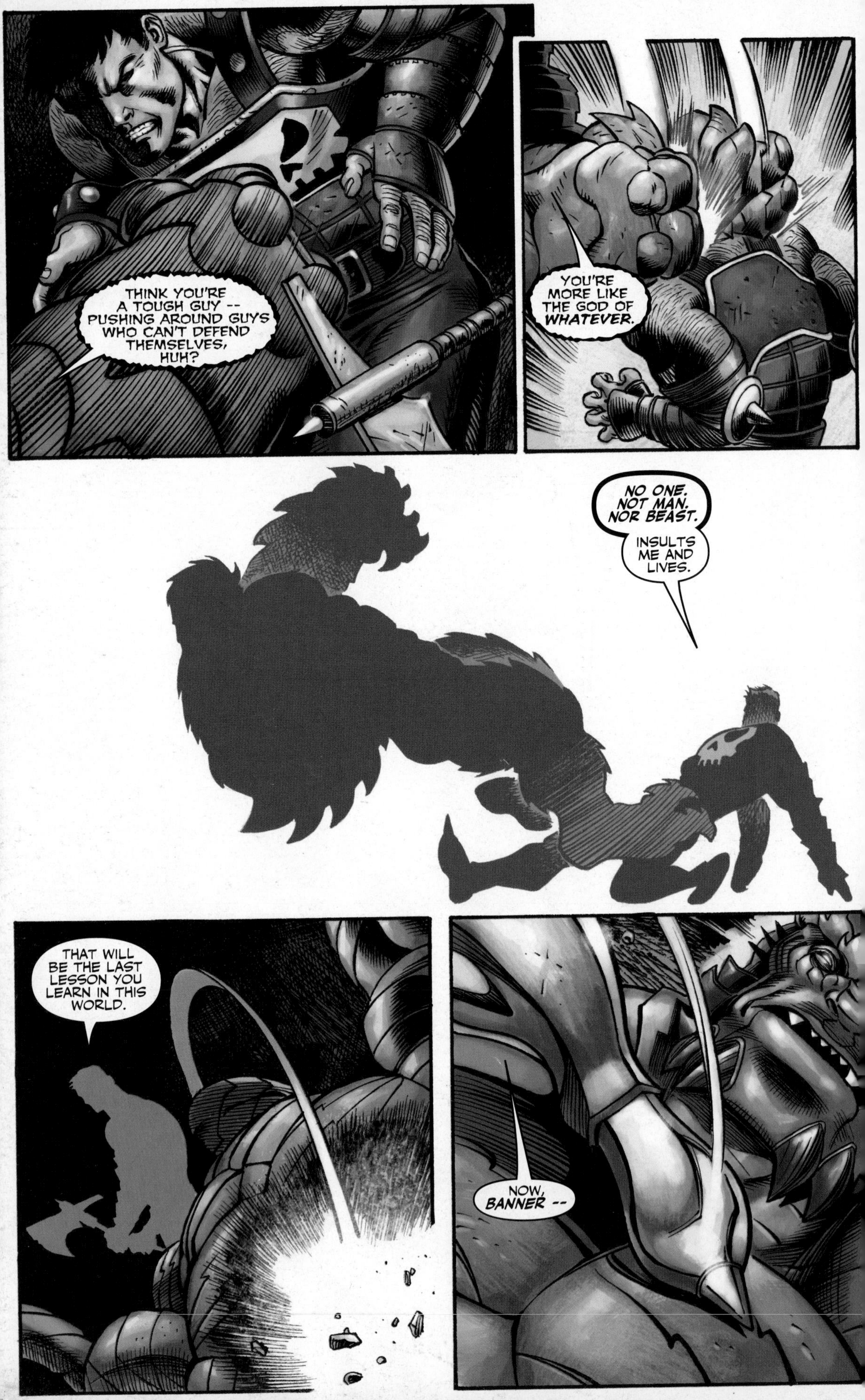
THINK YOU'RE A TOUGH GUY -- PUSHING AROUND GUYS WHO CAN'T DEFEND THEMSELVES, HUH?
YOU'RE MORE LIKE THE GOD OF WHATEVER.
NO ONE. NOT MAN. NOR BEAST.
INSULTS ME AND LIVES.
THAT WILL BE THE LAST LESSON YOU LEARN IN THIS WORLD.
NOW, BANNER --

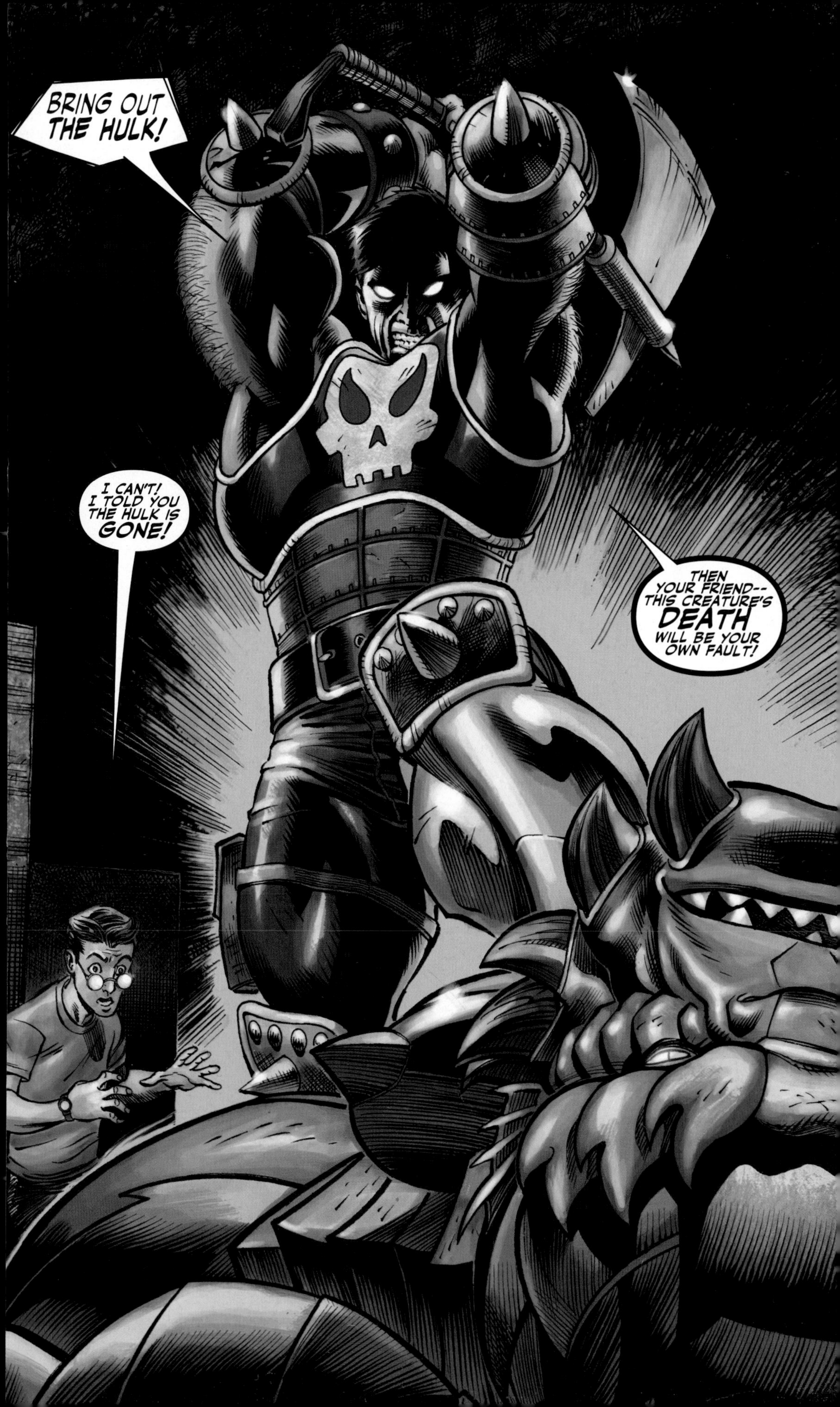
BRING OUT THE HULK!
I CAN'T! I TOLD YOU THE HULK IS GONE!
THEN YOUR FRIEND-- THIS CREATURE'S DEATH WILL BE YOUR OWN FAULT!

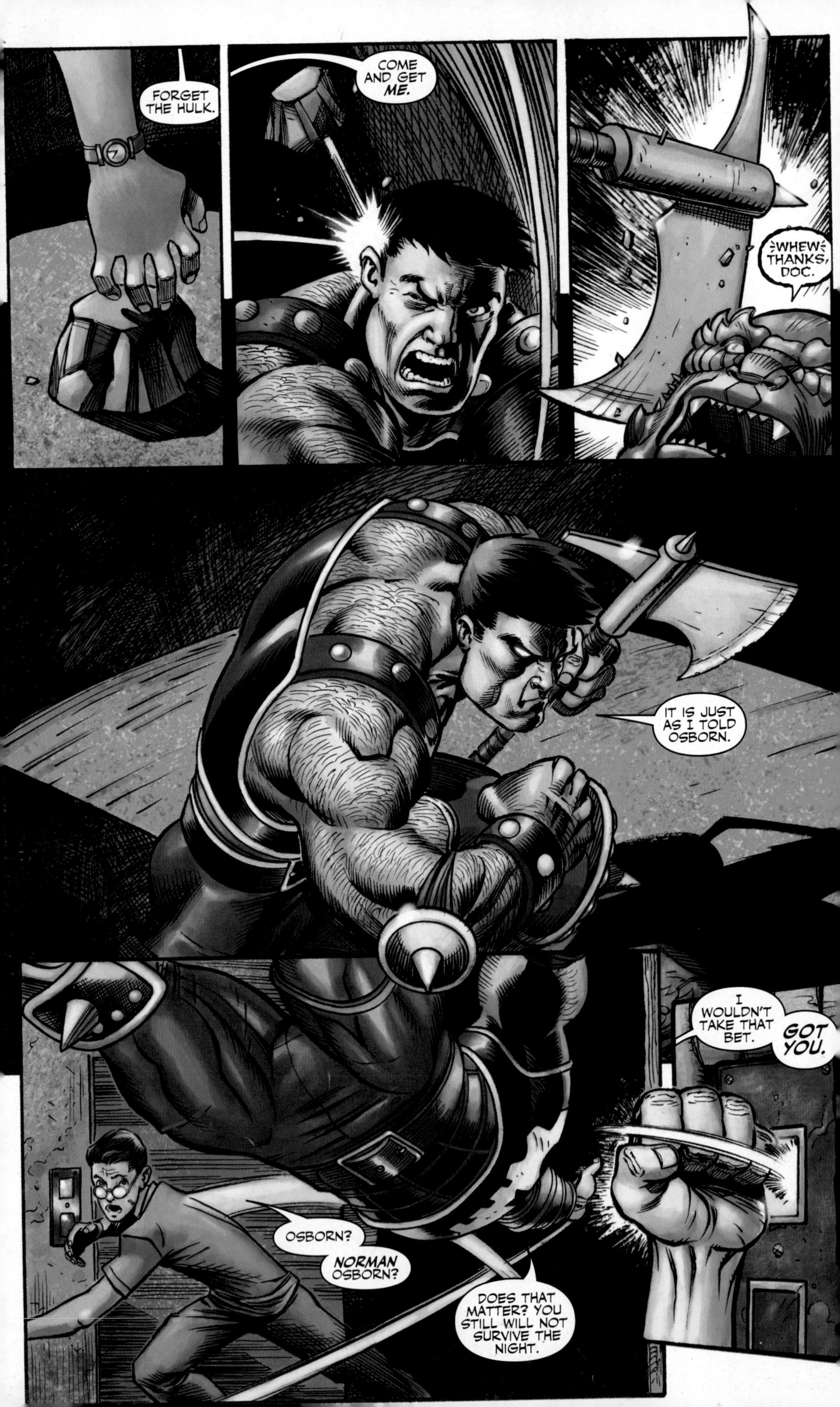
FORGET THE HULK.
COME AND GET ME.
WHEW THANKS, DOC.
IT IS JUST AS I TOLD OSBORN.
I WOULDN'T TAKE THAT BET.
GOT YOU.
OSBORN?
NORMAN OSBORN?
DOES THAT MATTER? YOU STILL WILL NOT SURVIVE THE NIGHT.

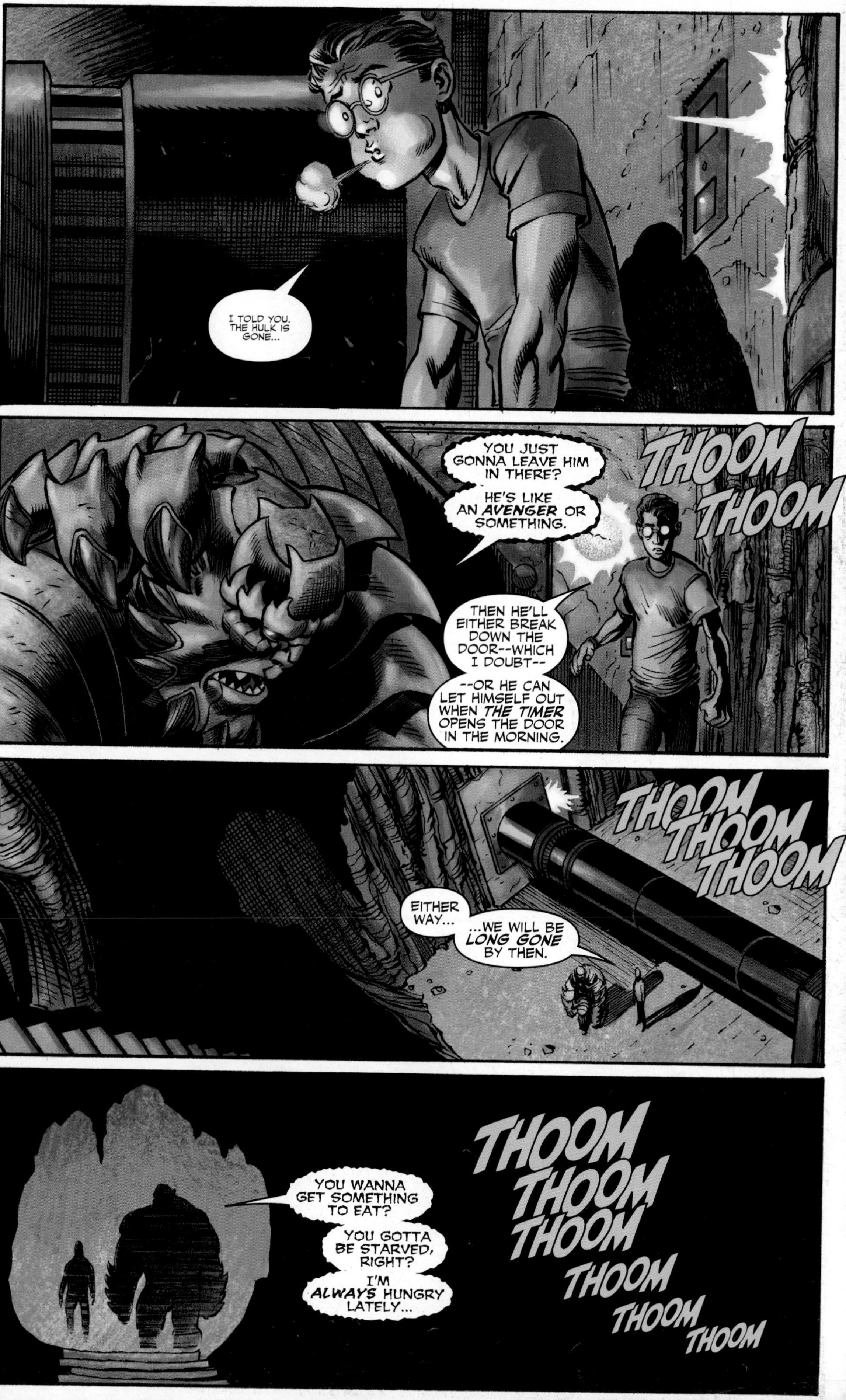
I TOLD YOU. THE HULK IS GONE...
YOU JUST GONNA LEAVE HIM IN THERE?
HE'S LIKE AN AVENGER OR SOMETHING.
THOOM THOOM
THEN HE'LL EITHER BREAK DOWN THE DOOR--WHICH I DOUBT--
--OR HE CAN LET HIMSELF OUT WHEN THE TIMER OPENS THE DOOR IN THE MORNING.
THOOM THOOM THOOM
EITHER WAY...
...WE WILL BE LONG GONE BY THEN.
THOOM THOOM THOOM THOOM THOOM THOOM
YOU WANNA GET SOMETHING TO EAT?
YOU GOTTA BE STARVED, RIGHT?
I'M ALWAYS HUNGRY LATELY...

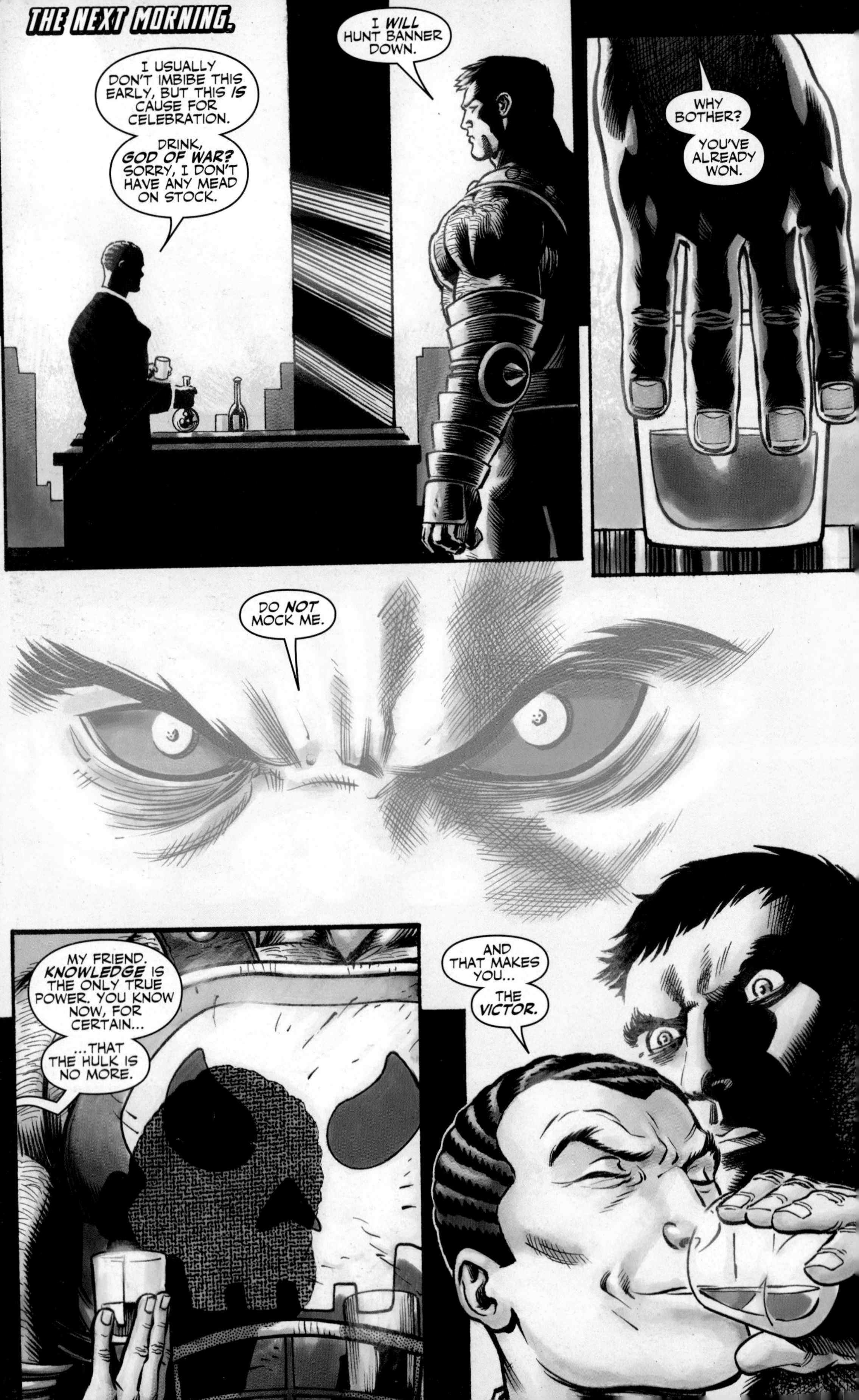
THE NEXT MORNING.
I USUALLY DON'T IMBIBE THIS EARLY, BUT THIS *IS* CAUSE FOR CELEBRATION.
DRINK, *GOD OF WAR?* SORRY, I DON'T HAVE ANY MEAD ON STOCK.
I *WILL* HUNT BANNER DOWN.
WHY BOTHER?
YOU'VE ALREADY WON.
DO *NOT* MOCK ME.
MY FRIEND. *KNOWLEDGE* IS THE ONLY TRUE POWER. YOU KNOW NOW, FOR CERTAIN...
...THAT THE HULK IS NO MORE.
AND THAT MAKES YOU... THE *VICTOR*.

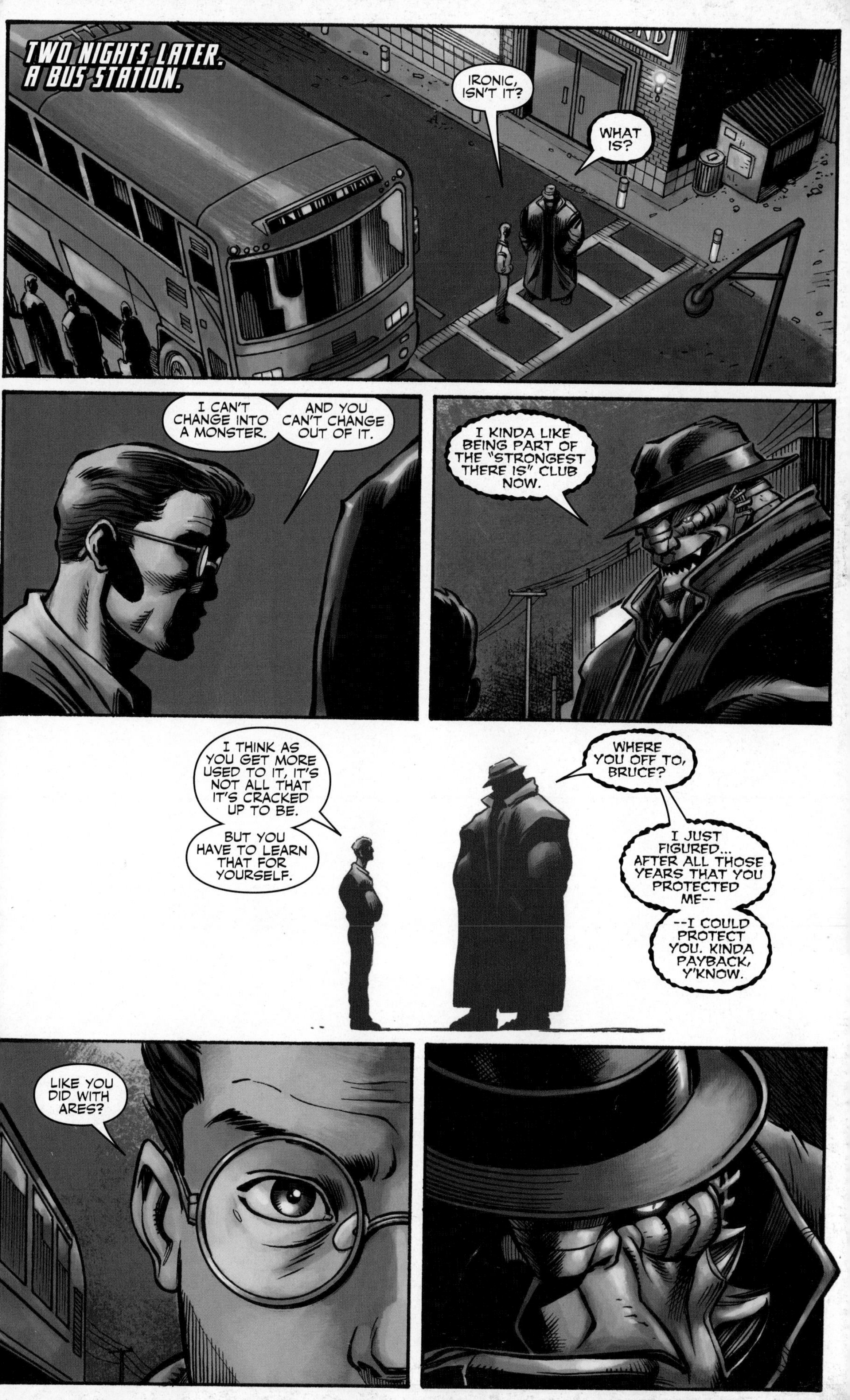
TWO NIGHTS LATER. A BUS STATION.
IRONIC, ISN'T IT?
WHAT IS?
I CAN'T CHANGE INTO A MONSTER.
AND YOU CAN'T CHANGE OUT OF IT.
I KINDA LIKE BEING PART OF THE "STRONGEST THERE IS" CLUB NOW.
I THINK AS YOU GET MORE USED TO IT, IT'S NOT ALL THAT IT'S CRACKED UP TO BE.
BUT YOU HAVE TO LEARN THAT FOR YOURSELF.
WHERE YOU OFF TO, BRUCE?
I JUST FIGURED... AFTER ALL THOSE YEARS THAT YOU PROTECTED ME--
--I COULD PROTECT YOU. KINDA PAYBACK, Y'KNOW.
LIKE YOU DID WITH ARES?

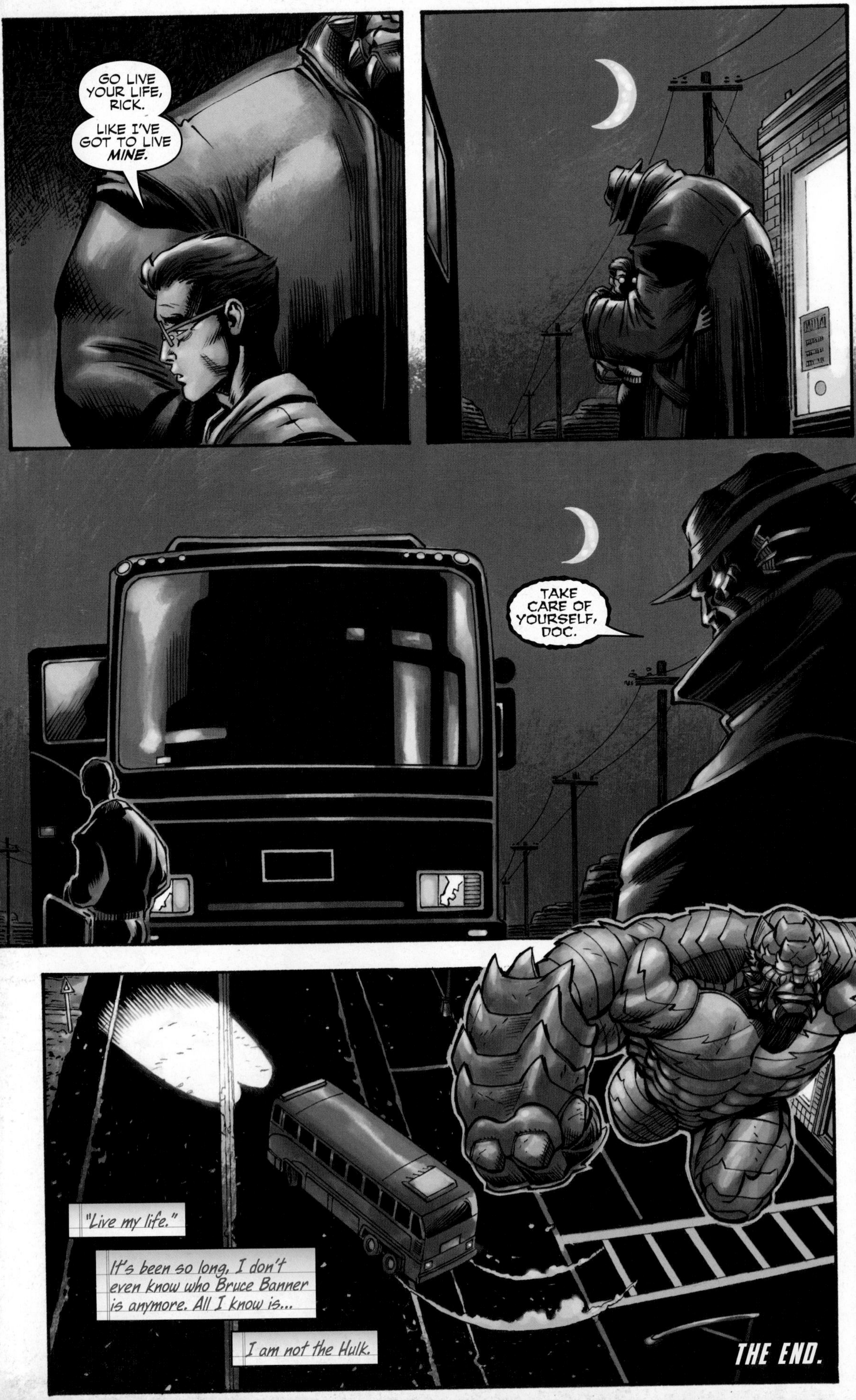
GO LIVE YOUR LIFE, RICK.
LIKE I'VE GOT TO LIVE *MINE.*
TAKE CARE OF YOURSELF, DOC.
"Live my life."
It's been so long. I don't even know who Bruce Banner is anymore. All I know is...
I am not the Hulk.
THE END.

★ EXTRAS ★

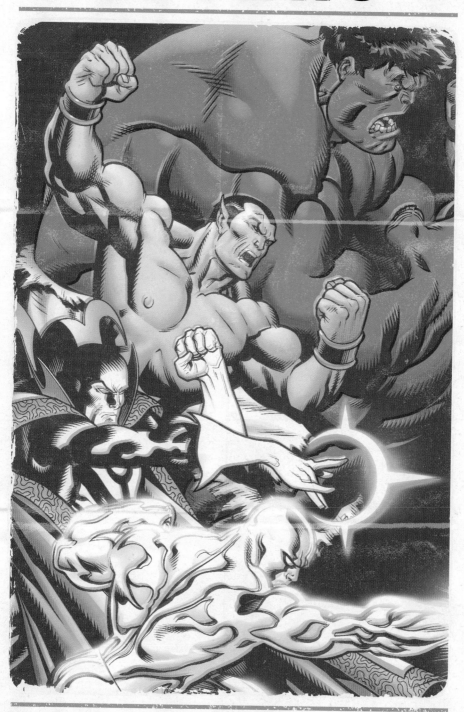

COVER GALLERY

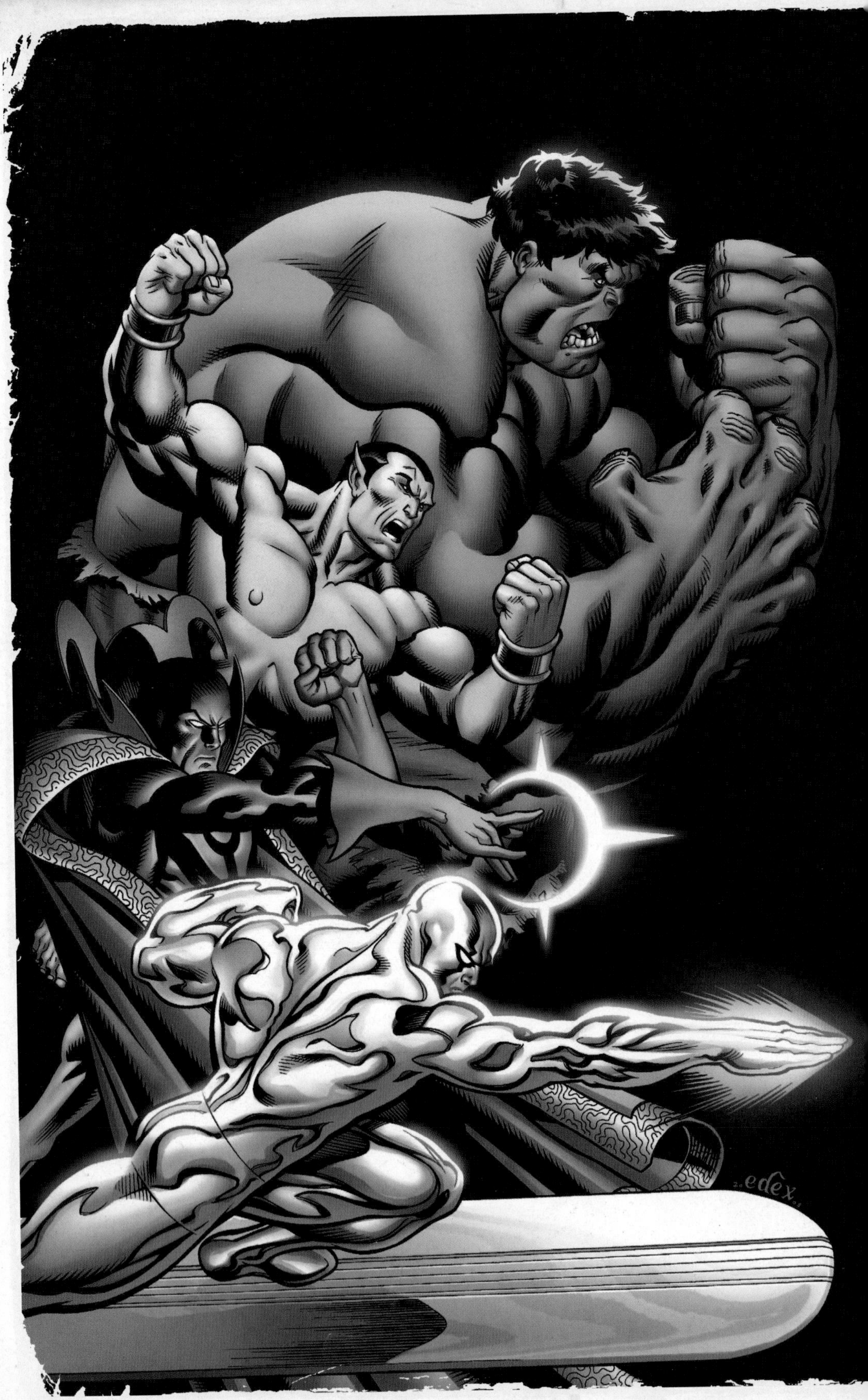
edex

★ ISSUE 10 COVERS

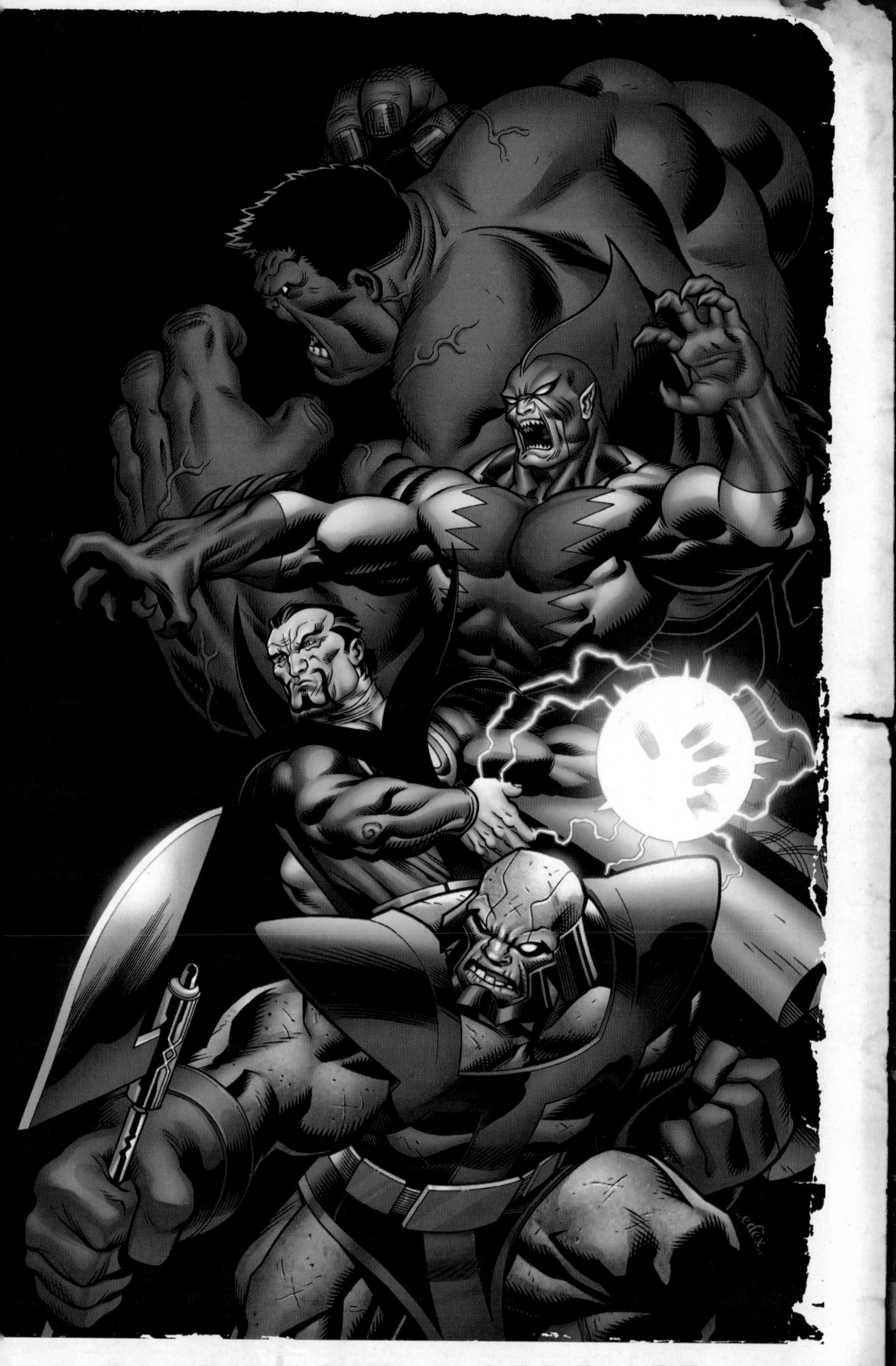

ED McGUINNESS & GURU eFX ★

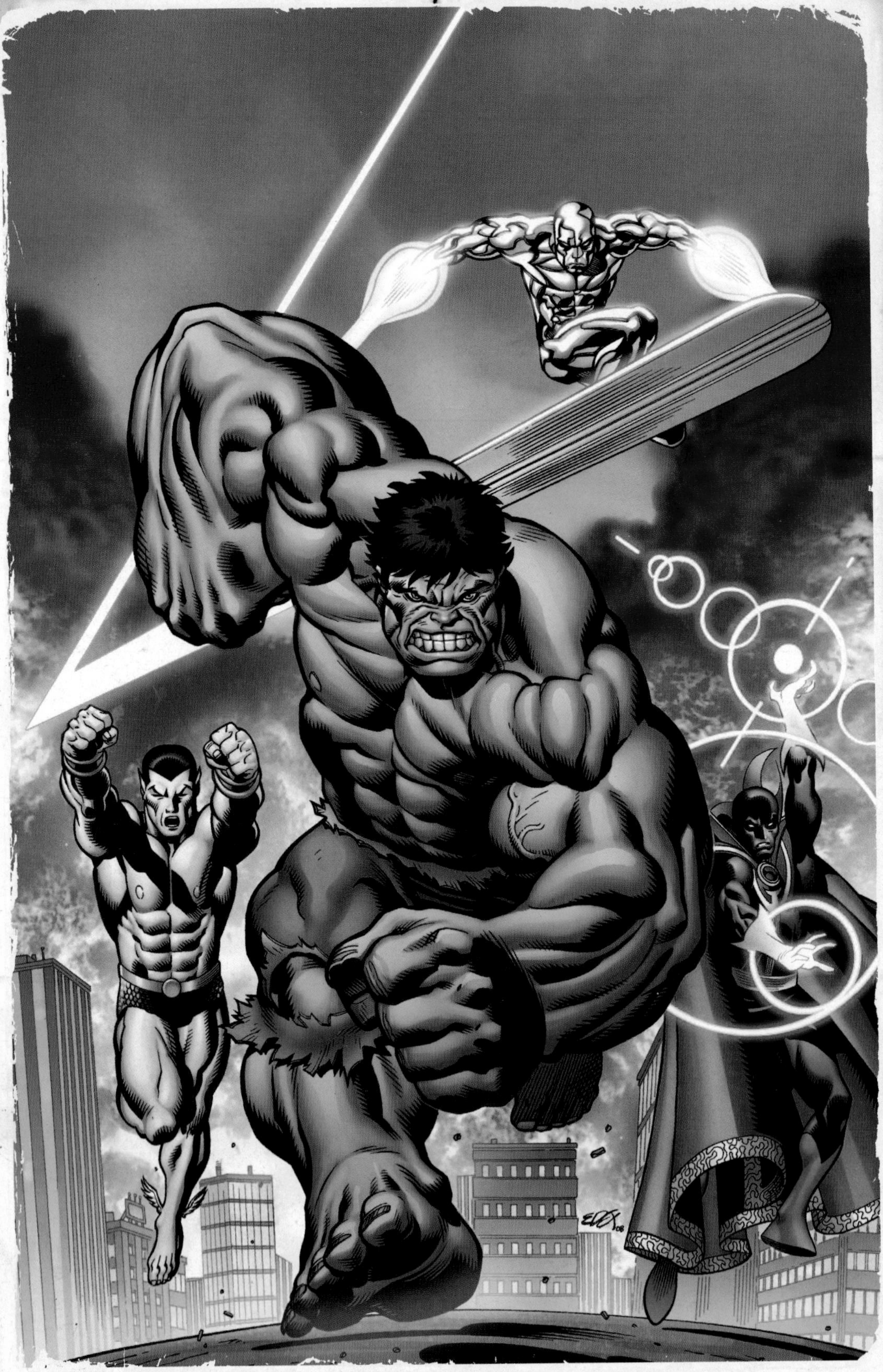

★ ISSUE 11 COVERS

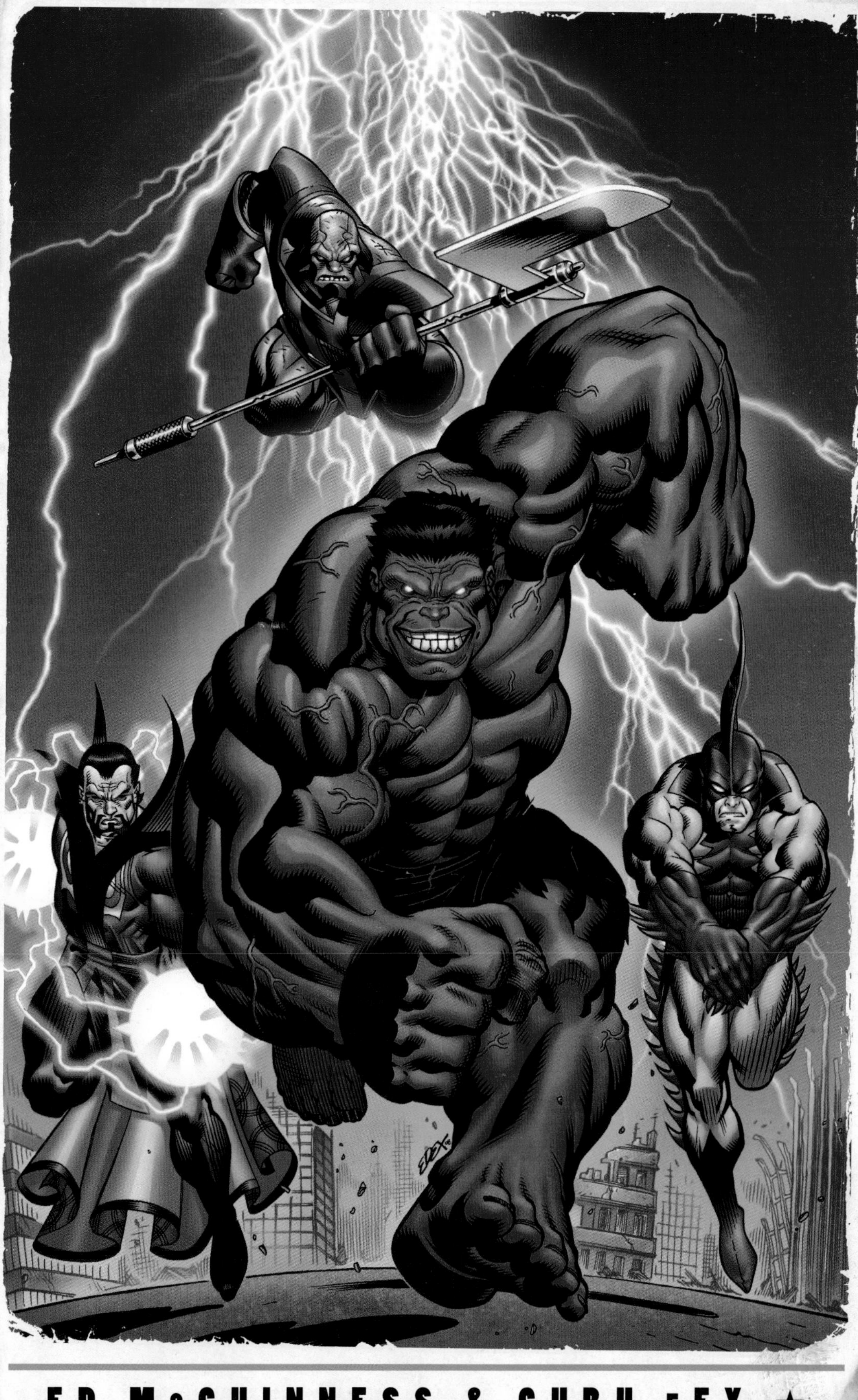

ED McGUINNESS & GURU eFX ★

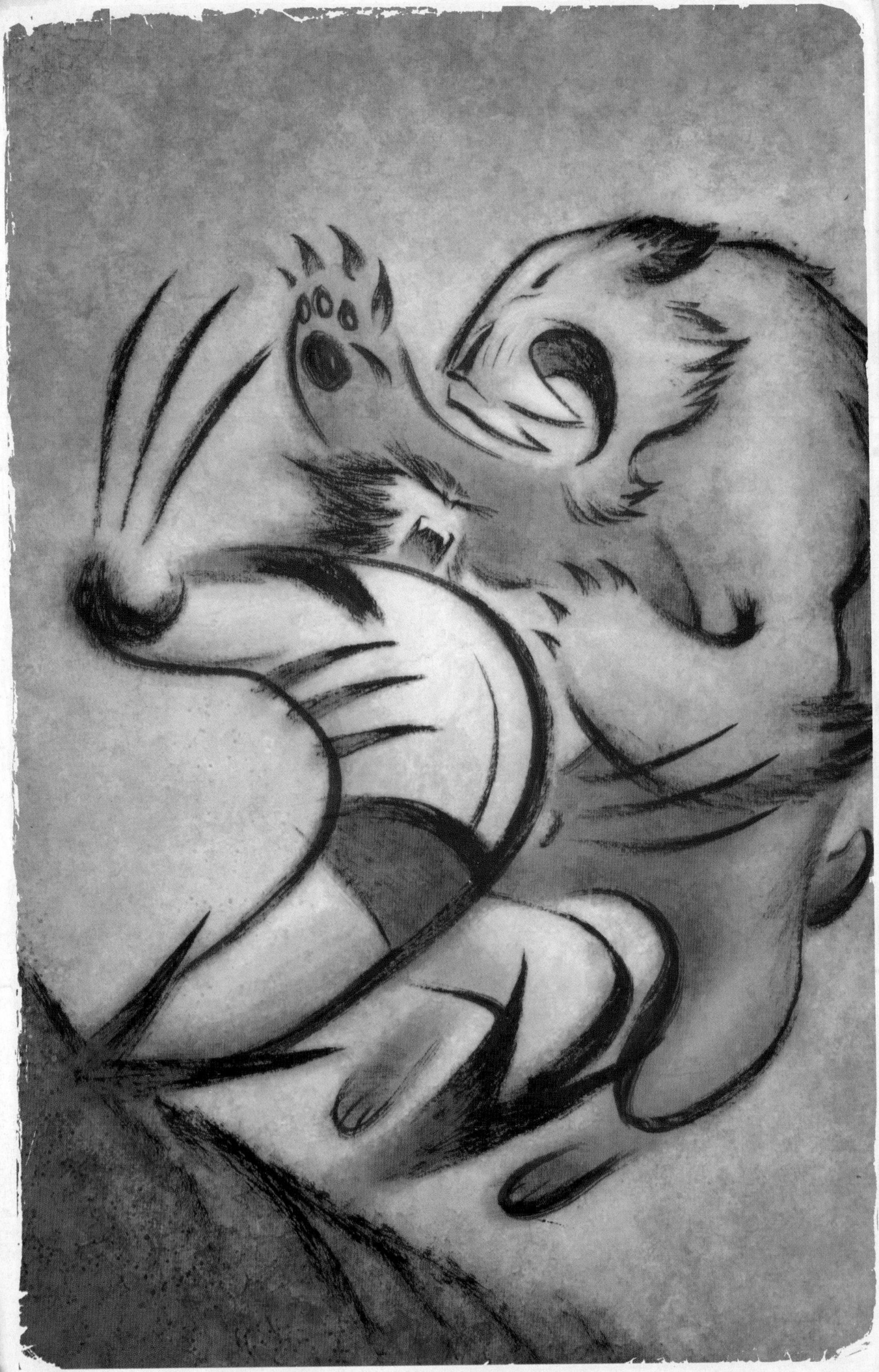

WOLVERINE ART APPRECIATION VARIANT ★ ED McGUINNESS & MORRY HOLLOWELL

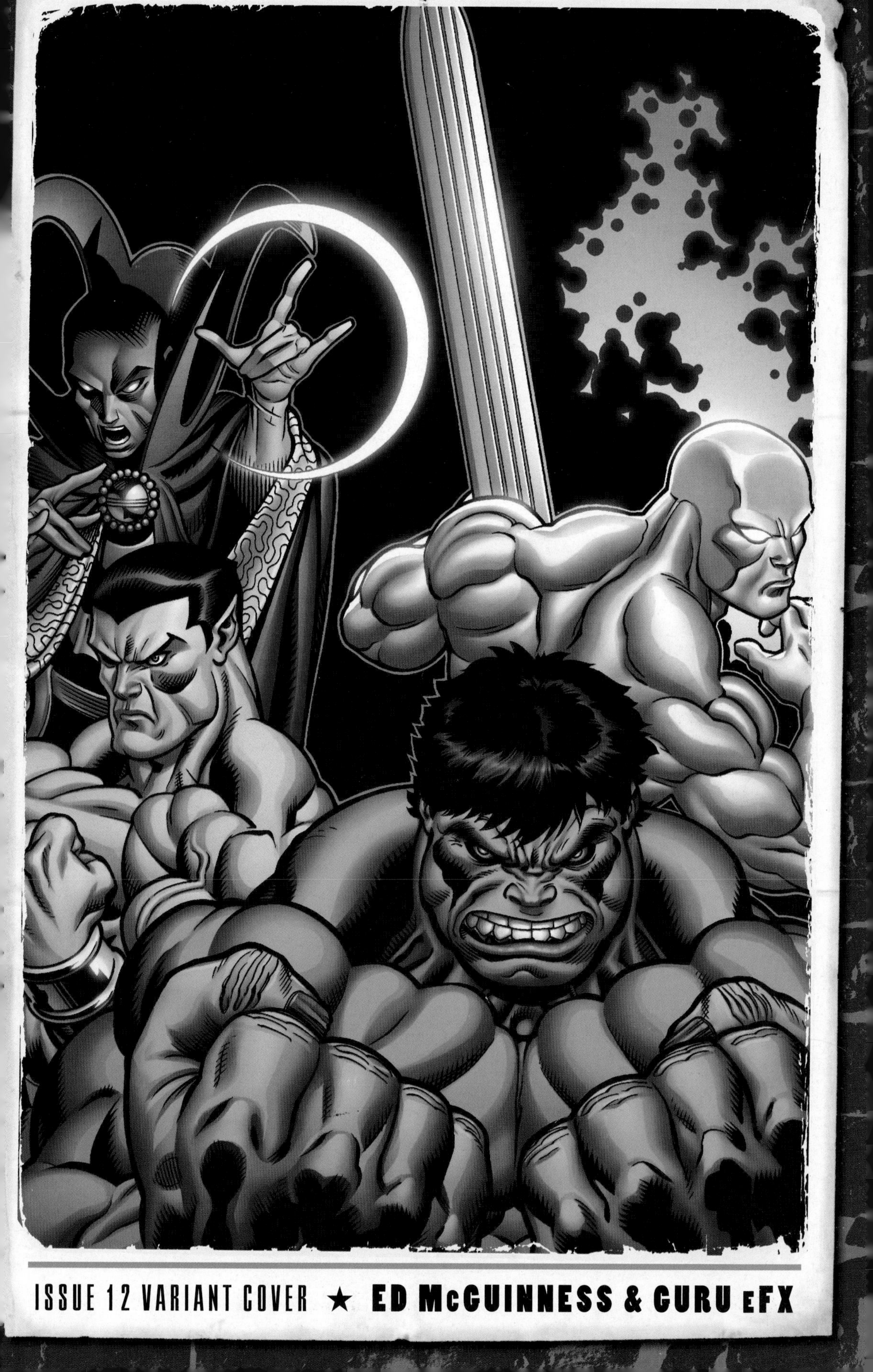

ISSUE 12 VARIANT COVER ★ ED McGUINNESS & GURU eFX

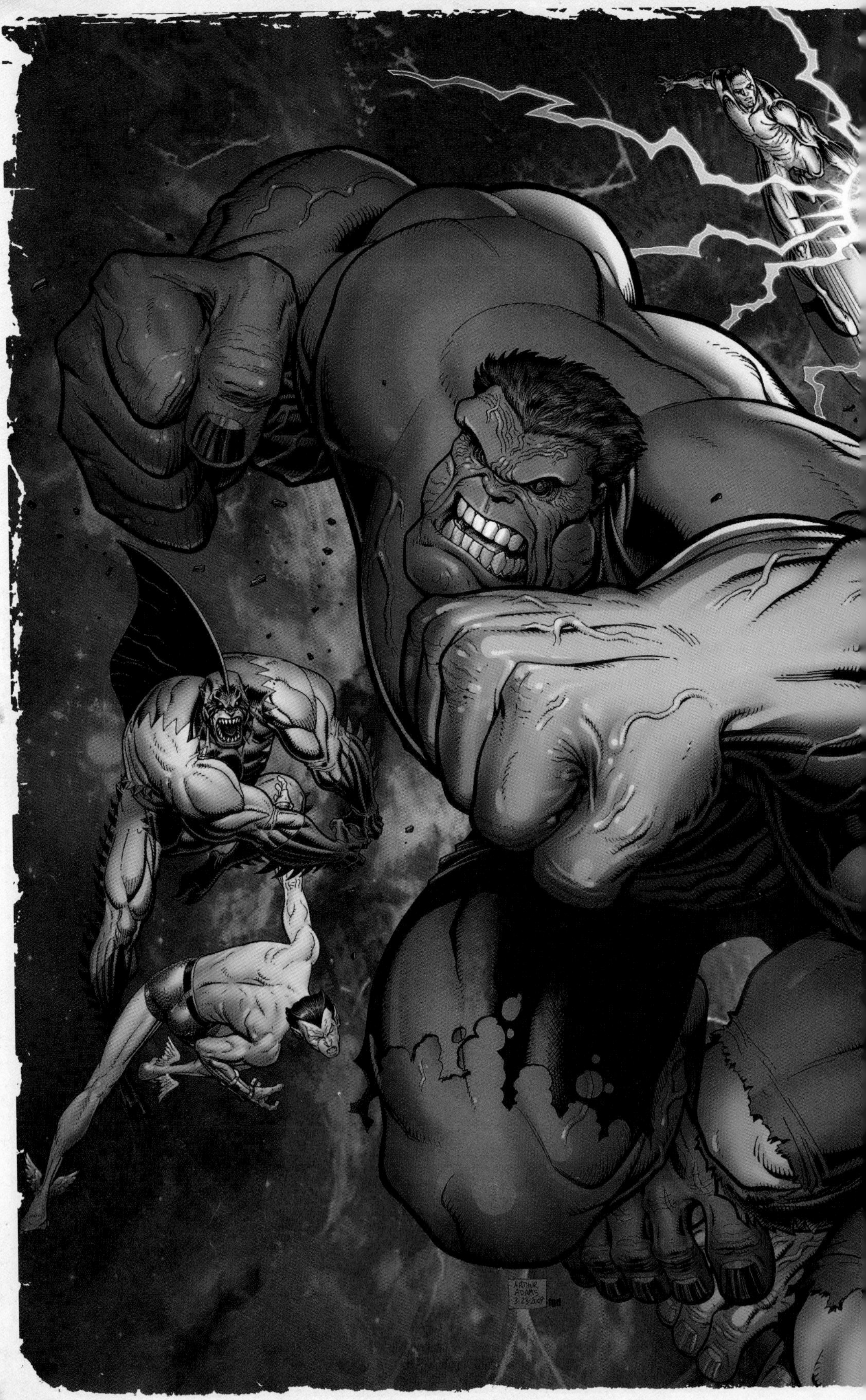
ARTHUR ADAMS 3.23.2008

★ ISSUE 12 VARIANT COVER

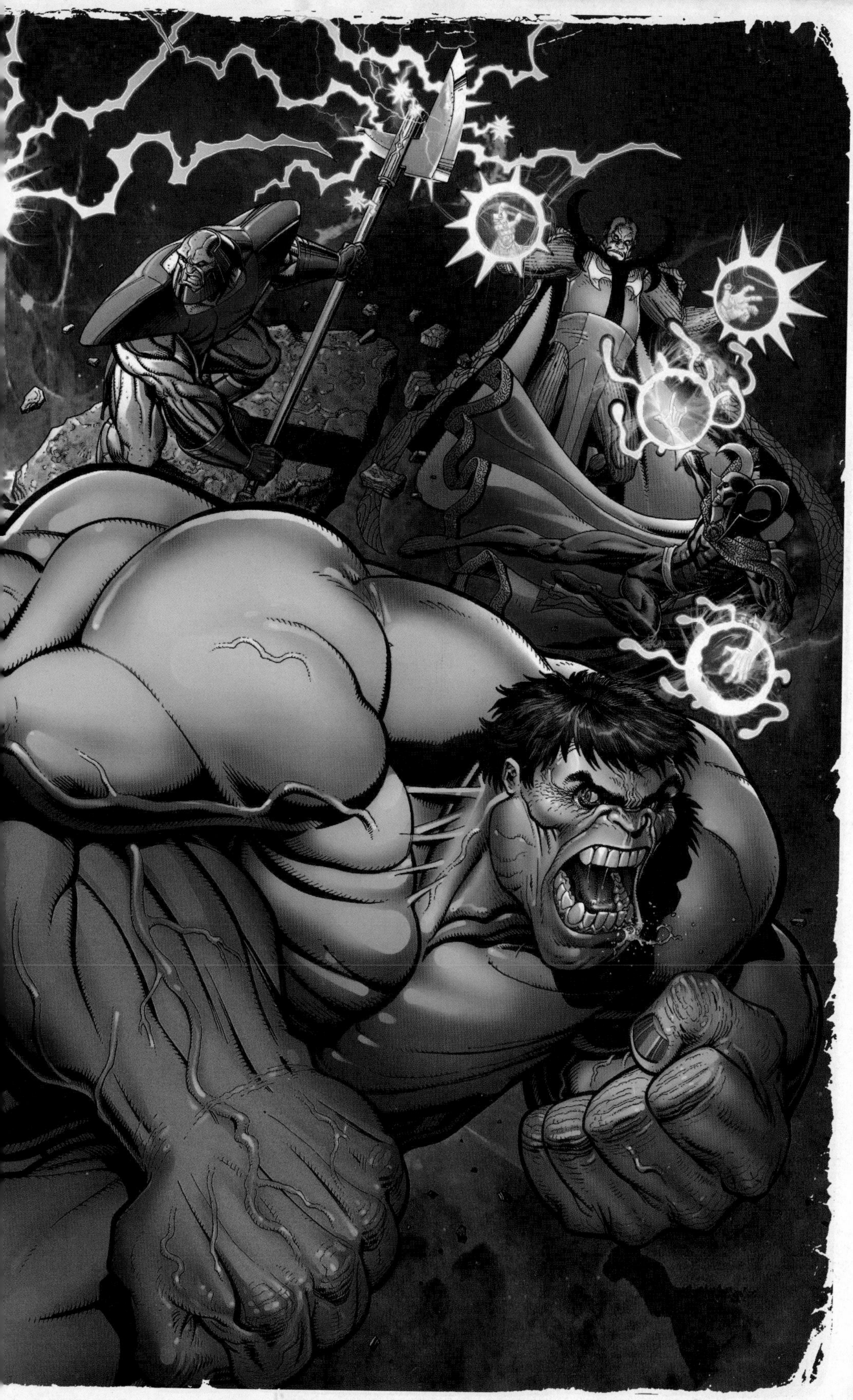

ARTHUR ADAMS & FERRAN DELGADO ★

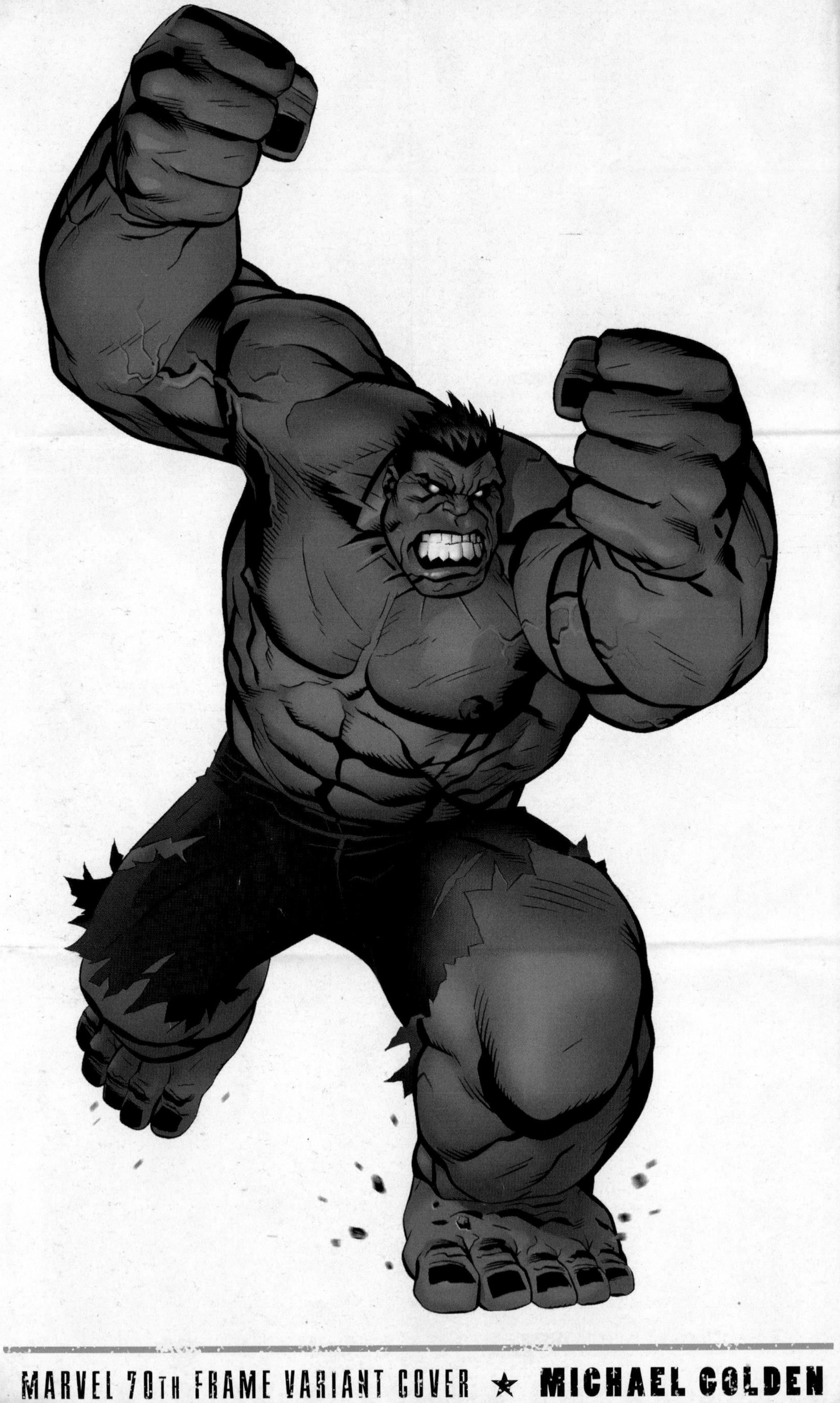

MARVEL 70TH FRAME VARIANT COVER ★ MICHAEL GOLDEN

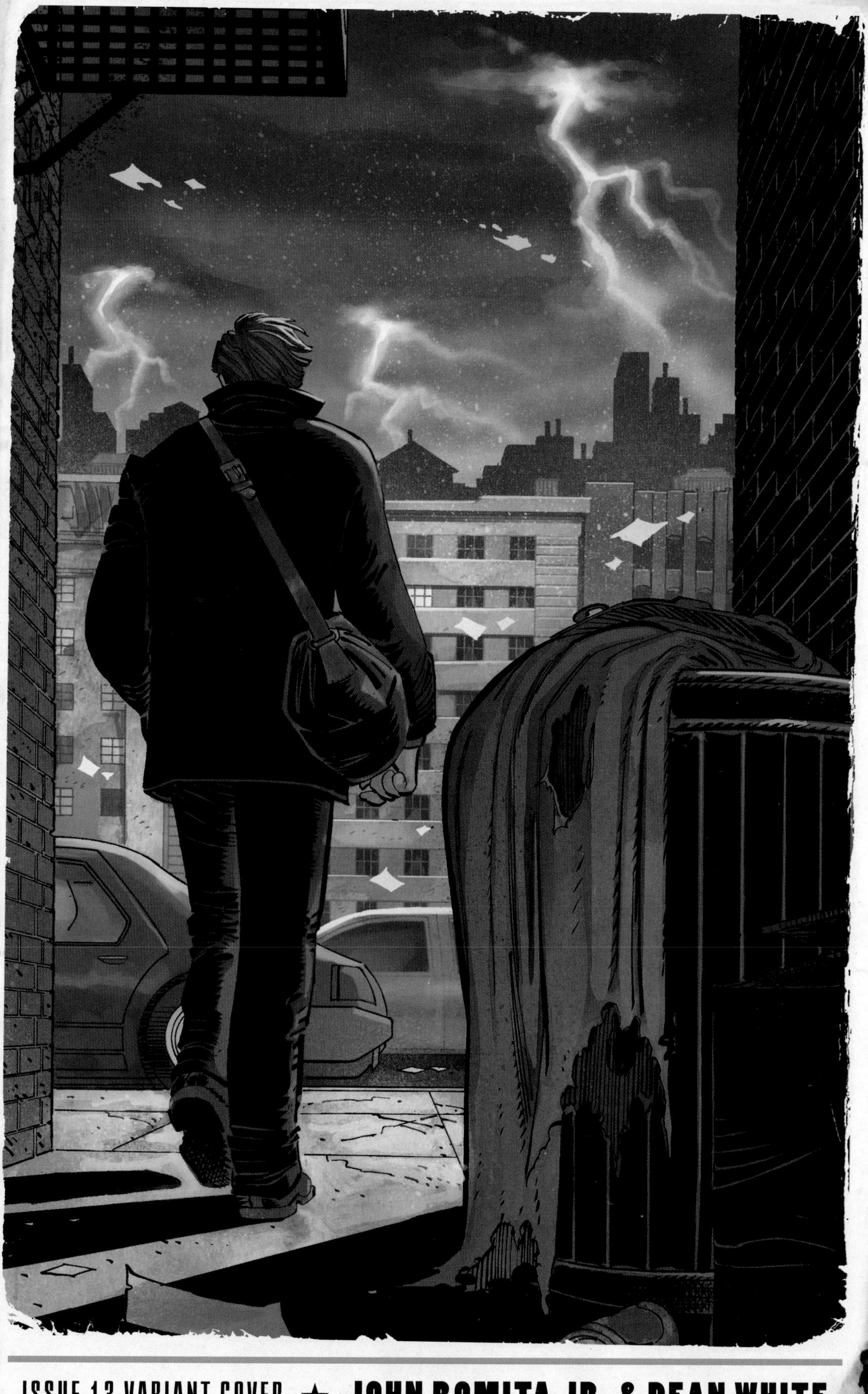

ISSUE 13 VARIANT COVER ★ JOHN ROMITA JR. & DEAN WHITE

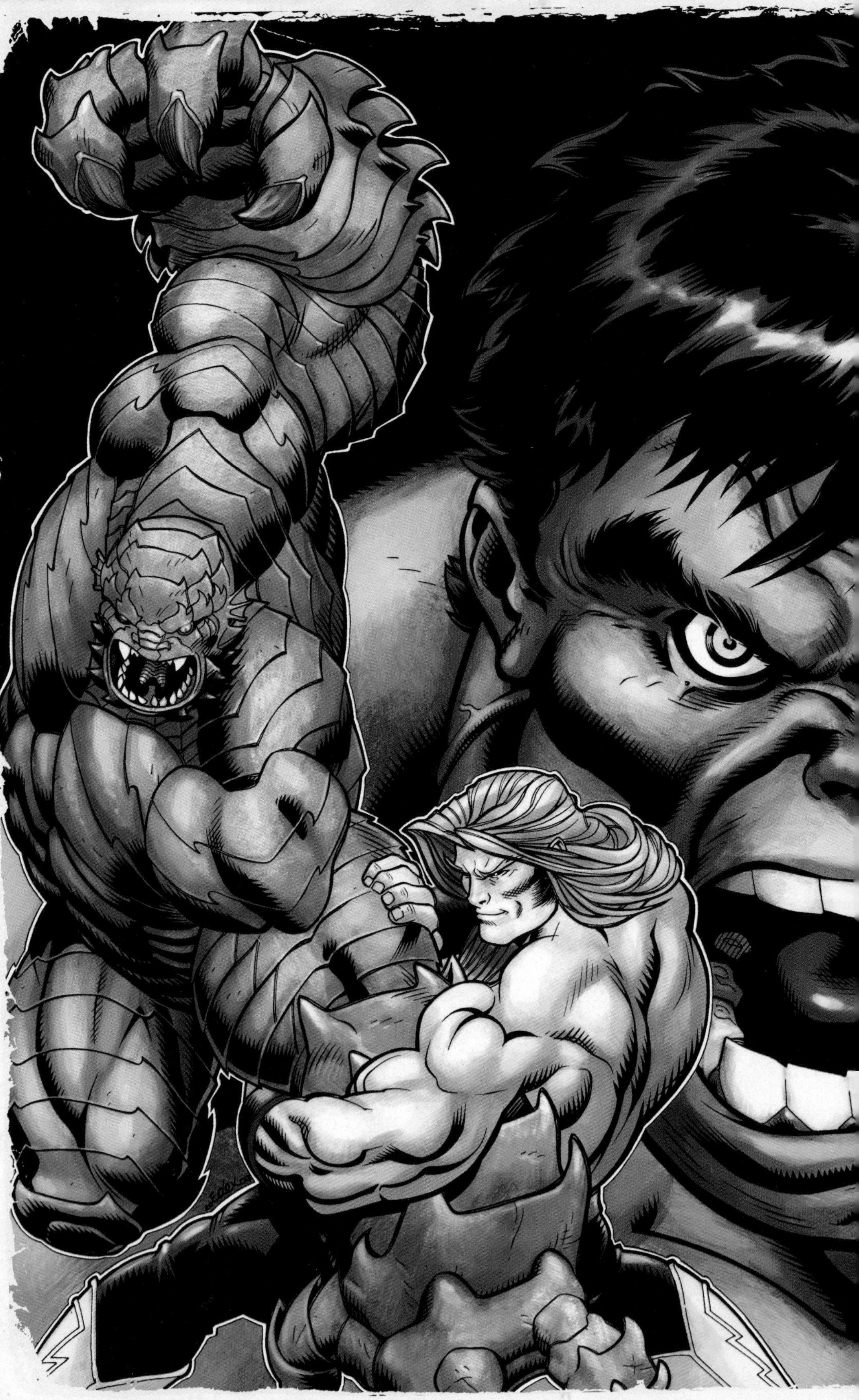

★ INCREDIBLE HULK 600 VARIANT COVER

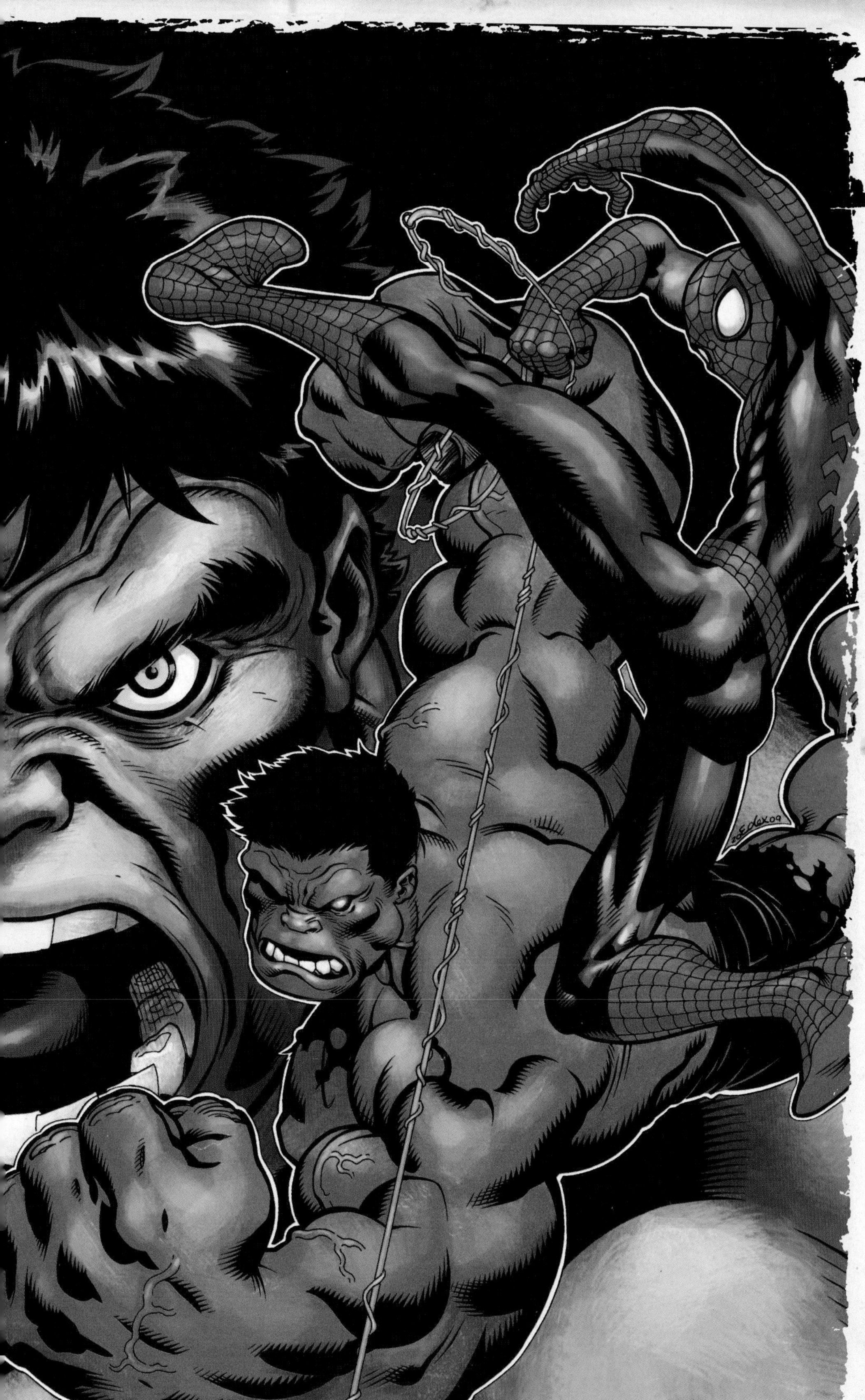

D McGUINNESS & DAN BROWN ★

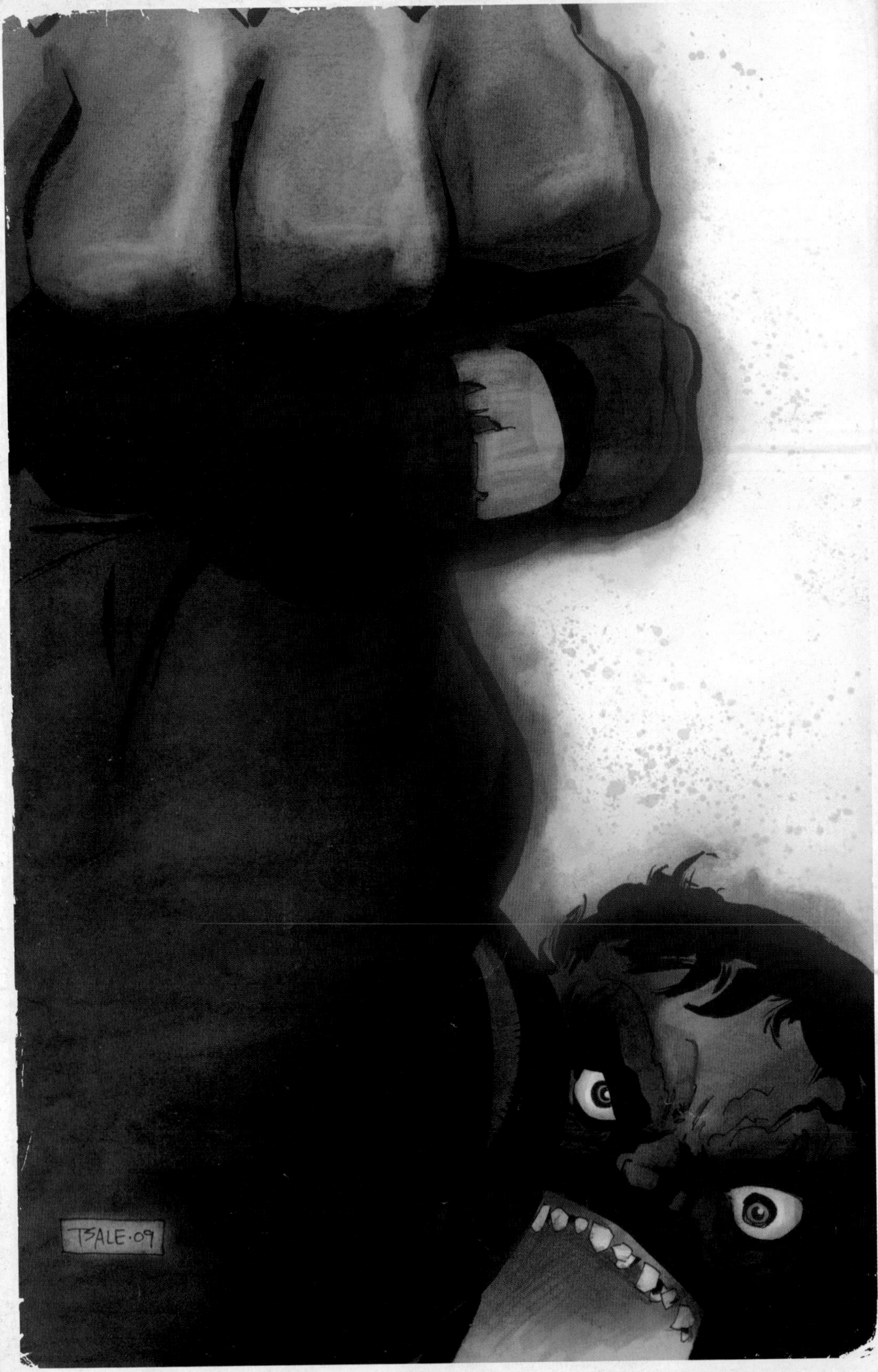
T. SALE·09

INCREDIBLE HULK 600 VARIANT ★ TIM SALE & DAVE STEWART

MINI MARVELS PRESENTS

HULK BEACH

WRITTEN BY AUDREY LOEB

ILLUSTRATED BY CHRIS GIARRUSSO chrisGcomics.com

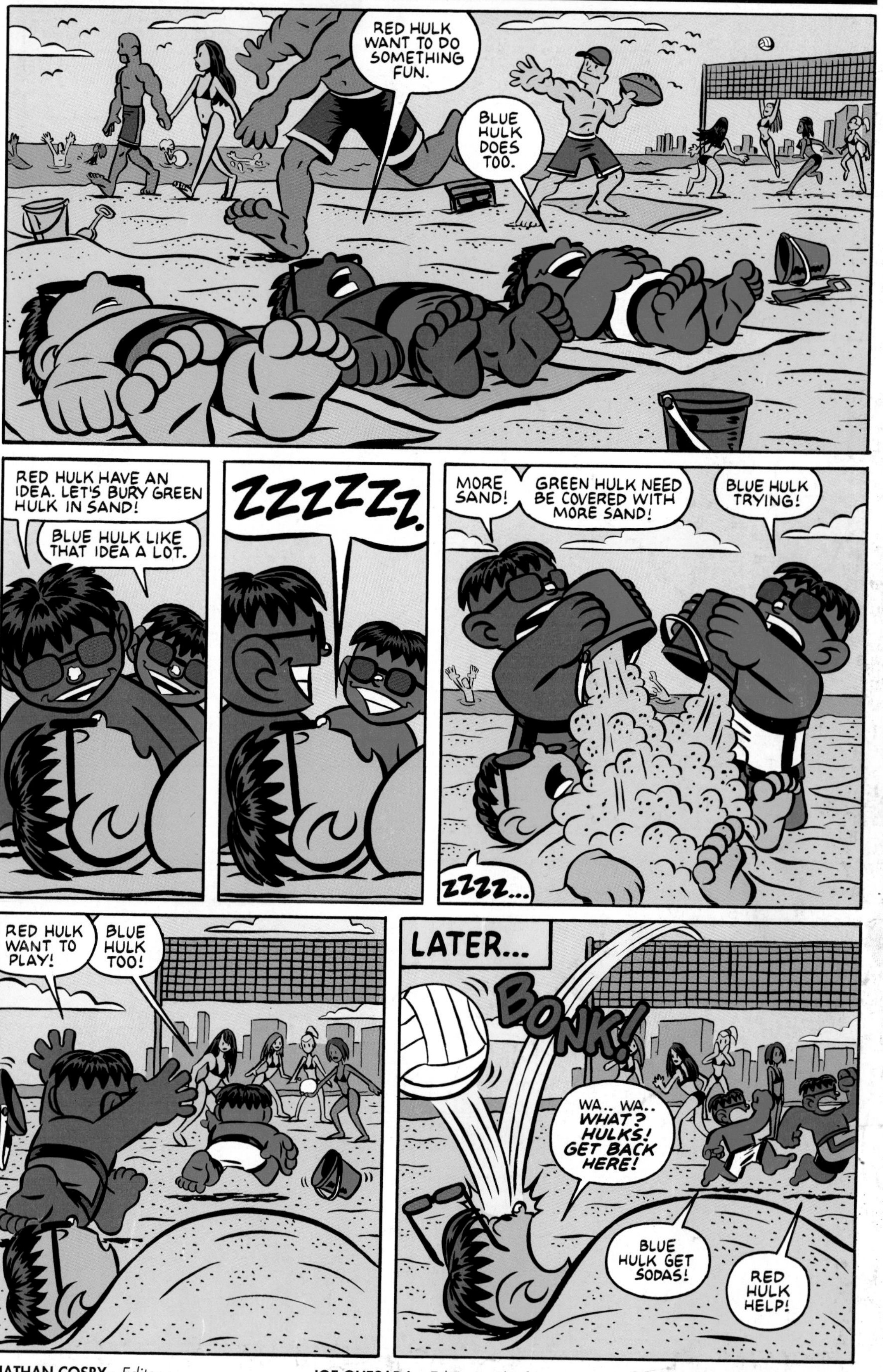

RED HULK WANT TO DO SOMETHING FUN.
BLUE HULK DOES TOO.
RED HULK HAVE AN IDEA. LET'S BURY GREEN HULK IN SAND!
BLUE HULK LIKE THAT IDEA A LOT.
ZZZZZZ.
MORE SAND!
GREEN HULK NEED BE COVERED WITH MORE SAND!
BLUE HULK TRYING!
ZZZZ...
RED HULK WANT TO PLAY!
BLUE HULK TOO!
LATER...
BONK!
WA.. WA.. WHAT? HULKS! GET BACK HERE!
BLUE HULK GET SODAS!
RED HULK HELP!

NATHAN COSBY - *Editor* JOE QUESADA - *Editor In Chief* DAN BUCKLEY - *Publisher*

HULK MAMA

WRITTEN BY **AUDREY LOEB**
ILLUSTRATED BY CHRIS GIARRUSSO chrisGcomics.com

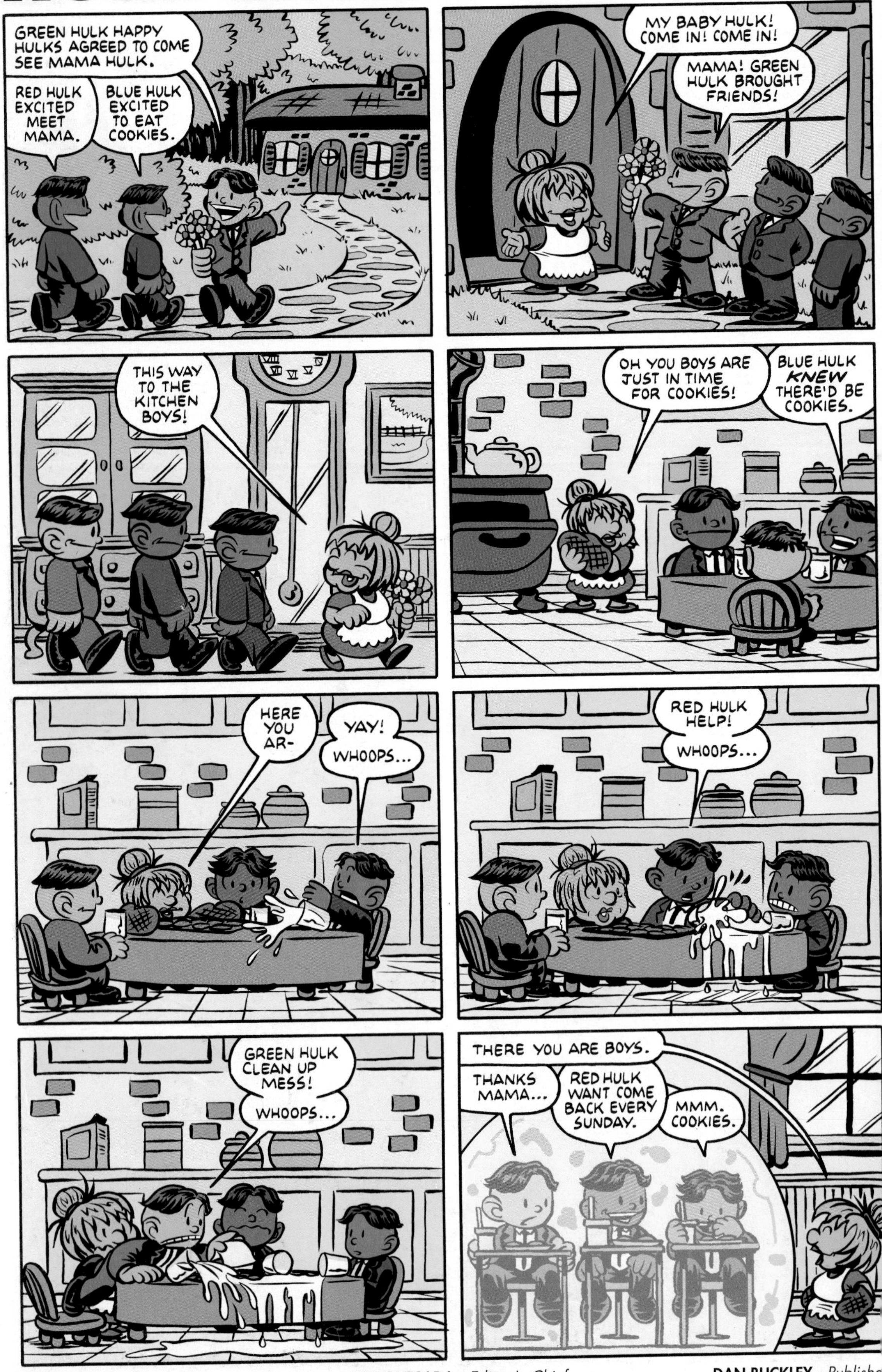

GREEN HULK HAPPY HULKS AGREED TO COME SEE MAMA HULK.
RED HULK EXCITED MEET MAMA.
BLUE HULK EXCITED TO EAT COOKIES.
MY BABY HULK! COME IN! COME IN!
MAMA! GREEN HULK BROUGHT FRIENDS!
THIS WAY TO THE KITCHEN BOYS!
OH YOU BOYS ARE JUST IN TIME FOR COOKIES!
BLUE HULK KNEW THERE'D BE COOKIES.
HERE YOU AR-
YAY!
WHOOPS...
RED HULK HELP!
WHOOPS...
GREEN HULK CLEAN UP MESS!
WHOOPS...
THERE YOU ARE BOYS.
THANKS MAMA...
RED HULK WANT COME BACK EVERY SUNDAY.
MMM. COOKIES.

JORDAN D. WHITE - *Editor* JOE QUESADA - *Editor In Chief* DAN BUCKLEY - *Publishe*

HULK CHEF

WRITTEN BY AUDREY LOEB

ILLUSTRATED BY CHRIS GIARRUSSO chrisGcomics.com

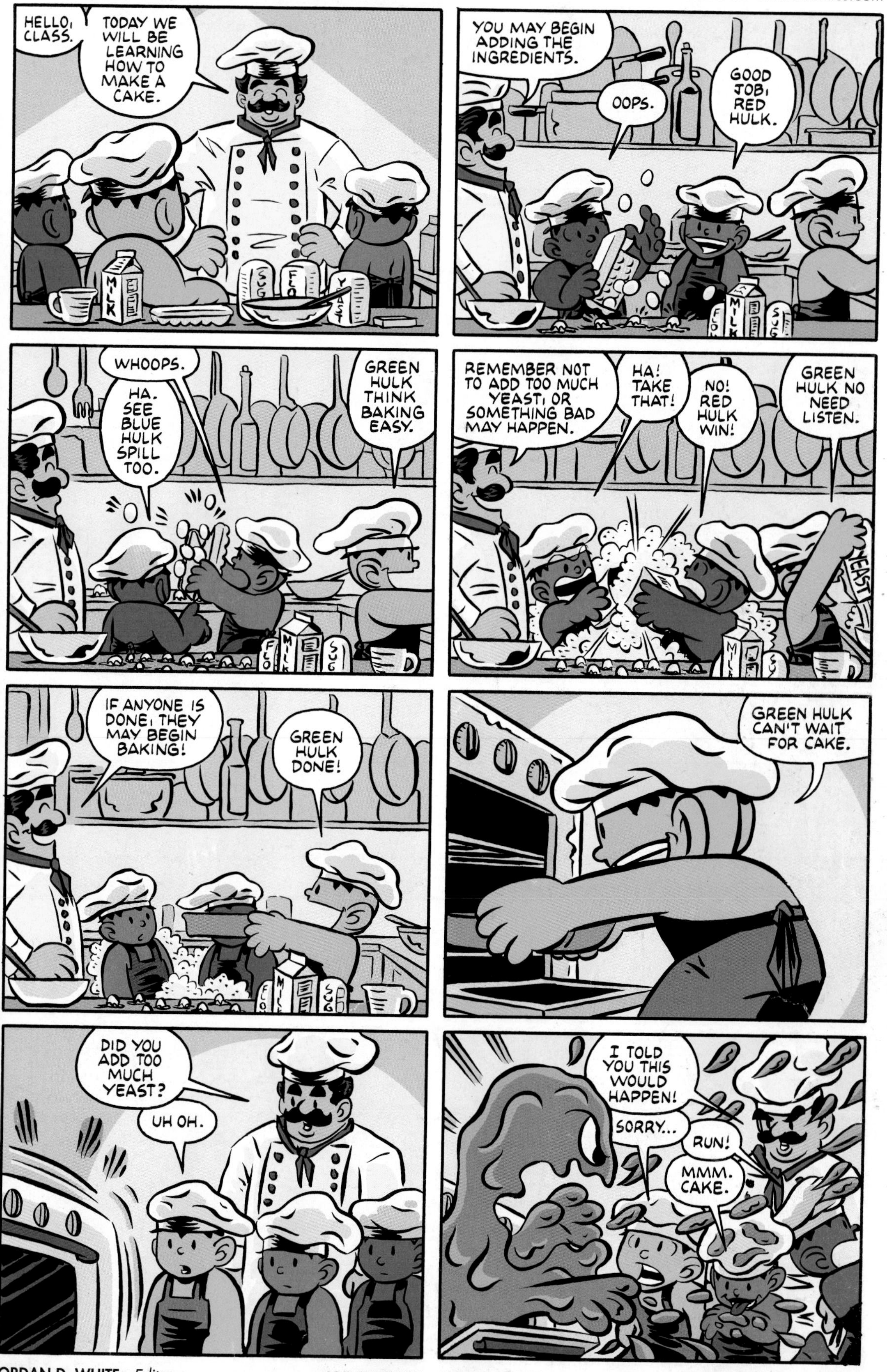

HELLO, CLASS.
TODAY WE WILL BE LEARNING HOW TO MAKE A CAKE.
YOU MAY BEGIN ADDING THE INGREDIENTS.
OOPS.
GOOD JOB, RED HULK.
WHOOPS.
HA. SEE BLUE HULK SPILL TOO.
GREEN HULK THINK BAKING EASY.
REMEMBER NOT TO ADD TOO MUCH YEAST, OR SOMETHING BAD MAY HAPPEN.
HA! TAKE THAT!
NO! RED HULK WIN!
GREEN HULK NO NEED LISTEN.
IF ANYONE IS DONE, THEY MAY BEGIN BAKING!
GREEN HULK DONE!
GREEN HULK CAN'T WAIT FOR CAKE.
DID YOU ADD TOO MUCH YEAST?
UH OH.
I TOLD YOU THIS WOULD HAPPEN!
SORRY...
RUN!
MMM. CAKE.

HULK DOG

WRITTEN BY AUDREY LOEB

ILLUSTRATED BY CHRIS GIARRUSSO chrisGcomics.com

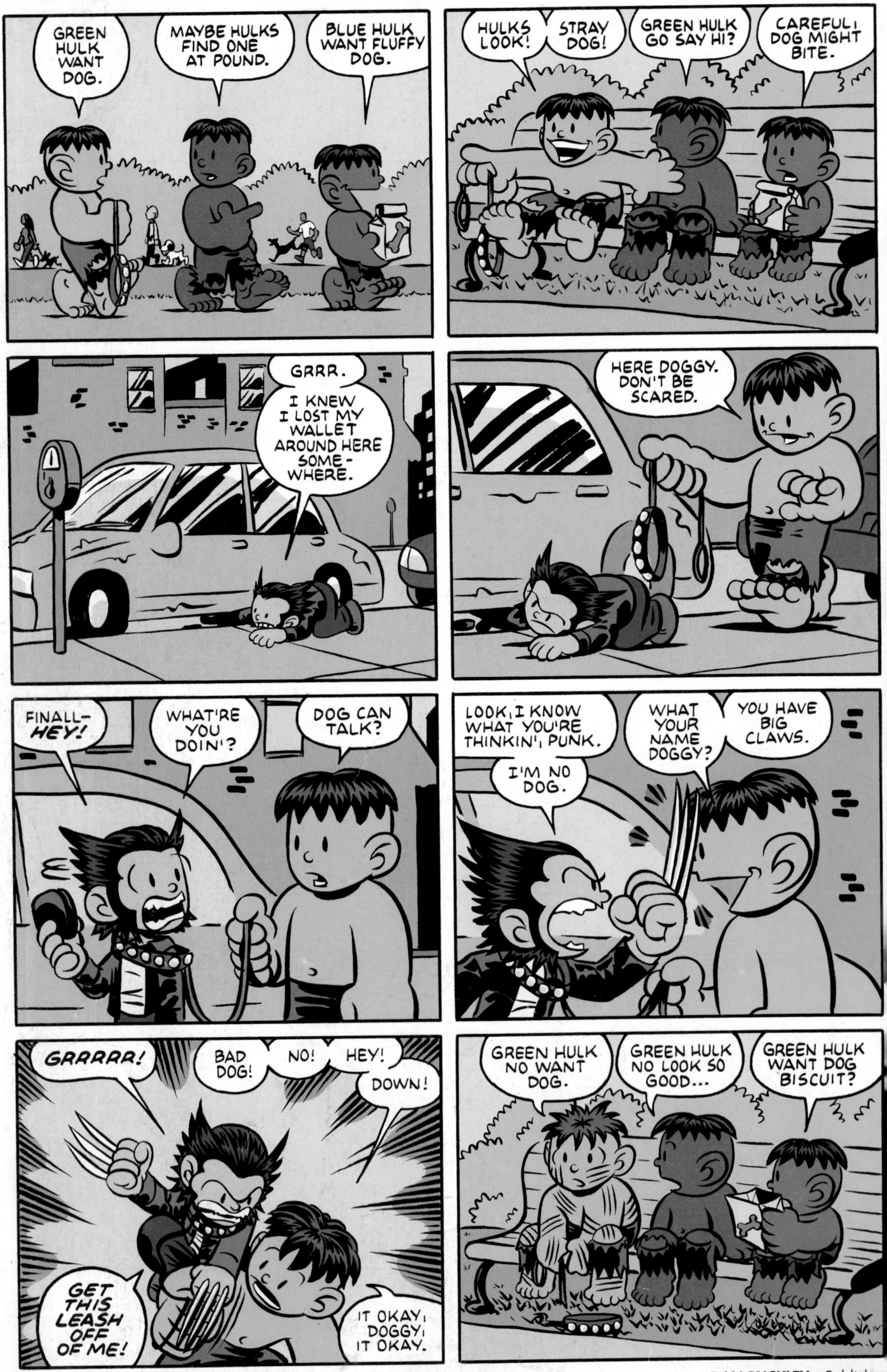
GREEN HULK WANT DOG.
MAYBE HULKS FIND ONE AT POUND.
BLUE HULK WANT FLUFFY DOG.
HULKS LOOK!
STRAY DOG!
GREEN HULK GO SAY HI?
CAREFUL, DOG MIGHT BITE.
GRRR.
I KNEW I LOST MY WALLET AROUND HERE SOME-WHERE.
HERE DOGGY. DON'T BE SCARED.
FINALL-
HEY!
WHAT'RE YOU DOIN'?
DOG CAN TALK?
LOOK, I KNOW WHAT YOU'RE THINKIN', PUNK.
I'M NO DOG.
WHAT YOUR NAME DOGGY?
YOU HAVE BIG CLAWS.
GRRRRR!
BAD DOG!
NO!
HEY!
DOWN!
GET THIS LEASH OFF OF ME!
IT OKAY, DOGGY, IT OKAY.
GREEN HULK NO WANT DOG.
GREEN HULK NO LOOK SO GOOD...
GREEN HULK WANT DOG BISCUIT?

JORDAN D. WHITE - *Editor* **JOE QUESADA** - *Editor In Chief* **DAN BUCKLEY** - *Publisher*